Cristy's Kitchen

𝓌𝓂
WILLIAM MORROW
An Imprint of HarperCollins Publishers

Cristy's Kitchen

More Than 130 Scrumptious and
Nourishing Recipes Without Gluten,
Dairy, or Processed Sugars

Cristina Kisner

FOREWORD BY BRANDON STANTON

PHOTOGRAPHS BY JIMENA AGOIS

ILLUSTRATIONS BY JULIETA GRACEY KISNER

FOR MY BELOVED DAUGHTERS,
Camila, Gala, Julieta, Josefina, and Hebe—
my driving force, my strength, my blessings,
and my greatest teachers.
May this book remind you that miracles exist,
and you only have to believe with all your heart.
Las amo con todo mi corazón.

contents

foreword

I FIRST MET CRISTY KISNER a couple of years ago, during a very scary time in my life. I'd just been diagnosed with an autoimmune disease. I was having frightening symptoms, including unexplained joint pain that was spreading through my body. And my bloodwork was quite concerning, to say the least. Perhaps the most disconcerting part of an autoimmune condition is that it comes from within. For my entire life I'd viewed my body as an ally—a partner in the fight against microbes, ailments, and maladies. It had always been us against the world, but not anymore. Suddenly, my body was working against itself. It had become its own worst enemy. And that was a frightening and disorienting prospect.

I'd discovered Cristy's café and bakery, Cristy's Kitchen, by chance a few months earlier. It was actually my wife who made the discovery, as she is constantly on the lookout for good organic food. We didn't live particularly close to the restaurant. It was a forty-five-minute drive from our house. But we decided to stop in one day on the way home from a hiking trip. I didn't meet Cristy that day, as she was back in the kitchen. But the food was delicious, and her husband, Sebastián, stopped by our table long enough for us to learn the family's story. Cristy's journey with food had begun with her own daughter's autoimmune disease, which had seemed incurable. And out of desperation for her daughter's health, she learned to cook delicious recipes with only the purest ingredients. Two things happened: her daughter's symptoms began to subside, and Cristy

became an expert in organic cooking. Not long afterward, Sebastián's furniture business failed and the family emigrated from Peru to America and opened Cristy's Kitchen. I was inspired by their story, and of course the food was delicious. So my wife and I made the long drive out to Roswell, Georgia, several more times. Eventually, I got to know Cristy quite well. And when I learned of my diagnosis, she was the first person I thought to call.

Cristy took charge immediately. I gave her complete control of my diet. For two months I hired her to prepare all my meals. But it wasn't just food that she was providing. She took time to give me comfort in many a late-night text thread. She spoke directly to the most difficult part of the diagnosis: the feeling that my body had become its own worst enemy, and I was all alone in the fight. *View your body as a friend*, she would say. *Love your body*. And most important: *Give your body what it needs*. And after years of research, Cristy seemed to know exactly what my body needed. With every dish that she delivered, Cristy gave me hope. And I've always felt that this is the most important thing she offers. Cristy gives hope; it just happens to come in the form of delicious and healthy food.

Over the next couple of months my symptoms subsided, without a single bit of medication. And they have yet to return. No more swelling. No more joint pain. The only remaining symptom is a mild annoyance: whenever it's below room temperature, my hands turn blue. And this I don't really mind. I almost view

it as a gentle reminder from my body to give it what it needs. I'm not as puritanical with my diet as I was in the immediate aftermath of my diagnosis. I don't eat completely clean. But I'm 90 percent better than I used to be, and my body is much better for it. I've lost nearly fifty pounds—weight I'd gained from years of care-less eating. Ironically, when I encounter people that I haven't seen in a long time, they seem worried by the weight loss. They'll inquire about my health in hushed tones, seeming to think that such a dramatic transformation could only be caused by a serious illness. And they're right.

It was caused by a serious illness. Just not in the way that they fear.

I cannot offer scientific proof that my body was healed by Cristy's food. I'm not a doctor. I haven't conducted any controlled clinical trials. But I do know one thing. Two years ago I found myself in a very dark place, and I felt there was no way out. Cristy offered to help, and she asked only that I believe in her food. I gave her that belief, and my body healed itself. Whether it was the food or the belief, I will never know. But Cristy gave me both. And it's hard to say which one I needed more.

—BRANDON STANTON

introduction

THIS IS A COOKBOOK, but beyond that, it's a book about my journey as a mother looking for a way to improve the health of my daughters through food.

I don't think of food just in terms of ingredients. For me, it has a much deeper meaning; it's been a miracle in our life, medicine for both the body and soul. Through research, intuition, and experimentation, I have been able to discover the power of food.

In this book you will find what I call "real and clean cuisine"—recipes that are gluten- and dairy-free, with vegan, vegetarian, paleo, and autoimmune protocol (AIP) options; are made from scratch; and that feature real, organic ingredients that nourish the body and soul. I don't have a degree in nutrition or even a certificate from a culinary academy, but I come from a long line of women cooks, and my family is living proof of food's power to heal.

If you have dietary restrictions, if you are fighting a disease, or if you just want to prevent sickness and feel great and healthy, I hope this book will help you create and enjoy preparing delicious food, even if you don't like to cook.

My goal is to bring joy and discovery into your kitchen and to help make every dish a complete experience, both physically and mentally. If you pay attention to your ingredients, taste them carefully in their most natural state, and are aware of their powerful benefits, you will discover instinctively what your body really needs. Remember to take your time when eating, to sit down calmly and enjoy each bite. You will not only enjoy your meal but help improve your digestion. Food can be both healthy and delicious—a perfect, natural match.

The ingredients I use are heavily influenced by my Peruvian heritage, as well as my research into the benefits they bring to your wellness; see page 1 for more details on some of my most commonly used and lesser-known ingredients.

I don't always list my ingredients as organic, but whenever possible I use organic, both at home and at the restaurant, and I encourage you to do the same. I've noticed that organic ingredients have a powerful, positive effect on my family's health. For me, wisdom comes from nature, and the less humans intervene, the purer the food will be—the planet benefits, too. It's also really important to understand how to read the labels on any package (see page 2).

I could write an entire memoir of my family's medical trials and tribulations, as well as the various other crises that we've survived, but this isn't the place. I will say that, from each member of my immediate family, I've learned something critical that has influenced my culinary outlook and approach. The changes and lessons in our life and kitchen came gradually, and I'm sure we will continue changing and learning, because that's what life is about, continuous learning.

From Camila, my eldest daughter, who suffered from a variety of ailments over the years (including eye problems, allergies, skin issues, and a rare autoimmune disease), I learned how important it is to choose quality organic ingredients, and what a huge difference it makes; how to cook dairy-free; and eventually, all about the autoimmune protocol (AIP) diet. I also learned to trust my intuition as a mother, and that the right diet and supplements have the power to eliminate the symptoms of disease and increase quality of life (or calidad de vida, as we say in Spanish). Through our experience managing Camila's ailments, we came to understand that we are not only what we eat but what we feel and think, too. We are complete and complex beings.

Camila has also learned to listen to her own body and identify which ingredients both increase and decrease inflammation, including when it comes to her emotions and thoughts (and I encourage you to do the same!).

From Gala, my second eldest, who suffered from allergies as well as chronic stomach issues due to gluten intolerance, I learned the chemistry of gluten-free cooking but also that everything is chemistry—we are molecules that react to other molecules. We have the power to make healing potions for the body and for the soul, because we transfer our energy and love to the food we cook. Cooking is a way of loving, and when you are sautéing, mixing, and beating ingredients, remember that your love and energy are your secret ingredients.

From Julieta, my third daughter, with whom I was pregnant when I contracted listeriosis due to contaminated food, I learned to become a label detective and understand the difference between a truly wholesome food and one that has not been made with real ingredients and the right processes.

Look at coconut cream, for example. Some brands contain the thickening agent guar gum, while others do not. When you refrigerate pure coconut cream, it becomes solid because the fat it contains solidifies when cold. When the cream is watery, that means it does not contain

enough coconut, or the natural fat provided by coconut, and it is necessary to add gums to improve the consistency. A good coconut cream is naturally thick and creamy and does not need added gums (see page 28).

Shrimp is another example. Why would a bag of frozen raw shrimp need a preservative? Freezing is itself a preserving method.

Organic and natural flavoring—what do they mean? These are questions we must ask ourselves of each box, envelope, or bag that comes into our house.

Do we really know what we are buying? Do we really want to take the risk of feeding it to our family? Is it real food?

From Josefina, my second youngest, who had no ailments but craved foods such as french fries and pizza, I learned to encourage healthy eating habits in more effective ways—that is, not through restrictions and prohibitions but rather by involving her in the process of gardening and cooking and by educating her about the properties of each ingredient. One of the best gifts we can give our children is contact with nature. If we can have a vegetable garden at home, or even a simple pot of tomatoes, and they can be part of the sowing and harvesting process, it nourishes them, physically and spiritually.

When children understand what real food is and where it comes from, I've found that they're more open to the idea of eating fruits and vegetables (while they learn how to take care of and love themselves). And in the process, we give them a fantastic gift. That contact with the soil helps them maintain varied and strong gut microbiota, which will be the basis of health for the rest of their lives.

Josefina inspired me to be creative in the kitchen and swap junk food for healthy recipes. For example, organic potatoes or yuca cut by hand and fried in coconut oil is an excellent alternative to fast-food french fries. A pizza made of quinoa flour and seeds with cashew mozzarella and uncured (and grass-fed) pepperoni is so much better than a conventional frozen pizza. These foods add to our health instead of taking it away.

From my youngest, Hebe, who was born with kidney and urinary issues, I learned about the world of the gut microbiota, the benefits of probiotics, and the importance of balance in that community of bacteria for the harmony of the whole body. Digestive problems, food intolerances, urinary tract diseases, autoimmune diseases, psychiatric diseases, cardiovascular diseases, behavior problems . . . everything, absolutely everything, improves when we solve problems in the microbiota.

From my husband, Sebastián (Sebas), who suffered a heart attack, I learned how powerful and harmful stress is to the body. We are built to deal with occasional stress. In ancient times when we had to escape from a predator, we generated a hormonal load that allowed us to run, fight, or hide—but then our body returned to its natural balance. Today we do not have to run from predators, but we have to face bills, traffic, school, work, mothers-in-law, politicians, and more, and our body does not understand which of these is a real enemy and when to stop responding to stress. And in that constant cascade of emotions and hormonal imbalances, diseases appear. I believe that the secret to dealing with life's stresses, as difficult as it may seem, is that no matter what happens in your outer world, to try to fill your inner world with so much peace and love that you do not need anything more in order to be happy. Your body will start to recover its balance, and the world around you will start to heal, too.

I grew up in Tacna, Peru, in a kitchen where my mom was a self-taught alchemist, creating recipes from empanadas and juices to the most elaborate sweets and desserts with incredible passion and perseverance—she even made my wedding cake, including sugar dough flowers. Her creations are as good as or better than those of a professional pastry chef. While I have always loved to cook, I didn't have her patience for the precise science of baking. But when my daughters started reaching school age, I realized I'd better fall in love with baking, because I would need to make everything for their lunch boxes, from sandwich bread to desserts, to avoid any unhealthy packaged food. The best way I could feed them was choosing healthy and organic foods, which were not readily available at the time in stores and supermarkets in Lima, where we lived. After a while, the other families at the school became interested in what I was baking, and some parents asked me to teach them.

This led to a year of teaching groups of parents in my dining room, after which a local bakery commissioned me to begin baking gluten-free breads and set us up with a small production kitchen. This was a blessing, since at that time we were going through a financial crisis with the business we owned, a luxury furniture factory. So starting a baking business became our backup plan, and with a lot of effort, we were able to open a small storefront café and bakery, which we called Huh! The name was an attempt to phonetically re-create an Icelandic soccer team's prematch Viking war chant that was my family's own personal chant for getting through anything. Unfortunately, this business wasn't profitable either.

Though I lived in Lima, I had always loved the United States and dreamed about living there. I had visited once at age twenty-one and had a magical time at Disney World in Orlando. Sebas's heart attack was the catalyst that convinced us to give up his furniture business, move near his brother's family in Roswell, Georgia, and begin again. And to further our motivation, there was a café for sale in Roswell, which we saw as a sign, a miracle, a clue as to which way to go. With the help of friends and family, we were able to purchase it and open up a second Huh! in Georgia in December 2019.

Three months later the pandemic hit. To make matters worse, a business partner in Lima backed out unexpectedly and we lost our original bakery. There were moments when I was tempted to give up, but after everything we'd been through, even with a pandemic, we could only be grateful to be here. Roswell and our restaurant were magic to us. Even when the city was shutting down, the restaurant dining room was closed, and the girls couldn't go to school, we were able to make the best of what we had. I found two free sofas through an online marketplace, my brother-in-law's brother-in-law gave us a used TV, and we put together a cozy little room for the girls in the restaurant so they could be with us all the time during the pandemic. We practically lived there.

We were able to offer takeout and delivery for the several months before the dining room could open, but it was not easy to get by. Many people have heard about the miraculous turn of events that followed and saved us from the brink of financial ruin, so I will summarize it only briefly here. It started with a family who had recently become regular customers. The husband, a writer, learned about our struggles to remain solvent during the pandemic, and offered to help us out, in part because he loved our food. First, though, he urged us to change the name of our restaurant (which people were mispronouncing all the time) to Cristy's Kitchen. I was hesitant to name the restaurant after myself, but once we did, it seemed to add new light and energy to our business.

That writer turned out to be Brandon Stanton, the photographer, writer, and creator behind Humans of New York (HONY), the wildly popular blog and social media sensation. Brandon, who was spending the pandemic in his home state of Georgia, proposed that I share my family's story with the world through HONY.

It is very scary to expose your heart to the whole world, but in our conversations the word "hope" always appeared, and finally that was our mission—to tell our story to help people who were in the same situation as us, with health, financial, or other problems, to see that there is always a light at the end of the tunnel—that there is always hope.

We were together at the bakery the day Brandon posted our story to HONY. While we were sitting there, a woman called from Maryland and said, "I have a sick son, and in my mother's heart I felt that I should try with the food, but I was in doubt, but now I know that I should follow my heart. I'd like to take the car and drive there to hug you and say, thank you for giving me hope."

With tears in my eyes and Brandon's gaze on me, I knew that everything that had happened in recent years—illnesses, bankruptcy, tears, and fears, the dawns of working very hard, the tests that God put us through, and the creation of every recipe—everything had been worth it after getting that call.

Humans of New York exists to remind us of how human we are, that we are all created out of pure love, and we just have to remember that, and through one another's stories we can connect and reconnect with each other and with ourselves.

I will never have enough words to thank Brandon for what he did for us. Thanks to the generosity and contributions of HONY's readers, we received more than enough funding to keep our restaurant open and give our daughters the life we dreamed of for them. As immigrants, we arrived here with empty hands but with a heart full of hope and dreams—dreams that have now come true.

We have been truly blessed. Life has given us so many lessons and miracles, and with those has come a mission to help other families find a safe place where they can eat together despite their various dietary restrictions, and where the food is just as delicious as cuisine without restrictions, so they don't miss out on anything.

People with medical issues, food sensitivities, allergies, and those who are simply looking to improve their health will find in our restaurant a place where they can connect with others in similar situations, and that is a gift to us. I hope what I have learned in my kitchen for my own family can help you in your own quest for health.

America is our home now, and we feel that we are a part of an incredible community that has welcomed us with great affection. We hope to return a piece of our hearts to all of you.

Our next step is to reach every home in America that needs real, organic, clean, and lovingly homemade food. I hope this book inspires you, comforts you, and makes you believe in yourself and the power you have in the kitchen to take care of yourself and those you love the most.

To close our story, I want to remind you:

You are bigger than your problems,
You are more love than your fears,
You are more light than shadow.

Hug yourself,
encourage yourself,
and be aware that your body is
perfect as it is to house your soul.
And when you heal, everything
around you will heal, too.

Try this: turn up the music, call your kids into the kitchen, and start chopping veggies. Sauté some mushrooms, blend a green smoothie, bake an almond cake. Give them a spatula with chocolate, sing together, smile together, set the table together. I assure you that you'll have the best food of your life.

Let's cook!

Love,

Cristy

special ingredients

CERTAIN FOODS AND BAKING INGREDIENTS are mentioned throughout this book and appear in many of my recipes. Some you may not have heard of before because they are more common in other parts of the world. Others you may already use, whether or not you're aware of their nutritional benefits. I included this section to provide descriptions of these ingredients, information on their nutritional benefits, and notes on where you can locate lesser-known items.

People have different opinions about organic foods—both on what exactly "organic" means and to what extent it affects our health. I am an advocate of organic food, of course, having personally observed the powerful, beneficial effects that it has had on my family's health, especially in comparison to a diet based on conventional ingredients.

Nature is wise, and we should let it guide and teach us instead of manipulating it. I believe that if we keep our eyes open, we can see how everything is connected; what the roles are of insects, birds, earthworms, animals, water; how every little detail in nature exists for a reason and has a purpose. I am a believer in doing the right thing—and not only when creating great food—to ensure the health of our planet and our communities, too, because we are all connected.

NOTE: I do not include the word "organic" in the list below because I understand that not all readers have access to organic foods, whether for physical or financial reasons. But for my family, everything we eat, put on our skin, or use to clean (and even, if we can find them, the clothes we wear) is as organic as possible.

acacia fiber

Harvested from the sap of the acacia tree (native to parts of Africa, Pakistan, and India), acacia fiber serves as a prebiotic food. Prebiotics are compounds in food that induce the growth or activity of beneficial microorganisms in the gut.

When the good bacteria in our gut (such as *Bifidobacterium* and *Lactobacillus*) are abundant, they don't leave enough room for the harmful ones (such as *Escherichia coli* and *Clostridium*) to overgrow—and that's when our microbiota come into balance.

It is likely that acacia's anti-inflammatory activities at the intestinal level help to prevent

or lessen metabolic disease. One study suggests that composite yogurt enriched with acacia fiber and *Bifidobacterium lactis* has greater therapeutic effects in patients with IBS than standard yogurt.

Acacia's soluble fiber comes in powder and capsule form; in our recipes we use the powder.

RECOMMENDED BRANDS: Anthony's, Micro Ingredients

WHERE TO BUY: Amazon, supermarkets (Whole Foods, Sprouts, Walmart, Kroger), vitamin stores

adaptogenic mushrooms

Adaptogenic substances are believed to have the capacity to normalize body functions and strengthen systems compromised by stress. Adaptogenic mushrooms like reishi, chaga, turkey tail, lion's mane, and cordyceps have been used therapeutically for centuries for their ability to help the body's natural healing processes. They support the immune system, help to reduce stress and restore hormonal balance, and have anti-inflammatory properties. Some studies suggest that they have anticancer, antiviral, and antibacterial properties as well. Adaptogenic

mushrooms are one of my favorite ingredients because they do just that—help your body adapt to different situations. I've been dealing with a lot of stress for many years, which has had huge repercussions for my body, including early menopause. But since I started consuming adaptogenic mushrooms, my symptoms have diminished, so I try to include them whenever I can. You can try adaptogenic mushrooms in my Cacao Smoothie Bowl (page 33).

You can find these mushrooms in various forms: capsule, tablet, powder, liquid, or even coffee. My favorite way to consume them is as a powder or liquid extract, but I also take them as a supplement.

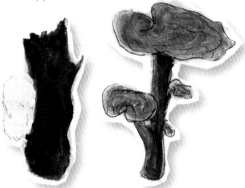

how to evaluate products and ingredients

Choose organic products whenever possible, especially those foods that appear on the Dirty Dozen list (see the Environmental Working Group website for details).

Ingredients on labels are listed in decreasing quantitative order; that is, the one with the highest volume in the product is listed first and the one used least appears last.

The front of the box is just for marketing the product. Always read the ingredient list, as simple as a product may seem (even products

professing to be "organic" may contain additives and nonsense ingredients).

If you can't pronounce a word in a product's ingredient list, avoid the product.

The fewer ingredients, the better.

Check information on allergens. A product may be produced or packaged in a plant that processes an ingredient you're allergic to, even if that ingredient isn't on the ingredient list.

WHERE TO BUY: supermarkets (Whole Foods, Sprouts, Thrive Market), Amazon

agar agar powder

A gel-like substance that comes from seaweed and can be used like a plant-based substitute for beef gelatin, agar agar comes in powder, flake, and bar form. I use the powder form in my recipes. It contains a high amount of fiber, which helps with regularity, and it may help to regulate blood sugar. It is a great source of iron and contains calcium, magnesium, potassium, and protein.

RECOMMENDED BRANDS: Living Jin, Now

WHERE TO BUY: Amazon, supermarkets (Walmart, Whole Foods)

aloe

The benefits of aloe have been recognized and taken advantage of throughout history. This low-calorie, fiber-, omega-, and vitamin-rich substance was used by Cleopatra as a beauty product, by other Egyptians as a medicine, and by the Hebrews as a laxative and remedy for skin conditions. According to Hippocrates, aloe's medical benefits include hair growth and the healing of tumors, stomach pains, and dysentery.

Today aloe's potential benefits include the reduction of cholesterol, fats, and tri-glycerides; antiviral, antibacterial, and laxative properties; protection against radiation and inflammation; and improvement of the immune system.

Aloin is the yellowish liquid found in the sap of the aloe plant. This compound, a molecule from the anthraquinones group, has amazing healing properties when used topically—but it is toxic when ingested, so the aloin must be removed before ingestion (see page 261). I do not recommend buying processed aloe products for consumption; start from a fresh aloe leaf to be sure of the quality.

You can find aloe in my Aloe Smoothie (page 261).

WHERE TO BUY: supermarkets (Whole Foods, Sprouts, Walmart, Kroger), Latin markets

apple cider vinegar

In ancient Greece around 400 BC, Hippocrates prescribed apple cider vinegar mixed with honey for a variety of ills, including coughs and colds. In addition to boasting antibacterial and anti-oxidant properties, apple cider vinegar helps to enhance the flavor of other ingredients.

RECOMMENDED BRAND: Bragg

aquafaba

The word *aquafaba* is the amalgamation of the Latin words for "water" and "bean"—and yes, it is literally bean water. Aquafaba can be made simply by boiling dried chickpeas (garbanzo beans) and reserving the cooking liquid. During the cooking process, many compounds transfer to the cooking liquid that help this magical liquid behave like egg whites and serve as a great replacement for eggs in vegan recipes.

(Remember, the longer you boil, the more viscous and like egg whites the liquid will be, so be patient!) Or you can also open a can of organic chickpeas and use the liquid (but remember that homemade is always better, and it's best to avoid aluminum cans).

You can find aquafaba in my Algarrobina Cocktail (page 274).

RECOMMENDED CANNED BRAND (IF YOU'RE IN A RUSH): Eden organic garbanzo beans

ashwagandha

Ashwagandha is an annual evergreen shrub in the Solanaceae, or nightshade family, that grows in India, the Middle East, and parts of Africa. Used in Ayurveda, it is an adaptogen that is believed to possess anti-inflammatory, antitumor, antistress, antioxidant, immune-supporting, anti-anxiety, and rejuvenating properties. It also appears to exert a positive influence on the endocrine, cardiopulmonary, and central nervous systems.

I use ashwagandha in powder form in my cooking. You can find ashwagandha in my Lúcuma and Algarrobina Fudge (page 228).

RECOMMENDED BRANDS: Organic India, Micro Ingredients, FGO

WHERE TO BUY: Amazon, supermarkets (Walmart, Kroger, Whole Foods, Sprouts)

avocado

I am convinced that avocados are the star food of healthy cooking. Eat an avocado daily and your heart will thank you. Avocado oil contains 71 percent monounsaturated fatty acids, 13 percent polyunsaturated fatty acids, and 16 percent saturated fatty acids, a balance that promotes a healthy blood lipid profile. This oil also improves the bioavailability of fat-soluble vitamins and phytochemicals in other fruits and vegetables when eaten together. Consuming avocados helps maintain cardiovascular health and supports weight management (since it provides satiety and energy) and healthy aging.

Both avocado fruit and avocado oil are great additions to our diets. For avocado oil, look for a brand that is organic, first cold press, extra virgin, and unrefined and that comes in a dark-colored bottle.

blue spirulina

Spirulina, a cyanobacteria commonly referred to as a blue-green algae, is one of the oldest life-forms on Earth. Spirulina grows in both fresh and saltwater sources and is known for its nutritional value: high protein; indispensable amino acids; vitamins (exceptionally high amounts of vitamin B12); beta-carotene and other pigments; minerals like iron, calcium, and phosphorous; essential fatty acids; and polysaccharides.

Blue spirulina helps with the proper functioning of the immune system by generating a balance in the gut microbiota. It contributes to the metabolism of fats and glucose, has antioxidant and anticancer properties, and reduces toxicity in our liver and kidneys.

RECOMMENDED BRAND: Incas by Asiya Life

WHERE TO BUY: Amazon

blue butterfly pea flower

Common in most Southeast Asian countries, butterfly pea flowers are used in Ayurvedic medicine as a brain tonic and memory enhancer, as well as an antistress, antianxiety, antidepressant, anticonvulsant, tranquilizing, and sedative agent. Further benefits include antimicrobial, antioxidant, and anti-inflammatory properties. Used as a dried flower in drinks or crushed into a powder, these flowers turn tea a beautiful blue color when hot water is added. If you add citrus to the tea, the pH level changes and the blue color miraculously and magically turns purple. Note that some herbalists do not recommend consuming it during pregnancy. You can find blue butterfly pea flour powder in my Blue Limonada (page 270).

RECOMMENDED BRAND: Incas by Asiya Life

WHERE TO BUY: natural food stores, Walmart, and Amazon

cabbage

Cabbage is one of my favorite ingredients in my kitchen. In addition to being super versatile and delicious both raw and cooked, it is believed that it prevents oxidative stress, induces detoxification enzymes, stimulates the immune system, and reduces the risk of cancers.

The fermented version, sauerkraut, is one of my family's favorite foods, and you can also find cabbage in my Turkey Cabbage Rolls (page 151).

cacao powder

Cacao, besides being delicious, is considered a superfood because it is a rich source of flavonoids, magnesium, zinc, iron, potassium, fiber, and proteins. Cacao has powerful antioxidant and anti-inflammatory agents that offer neuron protection, inhibit mental fatigue, and enhance cognition and mood. Other benefits include lowering immunoglobulin E release in allergic responses and positively affecting the immune response and bacterial growth at intestinal levels.

NOTE: It's important to look for cacao powder, not cocoa powder. Cacao powder is minimally processed and has superior nutritional properties and benefits, while cocoa powder is roasted at a higher temperature and typically supplemented with additives to cut the bitterness.

RECOMMENDED BRANDS: Zeal Superfoods, Zint, BetterBody Foods

WHERE TO BUY: Amazon, Walmart

the origin of cacao

Cacao was born in the Amazon jungle and spread north, entrancing everyone in its path. It is not clear exactly when or how it got to Central America, but there the Mesoamerican cultures transformed it into a mystical drink called xocolatl.

There are two types of cacao, common cacao and fine aroma cacao. The latter makes superior-quality chocolate, in which herbal, fruity, and even honey notes can be distinguished.

It is believed that the genetic origin of fine aroma cacao is southern Peru and that it was transported through the jungle on rivers. It is said that the first cacao beans were sent to Europe by Fray Jerónimo de Aguilar, along with the xocolatl recipe. It became popular throughout Europe, and cacao conquered the world!

how to recognize a good chocolate

A pure chocolate (100 percent) should have only the following in its list of ingredients: organic chocolate liquor. A chocolate with less than 100 percent chocolate liquor might include a sweetener (my favorite is organic coconut sugar) and organic cacao butter. Either way, the ingredient list should not contain any additives, artificial sweeteners, lecithins, dairy, soy, gluten, or ingredients that you cannot pronounce.

cacao nibs

Cacao nibs are fermented, dried, roasted, and crushed cacao beans. They are pieces of real chocolate in its purest expression—that is, without added sugar. Nibs contain all the nutrients and benefits of cacao powder and have a crunchy texture that enhances all sorts of recipes. Processing the nibs will yield cacao liquor, which is pure chocolate paste. You can find cacao nibs in my Chocolate Granola (page 43).

RECOMMENDED BRANDS: FGO, Anthony's, Zint, Terrasoul Superfoods

WHERE TO BUY: natural food stores, supermarkets (Whole Foods, Sprouts, Walmart, Kroger), and Amazon

camu camu

A native fruit of the Amazon that can be found in the wildest Peruvian jungle, camu camu is extremely acidic. In America it is generally sold in powder form or as a frozen pulp, but in Peru, where you can find it fresh, it can be processed into juices, smoothies, liqueurs, jams, and granitas. It is famous for being extraordinarily rich in vitamin C, which gives it a very high antioxidant capacity. In addition, it is an excellent source of minerals and has anti-inflammatory, liver-protective, and antibacterial properties.

Consuming camu camu is strongly associated with better health and higher bacterial diversity in the gut microbiota. You can find camu camu in my Homemade Protein Powder Mix (page 300).

WHERE TO BUY: supermarkets (Whole Foods, Sprouts, Thrive Market, Walmart), Amazon

carob

The carob tree is native to the Mediterranean region and the Middle East and has adapted to many other parts of the world. Both carob and algarrobo (plants of the same variety) can be processed into syrup and flour with a flavor that reminds us of chocolate, but they don't contain caffeine or theobromine. Carob is naturally high in fiber and contains vitamins A and B.

You can find carob in my AIP Chocolate Chip Cookies (page 213).

RECOMMENDED BRAND: Australian Carob Co.

WHERE TO BUY: Kroger, Amazon

cashews

Cashews are not only delicious to snack on by themselves; they're also one of the most versatile ingredients in healthy cooking and are often used to replace dairy. Cashews contain high-quality protein and monounsaturated fatty acids and are a great source of minerals such as copper, manganese, magnesium, and phosphorus. They help reduce triglyceride levels and lower blood pressure, which helps to reduce the risk of cardiovascular disorders. They are cholesterol-free, high in antioxidants, and—thanks to the amount of magnesium they contain—help reduce anxiety and migraines. Finally, they contain large amounts of tryptophan, the precursor amino acid for the synthesis of serotonin, a neurotransmitter that is associated with the feeling of well-being—so it might be said that eating cashews is totally heavenly.

coconut

Coconut is classified as a highly nutritious "functional food" and has been used in Ayurvedic medicine for thousands of years. Both coconut meat and coconut water have abundant medicinal and nutritional properties. Coconut water contains vitamins, minerals, electrolytes, amino acids, and phytohormones, making it a great replacement for commercial sports drinks, and coconut meat is a source of healthy fat, protein, and fiber, as well as some essential minerals.

coconut nectar

Coconut nectar is a syrup made from coconut sugar and water. It has a delicious caramel flavor and can be used in pancakes, waffles, or beverages, and as a replacement for any liquid sweetener in pastries.

RECOMMENDED BRAND: Wildly Organic

WHERE TO BUY: Amazon

coconut sugar

Palm sugar comes from the trunks of palm trees, while coconut sugar is harvested by tapping the flower sap of coconut palm trees. These two different sugars come with different harvesting methods. Even when organic, sugar is sugar, and less is always better. But I consider coconut sugar to be a great choice because it contains some iron, zinc, calcium, potassium, short-chain fatty acids, polyphenols and other antioxidants, and a fiber known as inulin.

RECOMMENDED BRANDS: Anthony's, Madhava, 365 by Whole Foods Market

WHERE TO BUY: Whole Foods, Amazon, Sprouts

green banana flour / plantain flour

Green banana flour comes from unripe bananas, and plantain flour comes from unripe plantains. Although they come from different varieties of the banana plant, the flours can be used interchangeably; green banana flour is just slightly darker and sweeter than plantain flour.

Both flours are sources of indigestible carbohydrates (also known as resistant starch) that serve as prebiotic food for the microorganisms of the intestinal microbiota, stimulating the growth of certain beneficial species (mainly bifidobacteria and lactobacilli). Remember that balance in our intestinal microbiota reduces inflammation and provides other health benefits, such as lowering blood sugar and improving insulin sensitivity. From my point of view, these benefits—along with the vitamins and minerals they contain—make them the healthiest flours that exist.

My favorite is plantain flour, since the color is lighter and it does not add as much flavor as the green banana flour. But I strongly recommend using green banana flour for the Spiced Green Banana Drink recipe (page 259) because there we need the sweet banana flavor to stand out. You can use green banana flour or plantain flour in my AIP Sandwich Bread (page 188), AIP Chocolate Chip Cookies (page 213), and Dark Cacao Tart with Berries (page 243).

RECOMMENDED BRANDS: Let's Do Organic green banana flour, LiveKuna organic plantain flour

WHERE TO BUY: Walmart, Amazon

guayusa

Guayusa is a native plant of the Amazon rainforest whose leaves are used primarily in the preparation of tea. The young leaves have the highest concentration of antioxidants (even more so than green tea) and have amazing antibacterial, anti-inflammatory, stimulant, and energy-enhancing properties. The flavor of guayusa is very similar to that of yerba mate, a strong tea that is one of my favorites. Both plants are members of the holly family, but from different species. Guayusa leaves contain magnesium, calcium, zinc, potassium, vitamins D and C, and high levels of caffeine, which is released slowly and evenly, helping to promote energy without the impact of a single big caffeine hit. Guayusa has a smooth flavor without bitterness. In addition, it contains stimulants such as theobromine and l-theanine that have a relaxing effect on the nervous system. You can find guayusa in my Guayusa Green Smoothie (page 262).

RECOMMENDED BRAND: Waykana Green Guayusa loose-leaf tea

WHERE TO BUY: Amazon

konjac (glucomannan)

Glucomannan (also known as konjac flour or konjac root powder) is a fiber extracted from the tubers of the konjac plant (*Amorphophallus konjac*). Glucomannan is the powdered root of the plant, created by slicing, drying, and then milling the corms. It has a neutral taste and adds an appealing gelatin texture. It has long been used in China, Japan, and Southeast Asia as both a food source and traditional medicine. It has wide-ranging effects, preventing many chronic diseases by regulating the metabolism. Clinical studies have shown that supplementing the diet with konjac fiber reduces levels of glucose, plasma cholesterol, and triglycerides and improves blood pressure and carbohydrate metabolism. This fiber also forms a defensive covering on the surface of the intestines, helping prevent constipation and improving the ecology of the colon, and it is a great source of prebiotic food for gut bacteria.

You can find glucomannan in my AIP Ravioli with Oxtail Sauce (page 139) or my AIP Sandwich Bread (page 188).

RECOMMENDED BRANDS: NOW supplements, Micro Ingredients Konjac Root Powder

WHERE TO BUY: Amazon

lúcuma

One of my favorite fruits, lúcuma is a native fruit of the Andes. Peruvians use it a lot in its fresh form. Its distinctive sweet flavor is perfect for smoothies, desserts, ice creams, and many other treats, and it can even be used as a sweetener (while providing many vitamins and minerals). If you can find it fresh, choose a fruit that is soft, has an intense orange color, and is so ripe that its skin opens like a flower. Today, lúcuma is available worldwide in powder form, and sometimes as frozen pulp in Latin markets and online. It is believed that the complex carbohydrates in lúcuma are more difficult to digest than simple carbohydrates and therefore produce fewer spikes in the blood, helping to keep blood sugar levels constant. Additionally, lúcuma contains insoluble dietary fiber, which helps to prevent constipation and serves as a prebiotic food for good intestinal health. You can try lúcuma in my Lucumoka drink (page 254).

WHERE TO BUY: powder: supermarkets (Whole Foods, Sprouts, Walmart, Kroger), Amazon; frozen: Latin markets

maca

Maca, a plant that grows at a very high altitude (about thirteen thousand feet) in Peru's Central Andes, is prized for its nutritional and medicinal properties. There are different varieties with different colors ranging from white to black.

Maca root is generally dried and consumed in powder form. The taste of maca is earthy and

nutty, and maca has favorable effects on energy and mood. It may help to reduce anxiety and improve sexual function, calm menopausal symptoms, and increase fertility. In addition, maca reduces glucose levels and has been linked to lower blood pressure and improved general health.

Due to its influence on hormone levels, I do not recommend that children or adolescents consume maca, but its benefits in adults can be enormous, especially during menopause. You can add maca to any smoothie, smoothie bowl, latte, chia pudding, and sweet treat. I love to use it in my Maca Power Coffee (page 255).

WHERE TO BUY: supermarkets (Whole Foods, Sprouts), Amazon

manuka honey

The manuka tree, a relative of the tea tree, grows abundantly throughout New Zealand. When hives are placed in areas where manuka trees abound, the bees feed on the nectar and produce manuka honey. The main antibacterial component of honey, methylglyoxal (MGO), is typically found in small amounts in regular honey, but in manuka honey it's found in high concentrations, turbocharging this special honey's antibacterial effect. The more MGO, the more powerful the antibacterial effect, so the antibacterial power of manuka honey is greater than in other varieties.

The unique manuka factor (UMF) rates the potency of honey—that is, how much MGO the honey contains. To be considered a therapeutic-grade honey, it must have a UMF greater than 10 (which usually means that it has more than 263+ MGO levels, but you can find options with much higher concentrations, such as one I found that was 2000+, a pharmaceutical grade).

Manuka honey also possesses antioxidant, anti-inflammatory, antimicrobial, and anticancer capabilities. Additional uses include the healing of wounds (especially those caused by diabetes), controlling gastrointestinal problems, fighting infections, and treating eczema, psoriasis, and acne.

The taste of manuka honey is mildly sweet and slightly bitter. I like to use it as a topping for my pancakes, crepes, and waffles. I also love to add it to my hot drinks or eat it directly, which is great if you are dealing with a cold or flu.

RECOMMENDED BRANDS: Wedderspoon Organic Manuka Honey UMF 16+, Biosota Organics

WHERE TO BUY: Supermarkets, Amazon

mct oil

MCT stands for "medium chain triglycerides." This is a type of fatty acid that is derived from coconut oil; yes, it is high in saturated fat, but it is the good kind. It has very potent antioxidant and antimicrobial properties that support your immune system, and it also provides antifungal, antibacterial, and even antiviral benefits.

MCT oil is widely used in ketogenic diets as a fuel for cells, as it is believed to increase both fat burning and mental clarity. Medium chain triglycerides are directly absorbed into the blood and are not stored as fat, but are quickly burned and converted into energy. If you are doing intermittent fasting, adding it to your morning coffee helps you start the day with energy and satiety.

RECOMMENDED BRAND: Bulletproof (Brain Octane C8 MCT Oil)

mesquite

Peruvian mesquite (called algarrobo) is a big legume tree that typically reaches more than sixty-five feet in height and can live for more than a millennium. The ripe fruits of the algarrobo are boiled to concentrate the natural sugars. They are then pressed, and the resulting extract is filtered and evaporated into a thick syrup. The syrup, called algarrobina, is a great food full of vitamins and proteins. Besides syrup, flour is made from the ground and dried pods of the tree; it's called mesquite flour in the United States and algarrobo flour in Peru.

Considered a superfood, mesquite can be substituted for cacao. It provides energy and succulent flavor and improves the mood. Mesquite contains lots of dietary fiber and protein and is low in fat and carbohydrates and rich in fatty acids; complex vitamins B, C, and E; and minerals such as magnesium, iron, calcium, zinc, iodine, selenium, and potassium. It is also a rich source of lysine, an amino acid that allows calcium to be better absorbed by our body. Mesquite has antioxidant, anti-inflammatory, antimicrobial, antifungal, antihyperglycemic, and antihypertensive effects and is believed to be an alternative and complementary medicine for the management of breast cancer—though *always* consult with your functional doctor before using for such cases.

You can find mesquite in my Mesquite Chocolate "Turrón" (page 219) and Algarrobina Cocktail (page 274).

RECOMMENDED BRAND: Zint (mesquite flour)

WHERE TO BUY: Amazon

moringa

Moringa is a perennial tropical tree native to the south of the Himalayan Mountains in northern India and distributed across many countries of the tropics and subtropics. I think of moringa as a superfood, like taking a bottle of multivitamins that grow in nature. The plant has multiple uses, whether in gastronomy, medicine, or nutrition. It contains many amino acids, antioxidants, vitamins, minerals, and flavonoids and is rich in iron and the essential nutrients necessary for iron metabolism, which makes it a great ally against malnutrition and could help to reduce anemia.

Although both the leaves and the seeds can be used, the highest concentration of nutrients is found in the leaves, which can be used fresh or in the form of capsules or powder. Its bitter, slightly sweet flavor resembles that of green tea. Add moringa to smoothies, juices, salads, stews, and soups, or use it in baked items such as my Superpowerful Brownies (page 210).

RECOMMENDED BRANDS: FGO, Organic India, Miracle Tree, Organic Veda

WHERE TO BUY: supermarkets (Sprouts, Whole Foods, Walmart, Kroger), Amazon

mulberries, dried

Mulberries, in addition to being delicious, are very nutritious and include abundant fatty acids, amino acids, vitamins, minerals, and bioactive compounds. They have been shown to have antioxidant, neuroprotective, anti-atherosclerosis, immunomodulatory, antitumor, antihyperglycemic, and hypolipidemic properties.

Mulberries are not always easy to find fresh, but you can buy them frozen. In this book I use them dried in my Sirloin and Blackberry Salad with Goldenberry Dressing (page 100) or Granola with Tigernuts, Mulberries, and Pineapple (page 41). They are also great as a snack, and you can toast them for a crunchy texture. Try them in salads, granola, cakes, energy bars, and more!

RECOMMENDED BRAND: Terrasoul, Anthony's

WHERE TO BUY: Amazon

noni juice

Noni is a tropical fruit from the Pacific Islands, Southeast Asia, Australia, and India. It has been used for thousands of years in Polynesia, both as a food source and for medicinal purposes. One of its great properties is that it helps to balance the immune system. When the immune system is overreacting, noni relaxes it, and when it is not working properly to protect the organism, noni activates it. Noni also has great anti-inflammatory and antioxidant power.

The fruit can be consumed raw or cooked in the form of juice, but noni fruit has quite an unpleasant "rotten" smell and taste for those who are not used to it, and the best way to take advantage of its properties is through fermentation. Fortunately, this fermented liquid is easy to find bottled online or at organic stores, so you don't need to ferment noni fruit at home. You can find noni juice in my Camila's Daily Noni Dose (page 277).

RECOMMENDED BRAND: Gopal's

WHERE TO BUY: supermarkets (Sprouts, Kroger, Walmart), Amazon

peruvian botija olives

Related to the Sevillian black olives from Spain, Peruvian botija olives are grown in the regions of La Libertad, Ica, Lima, Moquegua, Arequipa, and Tacna (where they are the best in flavor and size). Their name derives from the wooden botijas (pipes) in which they once were sold. Over the many years since it was first planted in Peru, this type of olive has undergone certain mutations, resulting in an olive with an incomparable and exquisite flavor. What's more, it is considered a superfood, full of monounsaturated fat (the good kind), vitamins A and E, calcium, and antioxidants.

Botija olives have a beautiful purple color and have a firmer, fleshy texture, and are larger in size than their Spanish predecessors. You can find Peruvian botija olives in my Olive, Raisin, and Rosemary Cauliflower Rice (page 94).

WHERE TO BUY: Latin markets, Amazon

potatoes

Potatoes are a staple of the Peruvian diet, as there are more than four thousand edible varieties grown in the country's Andean highlands. The International Potato Center in Lima has a gene bank that maintains—in vitro and in seeds—the world's largest collection of potatoes, sweet potatoes, and their wild relatives, as well as a unique collection of Andean roots and tubers, whose genetic, physiological, and biochemical attributes the scientific community has just begun to explore. The center holds that biodiversity in trust for humanity to ensure its availability for breeding and other uses, now and in the future.

In Puno, in southeastern Peru, there is a naturally freeze-dried potato called "chuño" (pronounced *chunio*). Chuño is prepared in June and July (winter in the Southern Hemisphere), when the cold reaches the high plateau of the Andes, at altitudes above 3,800 meters, and temperatures begin to drop at night to -5°C (23°F). The Andean communities take advantage of the contrast in temperatures between day and night to "mummify" (or freeze-dry) the potatoes: they are frozen at night and dehydrated in the sun during the day at temperatures that reach 18°C (64°F). The resulting potatoes, which are sweeter and lose any bitterness, are consumed a few months later, when the fresh potatoes run out. There are two varieties, black and also white, which is the same as the black but washed. As a child, my favorite chuño was the black one, and my mom was an expert at using it in her recipes.

Another fun fact about potatoes: through certain cooking techniques, we can completely transform and supercharge the type of starch from complex to resistant.

Resistant starch cannot be completely digested by our body because it is resistant to the enzymes that break down complex starches. Because of this resistance, it passes through our small intestines completely intact and acts as a prebiotic food for intestinal bacteria, increasing the "good" bacteria in our digestive system and protecting the intestinal mucosa. In addition, this starch does not convert to sugar, improving insulin response and making us feel more satiated. Overall, resistant starch can be a major tool in strengthening the immune system.

We can transform the starches in potatoes into resistant starches by baking or boiling them, then letting them cool in the fridge overnight. Another recommendation is to peel them before eating, because the peel contains the highest accumulation of solanine, an antinutrient (a substance that blocks the absorption of other nutrients).

A freshly cooked potato is not as nutritious as a potato that has been cooked and then refrigerated. Remember that when you want to prepare a delicious and super-healthy dish.

You can find potatoes in my Creamy Potato and Pea Salad (page 116).

quinoa

Quinoa (or quinua, as we call it in Peru) has been domesticated and cultivated in Peru for more than five thousand years. The Lake Titicaca basin is considered to be the primary center of origin of quinoa and the conservation center for the greatest biological diversity of this species.

A relative of both beetroot and spinach, quinoa is rich in proteins, lipids, fibers, vitamins, and minerals and contains an extraordinary balance of essential amino acids. It is an excellent source of thiamine, folic acid, and vitamin C. Its seeds contain high concentrations of calcium, phosphorus, magnesium, iron, zinc, potassium, and copper. In fact, its calcium, zinc, and iron content is the highest of any other cereal (quinoa is not technically a cereal but is often treated like one).

Because the outer layers of quinoa contain saponins, antinutrients that prevent the absorption of certain nutrients, before quinoa is packaged for sale these layers are removed through a traditional process of passing the quinoa through water and washing it several times. Even so, when preparing quinoa at home, I recommend washing it several times as well and then leaving it to soak overnight to eliminate any saponins that might remain. This method also starts the germination process, which will reduce quinoa's bitterness, enhance its nutritional value, and make it more digestible. You can find quinoa in my Quinoa Porridge (page 54) or Milky Quinoa with Shrimp (page 168).

WHERE TO BUY: supermarkets, Costco, Amazon

sacha inchi seeds

Sacha inchi is a superfood that is believed to have originated in the Amazon around three thousand years ago. It is native to and most abundant in the Peruvian jungle.

Its fruit is cultivated for its large, edible seeds, which are found in dark brown star-shaped pods (similar in appearance to anise pods but much larger). Sacha inchi seeds are very similar to nuts; they're also known as the peanut of the Incas, and you can eat them toasted plain as a snack, with salt, or with some dressing. In powder form, sacha inchi can be used in a variety of recipes or simply added to smoothies or lattes, or as a topping for nut yogurts. Additionally, oils can be extracted from the seeds and used in salad dressings and skin-care products.

Sacha inchi is considered to be one of the best vegan protein sources in the world, at 33 percent protein, far exceeding soy (23 percent) and sunflower (24 percent). It also has anti-inflammatory properties, so it is very useful for

people suffering from arthritis, rheumatism, and osteoporosis. It has high amounts of antioxidants and vitamins A and E, as well as high levels of omega-3, omega-6, and omega-9. Sacha inchi helps reduce high cholesterol and triglyceride levels. In addition, it helps to regulate blood pressure and prevent heart attacks, protecting the heart and shielding against metabolic syndrome. It is a great energizer, so it is an excellent tool for combating exhaustion, tiredness, insomnia, and stress. When I was pregnant, I was always looking for an omega supplement that would benefit my babies, and the ones I liked the most were fish oil and sacha inchi oil.

You can find sacha inchi in my Homemade Protein Powder Mix (page 300).

WHERE TO BUY: supermarkets (Kroger, Sprouts, Walmart), Amazon

salt

Salt is a very important mineral for our health, but it is important to remember to balance salt intake with potassium in order to maintain healthy blood pressure (too little potassium and too much sodium can cause high blood pressure). Normally if you are diagnosed with high blood pressure, a low-salt diet is recommended, but I think it's important to evaluate where the salt you consume comes from (and which sources of potassium you're including), since processed products are loaded with low-quality salt. A pure salt is not the same as what comes in, for example, cereal or fast food; different types of salt vary greatly in quality and nutrition. I recommend avoiding refined table salt, which typically contains additives. Instead, use real sea salt, Himalayan salt, or Maras salt. Better still, use a variety of these healthy salts, since they all have different proportions of minerals. So mix and match, and find your favorite salt combinations!

My preferred brand in the United States is Redmond Real Salt, but it's very expensive so I buy it only when it's on sale. Maras salt can be found on Amazon, and Himalayan salt is available everywhere. There are lots of quality salts to be found; just look for unrefined salt that's full of minerals.

RECOMMENDED BRANDS: Redmond Real Salt, Celtic Sea Salt, Himalayan salt, Maras salt

WHERE TO BUY: supermarkets (Whole Foods, Sprouts), natural food stores, Amazon

sauerkraut

Fermented foods (or beverages) are produced by controlled microbial growth and conversion of food components through enzymatic action. They provide many health benefits, including antioxidant, antimicrobial, antifungal, anti-inflammatory, antidiabetic, and anti-atherosclerotic (preventing the development of arterial plaque) activity. Sauerkraut is produced by lactic acid fermentation and is a big source of probiotics (lactobacilli). The fermentation process also increases the bioavailability of nutrients provided by cabbage.

It is important to include fermented items in our diet, and a good way to start is with sauerkraut. Choose a brand that has not been pasteurized and that contains only cabbage and salt.

You can find sauerkraut in my Smoked Salmon and Avocado Toast (page 65) and Stuffed Avocado (page 82).

tigernuts

Tigernuts are not actually nuts; they are small, brown, rough round tubers found on the roots of the herbaceous plant *Cyperus esculentus*. They can be found around the world but have origins in Africa going back at least two million years.

Tigernuts have a slightly sweet and starchy flavor and are high in good fats, fiber, biotin, vitamin B7, and essential minerals. They also contain arginine (an α-amino acid that is used in the biosynthesis of proteins and helps improve circulation and blood pressure); are a good source of carbohydrates, protein, and antioxidants; and help to lower cholesterol and triglycerides. The fat in tigernut milk consists of between 70 percent and 80 percent monounsaturated fatty acids (healthy fats), in particular oleic acid, which helps to strengthen cell membranes.

Sliced tigernuts replace oats in many AIP recipes. They are also available whole and peeled, sliced, and in the forms of flour and "butter." If using tigernut flour, you should sift it before using it, as it is usually very lumpy. One of the most popular forms of tigernut consumption in Spain is as horchata, essentially a spiced tigernut milk (although you can find drinks labeled "horchata" made from other ingredients). You can find tigernuts in my Granola with Tigernuts, Mulberries, and Pineapple (page 41) and Strawberry Tigernut Smoothie (page 267).

RECOMMENDED BRANDS: Anthony's, Organic Gemini

WHERE TO BUY: Amazon

turmeric

Turmeric is a spice that comes from the root of the *Curcuma longa* plant, a perennial in the ginger family. Its active ingredient, curcumin, gives turmeric its well-known yellow-orange color. Curcumin is high in antioxidants, has powerful anti-inflammatory properties, and plays an important role in the prevention and treatment of various conditions ranging from cancer to autoimmune, neurological, cardiovascular, and diabetic diseases. Since hidden inflammation is at the root of all chronic illness, turmeric helps manage conditions like metabolic syndrome, arthritis, lupus, and even anxiety and hyperlipidemia.

Ingesting curcumin by itself does not produce these health benefits due to its poor bioavailability, but combining it with other compounds can drastically increase its efficacy. For example, when combined with piperine (the main active component of black pepper), curcumin's bioavailability increases by 2,000 percent. Also, turmeric is fat soluble (it dissolves in fat), so consuming it with fat helps improve its absorption in your bloodstream.

RECOMMENDED BRANDS: I look for organic single-ingredient brands, including Anthony's, FGO, or Spice Train; you can find fresh turmeric, too, but its staining power is real!

yacon

Yacon, a tuber native to the Andean regions of South America, is an abundant source of fructooligosaccharides (FOS) and is used as a substitute for sugar. It contains a large amount of prebiotic fiber (inulin)—that is, it contributes to the growth of good bacteria that promote intestinal health while reducing the population of pathogenic bacteria. It also helps regulate the immune response, glucose levels, and fat metabolism.

The most common form of yacon (and the most delicious) is the syrup, but you can also find it as a flour and as an extract in capsule form. It can be used to replace any sweetener, such as maple syrup, agave, honey, sugar, and so on, offering a really low glycemic index. But if you can find it, I highly recommend trying fresh raw yacon root (my preferred way to eat it). You can eat it peeled and sliced and add as is to smoothies or juices, giving a delicious (and super-healthy) sweetness. Living in Lima, I liked to freeze it sliced, so I always had it on hand to add to my smoothies or juices. Jam can also be made from fresh yacon by grating it and cooking it with raw, unprocessed cane sugar; it's one of my family's favorite jams.

For a recipe using yacon syrup, see my Chocolate Granola (page 43).

WHERE TO BUY: Amazon, Latin markets

yuca

Yuca, or cassava root, is rich in starch content, an excellent source of energy, and a good source of vitamin C and A, thiamine, riboflavin, and niacin. Yuca contains a certain amount of free cyanide, which can result in sickness if not properly handled by peeling, soaking, and cooking well before consumption. The best way to process yuca is to remove and discard the center, which contains a fibrous vein that has high cyanide levels, then soak the rest for a couple of hours in water before cooking. You can also find cassava flour, which is a wonderful ingredient for gluten-free cooking. You can find yuca in my Yuca Crackers (page 198).

RECOMMENDED BRAND: Otto's (cassava flour)

WHERE TO BUY: fresh: supermarkets, Latin markets; cassava flour: supermarkets, online

a note on dietary plans

I WANT MY RECIPES to be accessible from a wide variety of dietary angles. Please note the following:

- *All the recipes in this book are gluten-free and dairy-free. For this to be assured throughout your diet, always check that the ingredients you use are 100 percent gluten-free and dairy-free.*

- *When a recipe is labeled as vegetarian, it means that it may contain eggs.*

- *When a recipe is labeled as vegan, it means that it does not contain any kind of food of animal origin, but it can include bee honey, which some vegans object to. As an alternative sweetener, I'd recommend coconut sugar, coconut nectar, pure maple syrup, maple sugar, date syrup, date sugar, agave, yacon syrup, or sucanat/panela (raw unprocessed cane sugar, which is in its most natural state).*

- *When a recipe is labeled as paleo (see below), in addition to being dairy- and gluten-free, it is free of grains, legumes, and processed ingredients.*

- *When the recipe is labeled AIP (see page 19), in addition to being dairy- and gluten-free, it is free of grains, legumes, eggs, nightshades, alcohol, processed ingredients, nuts, and seeds.*

what is the paleo diet?

The paleo diet is a way of eating that focuses on nutrient-dense ingredients and avoids all kinds of processed and refined foods. This diet is also known as the evolutionary diet or the hunter-gatherer diet and is based on the diet of humans during the Paleolithic Era, which occurred between ten thousand and two million years ago. During that time, humans ate insects, wild plants, fruits, tubers, roots, animals, eggs, fish, and shellfish.

The principles of the paleo diet are based on the belief that our bodies have not evolved to eat and digest the foods produced through agriculture (which appeared only ten thousand years ago in the Mesopotamian region), especially modern agriculture (which is fertilizer-based, with many ingredients grown rapidly and genetically modified), and that the inflammation created by modern food production has contributed to the prevalence of many chronic diseases, such as obesity, type 2 diabetes, and cardiovascular disease.

Paleo eating is based on foods such as 100 percent grass-fed and grass-finished beef, pastured chicken and eggs, pasture-raised heritage pork, wild-caught seafood, and fruits, vegetables, nuts, seeds, and fats in their most organic and natural forms. Contrary to what many people may think, it is not a meat-based diet but a diet balanced between the consumption of proteins (including beef, pork, poultry, seafood, lamb, game, and organ meats—any kind of real and well-raised animals), healthy fats, nuts, seeds, fruits, and—a guideline that is not well known—many, many vegetables.

what is the aip diet?

The AIP (autoimmune protocol) diet is based on the principles of the paleo diet and aims to reduce inflammation, pain, and other symptoms caused by autoimmune diseases, such as lupus, celiac disease, and rheumatoid arthritis, among others.

The best doctor to supervise this kind of diet (and the supplements involved in the treatments) is a doctor of functional medicine (check out the website of the Institute for Functional Medicine for more information). Usually, a very strict elimination phase is carried out for a month, and then different foods are introduced one by one to see how the body tolerates them and to identify those that cause the greatest reaction in each individual. Some people are able to include more foods than others after this phase.

Foods to avoid while following the AIP diet include gluten, dairy, grains, legumes, eggs, seeds, nuts, nightshades, alcohol, and absolutely all processed and refined foods.

recommended books

When I began to see food as my only tool to help improve my daughters' health, since nothing else was working, the first thing I did was research on the internet.

I have always liked to study. I was not lucky enough to be able to go to university, but I really enjoy researching and learning, so I started taking notes, cross-checking information, reading scientific research (because obviously not everything on the internet is true), and looking for experts who could shed light on what the path to follow should be.

One of my favorite authors and functional medicine doctors is Dr. Mark Hyman, whom I dream of talking with one day; he has experienced firsthand what it is like to have a disease and how food can change our lives. All his books are spectacular, but my favorite is perhaps *The Pegan Diet,* and of course, his podcasts are extremely enriching.

Dr. Frank Lipman is another leader in functional medicine whom I admire a lot and whose work was an incredible help in managing my early menopause; one of his books, *The New Rules of Aging Well,* has especially great information.

Dr. Terry Wahls is an amazing woman, an MS warrior with such a wonderful vision about food that always includes fermented foods. I recommend you read *The Wahls Protocol.*

Someone I admire very much from the Spanish-speaking world is Carlos Pérez, an expert in psychoneuroimmunology. He has some brilliant talks online, as well as a book called *Paleovida.*

Another book that helped me to understand how autoimmune diseases work is *The Paleo Approach* by Sarah Ballantyne, and I love the authenticity and accuracy of the work of Dave Asprey, creator of the Bulletproof brand and expert in intermittent fasting, especially his book *Fast This Way.*

And of course, we are complex beings, and to complete the tools that benefit our health, I am a big proponent of meditation. Scientific evidence shows that it can improve our physical health, and even modify our genes, in addition to helping us relax and calm the mind.

My favorite meditations are those of Dr. Joe Dispenza, whose website offers many amazing, guided meditations and all the scientific proof, done in conjunction with the University of California in San Diego, that shows how meditation can change our lives. His blog is well worth reading. He has written three *New York Times* bestselling books, and my favorite is *You Are the Placebo.*

a note on measurements

I CREATED MY RECIPES using grams as measurements. Peru uses the metric system, and beyond that, measuring in grams is the most accurate way to produce an error-proof recipe. Some ingredients are very difficult to measure in cups, especially when there are so many brands and varieties of the same ingredient. Even the amount of a cup can vary depending on the country you are in; in some countries one cup is 250 milliliters, and in other countries it is 236 milliliters, for example. Cup, tablespoon, and teaspoon measurements are included as they are the most commonly used system in the United States, but I highly recommend that you pick up a scale and try using grams if you haven't in the past, especially if you have perfectionist tendencies and do a lot of baking. My recipes call for nonstandard flours (e.g., almond, coconut, tigernuts, lúcuma), and different brands of these flours are ground differently; therefore an equal volume in cups may yield different weights, depending on the brand.

Another example—bananas can vary in size, and even when you cut them, the cuts can be larger or smaller, filling the measuring cups in different ways. Or when it comes to ice, different brands of ice makers or trays produce different sizes and shapes. And depending on the brand of frozen fruit, some pieces will be larger and others smaller, meaning that they won't fit consistently in a measuring cup.

I used "large" eggs to create these recipes, but I've found that they aren't always consistent in size. The eggs in these recipes weigh between 50 and 60 grams without their shells (the shell adds 10 grams to the egg).

Here's how I make smoothies easily: Set a blender container on a scale and weigh the ingredients as you put them in. You'll thank me when you have fewer messy cups and spoons to wash!

my favorite cooking tools

TO COOK HEALTHY and healing foods at home, having the right cooking equipment will make your life easier. The tools below are those that I consider indispensable and use regularly, both at Cristy's Kitchen and in my home kitchen.

coffee and spice grinder

Although I'm not a fan of drinking coffee, I do love the aroma of it freshly ground. I recommend using a coffee grinder for the best results, and you can find them with a little spice grinding attachment, which is very handy. While my preferred grinding option is the mortar and pestle (see page 24), certain spices are very hard to grind, and sometimes you just don't have that much time. In such cases, a spice grinder is just fantastic! A store-bought spice mix can never compete with your own home-roasted, freshly ground version.

RECOMMENDED BRAND: KitchenAid Blade Coffee and Spice Grinder Combo Pack

cold-press juicer

I often get asked what type of juicer I recommend. My favorite is a cold-press juicer because it slowly squeezes all the juice from fruit, vegetables, and herbs while maintaining their nutritional properties and benefits. With a cold-press juicer, you can obtain more nutrients and more juice as well, which saves money because you have less waste. If you're con-sidering buying a cold-press juicer, look for a stainless steel one.

If you're using a centrifuge juicer, I recommend drinking the juice immediately after making it, because the centrifugal extractors have metal blades that move at high speed, producing heat. This causes the ingredients to oxidize; as a result, the nutritional benefits begin to decline rapidly.

I love to use my cold-press juicer when making Green Juice (page 269).

RECOMMENDED BRANDS: Nama, Omega Juicer or, if your budget allows, the stainless steel Angel Juicer

dehydrator

Dehydrated food is a complex and complete world—and it's not just about dehydrated fruits and vegetables. I urge you to look into the amazing universe of modern dehydrated food recipes out there. As a bonus, if you dehydrate your favorite snacks yourself, you'll save lots of money. For an example of the joys of a good dehydrator, see my Coconut Bacon recipe (page 61).

RECOMMENDED BRAND: Excalibur

food processor

In healthy cooking we use a lot of nuts and seeds. The best way to chop them quickly is with a good-quality food processor. I use my

food processor for many other things as well— to make the base of a cheesecake, Cashew Parmesan (page 301), doughs, crusts, and purees, and to chop veggies as well. I recommend a large food processor that can hold between 11 and 14 cups and that comes with a separate smaller container, which allows you to make large or small batches. Some processors also include a spiralizer attachment, which is super useful for spiralizing vegetables that can be used to make veggie "pasta" or to spiralize fruit for a quick apple pie or a fruit salad made with apples and pears.

RECOMMENDED BRAND: Cuisinart

high-powered blender

A high-powered blender is one of the best investments you can make in kitchen equipment (when we came to the United States, we brought only clothes and my blender in our suitcases—that's how important it is to me). A high-powered blender enables you to extract all the juices and oils out of nuts, ensuring that nut milks come out rich and creamy. It also increases your control over the consistency of your blended mixtures, allowing you to create smoothies that range from super silky to ice cream–like. An example of the latter is the Spiced Pumpkin Smoothie Bowl with Caramelized Bananas (page 36).

RECOMMENDED BRAND: Vitamix

instant pot

The multiple functions of an Instant Pot will make your life easier. It can be used as a pressure cooker to speed up cooking times or as a slow cooker that can be left for hours or even overnight. I also like using it to air-fry food—and I absolutely love the yogurt function, which I use to make my Coconut Yogurt (page 50).

kitchen scale and gram scale

As mentioned on page 21, I strongly encourage you to purchase and use a regular kitchen scale, but a gram scale will allow you to weigh very small quantities (such as less than 1 gram and up to 100 g). This helps to achieve precise measurements, and given that a lot of these recipes use ingredients you may not be familiar with, I want you to be set up for success!

RECOMMENDED BRANDS:

KITCHEN SCALES: MyWeigh KD Kitchen and Craft Digital Scale (with adapter); GreaterGoods Digital Kitchen Scale (with batteries)

GRAM SCALE: Fuzion TU-X Digital Pocket Scale, 200g/0.01g

mortar and pestle

Among my favorite tools is the mortar and pestle, which has been used since at least the Neolithic era, if not before. I think there's a certain magic in using traditional utensils, but beyond that, I love the coarse, rustic texture that a mortar and pestle yields when grinding herbs, seeds, nuts, spices, and other ingredients. My favorite mortar-and-pestle sets are made of stone and porcelain, and I find that the most convenient sizes are 6 inches (2-cup capacity) and larger.

pots and pans

There's much discussion around whether aluminum pans are safe. Some people believe they cause neurotoxicity and neurobehavioral alterations or are even related to neurological diseases such as Alzheimer's and Parkinson's.

My grandmother used to say, "When the river sounds, it is because it brings stones." The closest English equivalent is probably "Where there's smoke, there's fire." In other words, if there are that many concerns about aluminum, there's most likely truth to some of them. Unfortunately, as it's one of the cheapest and most used materials in the world, aluminum is very difficult to get rid of, but we can make better choices. For example, we can avoid using aluminum foil, and we can choose cast-iron, stainless steel, ceramic, glass, and even clay cookware. I also avoid using nonstick pans and instead choose high-quality food-grade silicone molds; unbleached, chlorine-free, nontoxic, and eco-friendly paper liners; or parchment paper when baking.

RECOMMENDED BRANDS: cast iron—Le Creuset, Staub, Lodge; nonstick ceramic-coated pans—Our Place; crepe pan—de Buyer; silicone molds—Freshware; food storage and baking—Pyrex; liners and parchment paper—If You Care

a note on cleaning products and cosmetics

WHILE WE ARE CHANGING OUR DIET in order to have healthier bodies and minds, we should also focus on the cleaning products we use in our homes and the beauty products we put on our bodies. What we breathe and what we absorb through our skin influences our health more than you can imagine. So, just as you should be looking carefully at the ingredient lists of the foods you consume, it's important to review the ingredients in our cleaning products and cosmetics. In the process, you may come to realize you can cut way back on the number of products you use—and save a lot of money in the process. In our house, we use baking soda and vinegar to clean almost everything. And we don't need sprays, air fresheners, or artificial deodorizers; we can simply use essential oils, which also provide therapeutic benefits for us to enjoy.

At the bakery, regulations require that we use a dilution of water with chlorine for disinfection, and we don't need deodorizers because we always have delicious stuff in the oven making our kitchen smell great!

The same goes with skin, oral, and hair products; there are abundant excellent brands available today that use organic ingredients, and you can find many recipes online to make your own products. But I've come to realize that we usually don't need that many creams and lotions for our skin because the health of our skin comes from our gut. If our gut is in balance, our skin will look fantastic. Our skin (like part of the whole, perfect, and integrated machine that is our body) shows us signs that something is happening inside us. So we have to focus on what we put in our mouths before we go searching for an expensive anti-aging cream.

breakfast

a note on coconut cream

WHEN A RECIPE REFERS TO THE "SOLID PART" OF COCONUT CREAM:
If you're using homemade coconut cream, make the Coconut Milk recipe (page 307), but only with cold water, and refrigerate it until the fat separates, rises to the top, and is solid enough to scoop with a spoon.

If you're using canned coconut cream, make sure you buy organic without guar gum. Refrigerate the can overnight or for a few days (depends on the brand, as some need more time to thicken than others) before using to ensure that the cream layer solidifies. (Even pure coconut cream contains some water.) I always have two cans in the fridge ready to use. Don't shake the can before opening to ensure that the cream and water remain separate. From there, you can open the can and scoop out the solid cream layer.

RECOMMENDED BRANDS:
Let's Do Organic,
Native Forest

golden milk pancakes

MAKES 12 PANCAKES, TO SERVE 4 TO 6

Golden milk is a medicinal drink from Ayurvedic cuisine with enormous anti-inflammatory properties. In my house, when someone gets sick, especially with a respiratory illness like the flu, I prescribe two or three glasses of golden milk daily. However, golden milk has quite a strong flavor, making it difficult to convince my younger daughters to take their medicine. So I'm always thinking of other ways to give them this anti-inflammatory blend, and these pancakes are a winning recipe and a delicious addition to our morning repertoire.

IN a high-powered blender, combine the cashew flour, almond flour, shredded coconut, baking powder, baking soda, vinegar, turmeric, cinnamon, pepper, coconut cream, eggs, banana, and maple syrup and blend until very smooth and lump-free.

HEAT a large cast-iron skillet or griddle over medium heat and melt 1 teaspoon of coconut oil. Form pancakes by pouring or scooping ¼-cup portions of the batter onto the skillet, leaving enough room between each pancake to avoid contact. Let cook until the bottom turns light brown and becomes firm enough to flip over, about 1 minute. Flip and continue to cook until golden brown in spots and cooked through, another minute or so.

REPEAT with the remaining batter, adding more coconut oil to the pan if your pancakes start to stick.

SERVE with honey and fresh berries. To freeze the pancakes, let cool to room temperature, then freeze in freezer-safe bags or containers for up to 4 months.

½ cup (60 g) cashew flour

½ cup (60 g) superfine blanched almond flour (such as Bob's Red Mill brand)

½ cup (50 g) unsweetened shredded coconut (such as Let's Do Organic brand)

1 teaspoon Homemade Baking Powder (page 297)

½ teaspoon baking soda

½ teaspoon apple cider vinegar (see page 3)

1 teaspoon ground turmeric (see page 16)

½ teaspoon ground cinnamon

Pinch of freshly ground black pepper

⅓ cup (83 g) coconut cream without guar gum (such as Let's Do Organic), solid part only (see Note on page 28)

5 large eggs, at room temperature

⅓ cup (45 g) small-diced banana

1 tablespoon pure maple syrup

Organic extra virgin coconut oil, as needed to cook the pancakes

½ cup honey, for drizzling

Fresh berries, such as strawberries, blueberries, or raspberries, for serving

lúcuma pancakes

MAKES 10 PANCAKES, TO SERVE 5

5 large eggs, at room temperature

½ cup plus 2 tablespoons (80 g) superfine blanched almond flour (such as Bob's Red Mill brand)

⅓ cup (50 g) lúcuma powder (see page 9)

¼ cup (28 g) coconut flour (such as as Let's Do Organic brand)

⅓ cup (85 g) unsweetened applesauce

1 tablespoon pure maple syrup

1 teaspoon Homemade Baking Powder (page 297)

½ teaspoon baking soda

1 teaspoon apple cider vinegar (see page 3)

Pinch of sea salt

Organic extra virgin coconut oil, as needed to cook the pancakes

Yacon syrup, for serving (see page 17)

2 bananas, peeled and sliced, for serving

My favorite places in any town are the local markets; they are the heart of a city, a beacon of culture, and a treasure trove in the form of fruits and vegetables. When I lived in Lima, there was a very traditional market where you could buy a huge variety of fruits and vegetables, which were usually abundant throughout the year. This was the best place to find the most perfect lúcuma fruit in the whole city, with the freshest, sweetest, and creamiest flesh, which invited you to bite right into it. Finding these fresh treasures in the United States is a bit difficult, but we are lucky to be able to find lúcuma in powder form in any health-food store. The flavor of the powder harmonizes with any recipe, giving it a dessert-like flavor.

IN a high-powered blender, combine ⅓ cup (80 g) water, the eggs, almond flour, lúcuma powder, coconut flour, applesauce, maple syrup, baking powder, baking soda, vinegar, and salt and blend until smooth.

HEAT a large cast-iron skillet or griddle over medium heat and melt 1 teaspoon of coconut oil. Form pancakes by pouring or scooping ¼-cup portions of the batter onto the skillet, leaving enough room between each to avoid contact. Let cook until the bottom turns light brown and becomes firm enough to flip over, about 1 minute. Flip and continue to cook until golden brown in spots and cooked through, another minute or so.

REPEAT with the remaining batter, adding more coconut oil to the pan if your pancakes start to stick.

SERVE with yacon syrup and sliced bananas. To freeze the pancakes, let cool to room temperature, then freeze in freezer-safe bags or containers for up to 4 months.

blue smoothie bowl

MAKES 1 SERVING

smoothie bowl

9.5 ounces (270 g) frozen banana chunks (about 3 medium bananas)

2.5 ounces (70 g) frozen diced avocado

3.5 ounces (100 g) frozen pineapple chunks

1 cup (240 g) Coconut Milk (page 307) or canned organic coconut milk without guar gum (such as Native Forest's Simple)

2 teaspoons blue spirulina powder (see page 4)

optional toppings

Sliced banana

Fresh berries, such as raspberries, blueberries, strawberries, and blackberries

Fresh dragon fruit, peeled and diced

Fresh kiwi, peeled and diced

Granola with Tigernuts, Mulberries, and Pineapple (page 41)

You can make this recipe as you would a work of art, and if you have kids, they'll love the creative process. Playing with different fruits and colors is a wonderful way to introduce children to new flavors and textures that they might not usually dare to try. Let them cut their fruit into different shapes and encourage them to decorate their bowls in the most imaginative way they can. There's nothing more energizing than starting the day with a wide variety of colors and nutrients along with a heaping spoonful of creativity. You can even eat this smoothie bowl for lunch as a midday pick-me-up!

IN a high-powered blender, combine the banana, avocado, pineapple, coconut milk, and spirulina. Blend, using the tamper to press down as needed, until the mixture has a very smooth, ice cream–like texture.

TRANSFER the mixture to a serving bowl and, if desired, decorate with sliced bananas, berries, dragon fruit, kiwi, and granola, keeping some of the surface bare so you can see the blue color of the smoothie underneath. Serve immediately.

See the photo on page 34.

cacao smoothie bowl

MAKES 1 SERVING

How right romantics are in giving chocolate to those they love: cacao is literally good for our hearts and happiness. Frozen bananas are normally used to add creaminess to a smoothie bowl, but here, neutral-flavored zucchini adds creaminess without overshadowing the wonderful chocolate flavor. I often make smoothie bowls, but there are smoothie bowls and there is *the* smoothie bowl, and when I add cacao, Sebas knows it's a special breakfast that comes with extra love and care for his heart. Remember, if you want to give love, a cacao bowl is a glorious offering!

IN a high-powered blender, combine the zucchini, avocado, coconut milk, MCT oil, cacao powder, nut butter, cacao nibs, mushroom powder, dates, and protein powder (if using). Blend, using the tamper to press down as needed, until the mixture has a very smooth, ice cream–like texture.

TRANSFER the mixture to a serving bowl and top with the granola, bananas, and blueberries. Serve immediately.

See the photo on page 35.

smoothie bowl

3.6 ounces (104 g) frozen peeled, diced zucchini

1.7 ounces (50 g) frozen diced avocado

1 cup (240 g) Coconut Milk (page 307), canned organic coconut milk without guar gum (such as Native Forest's Simple), or Almond Milk (page 304)

1 tablespoon MCT oil (see page 10)

2 tablespoons (15 g) cacao powder (see page 5)

1 tablespoon nut butter of your choice, such as raw almond butter, cashew butter, or mixed nut butter

1 teaspoon cacao nibs (see page 6)

1 teaspoon adaptogenic mushroom powder (see page 2)

2 Medjool dates, pitted and finely chopped

1 serving (6 tablespoons/60 g) Homemade Protein Powder Mix (optional; page 300)

suggested toppings

Chocolate Granola (page 43)

Bananas, peeled and sliced

Fresh blueberries

spiced pumpkin smoothie bowl with caramelized bananas

MAKES 1 SERVING

toppings

1 tablespoon organic extra virgin coconut oil

1 firm but ripe banana, cut into 1-inch slices

2 teaspoons maple sugar (such as Coombs Family Farms brand)

Pinch of Pumpkin Spice Mix (page 299)

Pumpkin Granola (page 38), for serving

smoothie bowl

½ cup (125 g) homemade or canned pumpkin puree

4.8 ounces (135 g) frozen banana, sliced in three large pieces

2 tablespoons (50 g) raw almond butter

2 Medjool dates, pitted and finely chopped

⅓ cup (80 g) Almond Milk (page 304)

½ cup (70 g) ice cubes

1½ teaspoons Pumpkin Spice Mix (page 299)

Living in Georgia and enjoying the four seasons for the first time has been very exciting for me. I grew up in a place with no fall season, with weather that is gray and boring most of the year. If you grew up in a wonderful place like Georgia, perhaps you are used to the colors of autumn and the leaves falling synchronously from the trees like a symphony. But for me, every drifting leaf thrills me and every vibrant pumpkin takes my breath away, filling me with a deep sense of gratitude for life.

As soon as pumpkins begin to appear in grocery stores, I become ecstatic knowing that autumn has arrived—I can practically smell the spices! Soon, my kitchen begins to fill with pumpkin recipes. I could eat pumpkin by the spoonful, but I wanted it a bit sweeter—so I made a scrumptious version that is almost a dessert. Have a bite, close your eyes, and enjoy a cozy fall day.

FOR THE TOPPINGS: Melt the coconut oil in a skillet over medium heat.

ADD the banana slices to the skillet and sprinkle with 1 teaspoon of the maple sugar. Cook until the sugar melts and caramelizes the bananas, 2 to 3 minutes. Flip gently with a spatula and again sprinkle with the remaining teaspoon maple sugar. Cook until caramelized on the second side, 2 to 3 minutes.

TRANSFER the bananas to a plate and sprinkle a pinch of pumpkin spice mix on top.

FOR THE SMOOTHIE BOWL: In a high-powered blender, combine the pumpkin puree, bananas, almond butter, dates, almond milk, ice cubes, and pumpkin spice mix. Blend, using the tamper to press down as needed, until the mixture has a very smooth, ice cream–like texture.

TRANSFER the mixture to a bowl and top with the caramelized banana and granola. Serve immediately.

TO MAKE THIS RECIPE AIP

for the smoothie bowl

Use coconut butter in place of
the almond butter.

Use coconut milk in place of
the almond milk.

Use 1 teaspoon ground cinnamon
and ⅛ teaspoon ground cloves in
place of the Pumpkin Spice Mix.

for the toppings

Use Granola with Tigernuts,
Mulberries, and Pineapple (page 41)
in place of the Pumpkin Granola.

Use ground cinnamon in place
of the Pumpkin Spice Mix.

pumpkin granola

MAKES 8 CUPS

2 cups (332 g) hulled raw pumpkin seeds

2 cups (280 g) coarsely chopped raw walnuts

4 cups (200 g) unsweetened coconut flakes (not shredded coconut; such as Let's Do Organic brand)

1 tablespoon plus 1 teaspoon (11 g) Pumpkin Spice Mix (page 299)

½ cup plus 2 tablespoons (200 g) pure maple syrup

⅓ cup plus 1 tablespoon (100 g) homemade or canned pumpkin puree

¼ cup (80 g) raw cashew butter

2 tablespoons (32 g) organic extra virgin coconut oil

Whipped coconut cream (see Note on page 28) or Coconut Yogurt (page 50), for serving (optional)

When I was creating my Spiced Pumpkin Smoothie Bowl (page 36), I had an idea spinning in my head that would take it to the next level: adding crunchy pumpkin seeds bathed in the flavors of pumpkin pie. This would harmonize with the creaminess of the pumpkin bowl and the hot golden spiced bananas, resulting in a dish that really hugs you.

Here it is—the perfect pumpkin granola to go with the perfect pumpkin bowl. But it's great on its own, too!

PREHEAT the oven to 325°F. Line a sheet pan with parchment paper.

IN a large bowl, combine the pumpkin seeds, walnuts, coconut flakes, and pumpkin spice mix.

IN a small saucepan over low heat, combine the maple syrup, pumpkin puree, cashew butter, and coconut oil. Melt until smooth, stirring occasionally.

POUR the melted mixture into the pumpkin seed mixture and stir until well coated.

SPREAD the granola evenly on the prepared sheet pan. Bake for 15 minutes. Stir to redistribute the granola. Lower the heat to 250°F and continue baking until the granola is medium golden brown and fragrant, about 5 more minutes, taking care not to overtoast the granola.

LET the granola cool completely in the pan; it will get crispy when it cools. Store in a jar at room temperature for up to 2 months.

SERVE it with yogurt or whipped coconut cream or on top of my Spiced Pumpkin Smoothie Bowl (page 36), or eat it as a snack.

granola with tigernuts, mulberries, and pineapple

MAKES 8½ CUPS

I created this recipe for my friend (and creator of Humans of New York) Brandon Stanton, who was looking to try a cleaner, lower-sugar, more nutrient-packed diet. I started cooking for him, and we decided to almost completely eliminate sweets, even the healthiest ones like alfajores, Peruvian cookies made with dulce de leche, which Brandon could eat one after another without stopping. Eventually, I put together this fragrant, almost dessert-like granola, which allows him to include a sweet treat in his diet. Now, every time I make it for him, instead of waiting to eat it in a smoothie bowl or with coconut milk, he just lunges for the jar, opens it, and starts gobbling it down straight. It makes me happy to know that the huge portions I make for him last only a couple of days . . . if that. Maybe it's the delicate sweetness, or the crunchiness, or perhaps just the clean, wonderful ingredients that make this sin-free granola so highly addictive.

4½ cups (250 g) unsweetened coconut flakes (not shredded coconut; such as Let's Do Organic brand)

2 cups (170 g) sliced tigernuts (see page 16)

1 cup (100 g) dried white mulberries (see page 12)

1¾ cups (165 g) dried pineapple, cut with scissors into ½-inch pieces

½ cup (115 g) coconut butter (such as Nutiva brand)

½ cup (155 g) pure maple syrup

2 tablespoons plus 1 teaspoon (35 g) organic extra virgin coconut oil

PREHEAT the oven to 325°F. Line a sheet pan with parchment paper.

IN a large bowl, combine the coconut flakes, tigernuts, mulberries, and pineapple.

IN a small saucepan over medium-low heat, combine the coconut butter, maple syrup, and coconut oil. Warm, stirring occasionally, until the mixture is completely melted.

POUR the melted mixture into the dry ingredients, stirring to coat.

SPREAD the granola evenly on the prepared sheet pan. Bake for 15 minutes. Stir carefully to redistribute the granola and continue baking until the granola is a soft golden color, about 8 more minutes, taking care not to overtoast the granola.

LET the granola cool completely on the sheet pan; it will get crispy as it cools. Store in an airtight container at room temperature for up to 2 months—but you're probably going to have to make another batch long before that.

chocolate granola

MAKES 8 CUPS

This granola is Gala's favorite; she loves chocolate in all its forms. When she was ten years old, I told her to choose a topic and research it thoroughly. I do this with all my children and encourage them to have fun with it, to be curious and discover the joy of finding their own truths through investigation. And, of course, Gala chose chocolate. She gave me an incredible PowerPoint about cacao, its benefits, its phytochemical properties, and—the most important thing for her—how to use it step-by-step to make real chocolate.

Don't be afraid of chocolate, the real cacao—it's totally good for you. In this recipe you can taste the wonderful contrast between the sweetness of the cacao powder with the maple syrup, and the bitterness of the cacao nibs. Crunchy, delicate, and packed with powerful nutrients, this granola is perfect for chocolate lovers.

PREHEAT the oven to 325°F. Line a sheet pan with parchment paper.

IN a large bowl, combine the hazelnuts, cashews, almonds, pecans, sunflower seeds, cacao powder, and cacao nibs.

IN a small saucepan over low heat, melt the almond butter, coconut oil, and maple syrup, stirring occasionally. When the mixture is fully melted, scrape it into the nut mixture, stirring well to coat.

SPREAD the granola evenly on the prepared sheet pan. Bake for 15 minutes. Stir carefully to redistribute the granola and bake until the granola smells fragrant and the nuts are lightly toasted, about 5 more minutes, taking care not to overtoast the granola.

LET the granola cool completely on the sheet pan; it will get crispy as it cools. Store in an airtight container at room temperature for up to 2 months.

2 cups (320 g) coarsely chopped raw hazelnuts

1⅓ cups (200 g) coarsely chopped raw cashews

3 cups (300 g) sliced raw almonds

1 cup (120 g) coarsely chopped raw pecans

½ cup (90 g) raw shelled sunflower seeds

¼ cup plus 1 tablespoon (30 g) cacao powder (see page 5)

1 cup (140 g) cacao nibs (see page 6)

½ cup (150 g) raw almond butter

¼ cup (60 g) organic extra virgin coconut oil

¼ cup (80 g) pure maple syrup or yacon syrup (see page 17)

apple, banana, and chocolate muffins

MAKES 6 LARGE MUFFINS

½ cup plus 1 tablespoon (60 g) superfine blanched almond flour (such as Bob's Red Mill brand)

2 tablespoons (20 g) coconut flour (such as Let's Do Organic brand)

⅓ cup (30 g) unsweetened shredded coconut (such as Let's Do Organic brand)

1 teaspoon Homemade Baking Powder (page 297)

½ teaspoon baking soda

½ teaspoon ground cinnamon

2 large eggs, at room temperature

½ cup (80 g) coconut sugar (see page 7)

¾ cup (180 g) mashed banana (about 2 small bananas)

¾ cup (125 g) peeled, cored, and grated red apple (such as Gala; about 1 apple)

¼ cup (55 g) extra virgin olive oil

¼ cup (60 g) organic extra virgin coconut oil, melted

1 teaspoon pure vanilla extract

½ cup (75 g) paleo 70% chocolate chips or gems (such as HU brand) or carob chips

¼ cup plus 2 tablespoons (50 g) coarsely chopped raw pecan halves

In the town where I was born and spent my childhood, teatime was an afternoon tradition. It was likely a custom inherited from the English settlers, modified by the Tacneños by adding their famous marraqueta bread and incredible olives. I have beautiful memories of the hour of lonche, when my mom served coffee with milk, bread, butter, fresh artisan cheese, homemade jam, and, of course, her best baked goodies, including loaf cakes, cookies, and muffins. It's amazing how we create such vivid memories around food.

Just like my family's lonches growing up, these apple, banana, and chocolate muffins are a piece of heaven for me. They can be enjoyed not only for breakfast but at any time of day—in a lunch box or as a dessert, and of course, they are worthy of building new family memories around.

PREHEAT the oven to 350°F. Line a large muffin tin with 6 baking cup liners.

IN a medium bowl, whisk the almond flour, coconut flour, shredded coconut, baking powder, baking soda, and cinnamon.

IN a large bowl, whisk the eggs lightly. Add the coconut sugar and continue to whisk until combined, making sure not to overmix the ingredients. Add the mashed banana, apple, olive oil, coconut oil, and vanilla and stir well to combine.

ADD the dry ingredients to the wet ingredients and stir until smooth, taking care not to overmix. Fold in the chocolate chips and pecans.

USING an ice cream scoop or two spoons, divide the batter evenly among the prepared muffin wells. Bake for 30 to 35 minutes, until a toothpick inserted in the center comes out clean (except for the melted chocolate).

TRANSFER the pan to a wire rack and let cool about 15 minutes, then remove the lined muffins and place them on the rack to cool completely.

EAT the muffins immediately or store in an airtight container in the fridge for up to 5 days. You can freeze them for up to 4 months.

blackberry muffins

MAKES 6 LARGE MUFFINS

There's an important rule in my house: we can eat all the berries we want at any time. I love that my girls are constant berry eaters because berries are incredibly healthy fruits—full of antioxidants and low in sugar. But in the summer when blackberries are in season, they are particularly huge, firm, sweet, and highly addictive, so they usually disappear from the fridge before I can cook with them! In order to create this recipe, I had to hide a few boxes in the deepest part of our fridge's produce drawer, but the result was totally worth it: six soft, fluffy, blackberry-filled muffins, perfect for a lunch box.

PREHEAT the oven to 350°F. Line a large muffin tin with 6 baking cup liners.

IN a large bowl, combine the coconut milk and vinegar. Let stand until it has turned into "buttermilk," about 10 minutes. Add the coconut sugar and stir until combined.

ADD the olive oil, applesauce, and vanilla and stir until just combined, taking care not to overmix the ingredients.

IN a medium bowl, whisk the cassava flour, tigernut flour, arrowroot flour, baking powder, and baking soda until combined.

USE a fine-mesh strainer or sifter to sift the dry ingredients into the wet ingredients, folding them in gently to combine. Stir in the shredded coconut and blackberries.

DIVIDE the batter evenly among the prepared muffin wells.

BAKE for 40 to 45 minutes, until a toothpick inserted in the center of a muffin comes out clean or with only some blackberry juice.

TRANSFER the pan to a wire rack and let cool for about 15 minutes, then remove the lined muffins and place them on the rack to cool completely.

EAT the muffins immediately or store in an airtight container in the fridge for up to 3 days. You can also freeze them for up to 3 months.

1 cup (240 g) Coconut Milk (page 307) or canned organic coconut milk without guar gum (such as Native Forest's Simple)

1 tablespoon apple cider vinegar (see page 3)

¾ cup plus 2½ tablespoons (150 g) coconut sugar (see page 7)

½ cup (125 g) extra virgin olive oil

⅓ cup plus 1 tablespoon (105 g) unsweetened applesauce

2 teaspoons pure vanilla extract

¾ cup plus 2½ tablespoons (134 g) cassava flour (see page 17)

½ cup plus 2 tablespoons (70 g) sifted tigernut flour (see page 16)

⅓ cup plus 1 tablespoon (50 g) arrowroot flour (also known as starch or powder)

1 tablespoon Homemade Baking Powder (page 297)

½ teaspoon baking soda

¾ cup (65 g) unsweetened shredded coconut (such as Let's Do Organic brand)

1¼ cups (150 g) fresh or frozen blackberries

pineapple-coconut muffins

MAKES 6 LARGE MUFFINS

3 large eggs, at room temperature

½ cup (85 g) coconut sugar (see page 7)

1 tablespoon pure coconut extract (such as Flavorganics brand)

2 teaspoons tequila (organic is always better, even here)

1½ cups (150 g) unsweetened shredded coconut (such as Let's Do Organic brand), plus more for topping

⅓ cup plus 1 tablespoon (50 g) arrowroot flour (also known as starch or powder)

1 teaspoon Homemade Baking Powder (page 297)

¼ teaspoon salt (see page 15)

½ cup (115 g) avocado or extra virgin olive oil

½ cup (45 g) unsweetened dried pineapple, cut with scissors into ½-inch pieces

When I first began creating my recipes in Lima, there were no health-food stores like there are now, so it was very difficult to find certain quality ingredients, like pure vanilla extract. Only a few brands of artificial flavoring were available in the markets, and finding an actual vanilla pod was mission impossible. Of course, using those little bottles of flavoring went against my whole being, so I decided to omit vanilla from my recipes altogether and used pisco (a Peruvian brandy) as a healthy alternative for adding flavor and aroma.

Now, it's a bit difficult and very expensive to buy pisco here in the United States, so I've explored an alternative ingredient to flavor my muffins—tequila! Not only can you find it everywhere (and it's organic!), but people love it. Once I thought of using tequila in these muffins, a pineapple margarita came to mind, so I added dried pineapple—and voilà! Enjoy these wonderful flourless tequila, coconut, and pineapple muffins.

PREHEAT the oven to 350°F. Line a large muffin tin with 6 baking cup liners.

IN a high-powered blender, blend the eggs until foamy, 2 to 3 minutes. Add the coconut sugar and continue blending until thick and smooth, about 30 seconds. Add the coconut extract and tequila, then blend again for a few seconds until mixed well. Add the shredded coconut, arrowroot flour, baking powder, and salt and blend until the coconut has completely liquefied. Add the avocado oil and blend for just a few seconds to integrate.

TRANSFER the batter to a large bowl and stir in the pineapple.

USING an ice-cream scoop or two spoons, divide the batter evenly among the prepared muffin wells. Sprinkle some shredded coconut on top.

BAKE for 35 minutes, or until a toothpick inserted in the center of a muffin comes out clean.

TRANSFER the pan to a wire rack and let cool about 15 minutes, then remove the lined muffins and place them on the rack to cool completely.

EAT the muffins immediately or store in an airtight container in the fridge for up to 5 days. You can also freeze them for up to 3 months.

coconut yogurt

MAKES ABOUT FIVE 6-OUNCE SERVINGS

One 13.5-ounce (398 g) can coconut cream without guar gum (such as Let's Do Organic; see Note on page 28)

1¾ cups (400 g) Coconut Milk (page 307) or one 13.5-ounce (398 g) can coconut milk without guar gum (such as Native Forest's Simple)

3½ tablespoons (35 g) tapioca flour

2 tablespoons (40 g) pure maple syrup

½ teaspoon acacia fiber (such as Anthony's brand; see page 1)

½ teaspoon agar agar powder (see page 3)

2 probiotic capsules (best if it includes *S. thermophilus*, *L. acidophilus*, *L. casei*, *L. bulgaricus*, and/or *B. lactis*, such as Terranics brand)

special equipment needed

32-ounce mason jar with a lid, food thermometer, cheesecloth, and rubber band, Instant Pot (optional)

Eighty percent of our immune system is found in our intestines. If our gut is in balance, our whole body functions properly. The intestinal microbiota is the population of microorganisms that inhabit our intestines. The amount varies from person to person and is dependent on many factors such as how you were born (natural labor or via C-section), whether you were breastfed, the environment you grew up in, and above all, your diet.

Hebe, my youngest daughter, was born with a congenital kidney problem that caused her to suffer from constant urinary tract infections starting when she was just a year and a half. The doctors' solution was surgery, which I refused. Instead, I dedicated myself to researching the relationship between microbiota and her infections, and I found a fascinating world of information. Since then, she takes probiotics daily, and she eats a lot of dairy-free yogurt and fermented vegetables and drinks. I also encourage her to play in the garden and get dirty so that she is exposed to the wonderful microbes provided by the earth.

Supplementing your diet with probiotics (and the prebiotics that feed them) can help to create a healthy balance within your body's unique community of microorganisms. This yogurt has an incredible creamy texture and is slightly acidic. Also, carefully chosen probiotic capsules will not only do wonders to improve your gut microbiota but it can also enhance the flavor of your yogurt.

PLACE a 32-ounce mason jar in a large pot and cover it with water. Bring the water to a boil and continue to boil for at least 10 minutes. Remove the jar from the water and let it air-dry.

IN a medium saucepan, combine the coconut cream, coconut milk, tapioca flour, and maple syrup. While whisking, sprinkle in the acacia fiber and agar agar. Whisk until all the ingredients dissolve completely.

STIRRING constantly, bring the coconut milk mixture to a boil over medium heat. Once it starts to boil, continue cooking and stirring for exactly 3 minutes.

REMOVE from the heat and stir occasionally while the mixture cools. When it is 98°F or lower, open the probiotic capsules and stir in the powder until it dissolves.

POUR the coconut milk mixture into the sterilized jar, cover the top with cheesecloth, and secure it with a rubber band.

TRANSFER the jar to an Instant Pot and select the yogurt option for 20 hours, or let the jar sit out in a warm spot in the kitchen (about 72°F) for about 20 hours.

WHEN the yogurt is ready, seal the jar with its lid and refrigerate overnight before eating.

NOTE

You don't have to use an Instant Pot or yogurt maker for this recipe, but there are additional benefits if you do. These appliances allow the yogurt to cook at a constant temperature, eliminating any chance for the product to spoil or to grow harmful bacteria.

kefir cashew yogurt

MAKES ABOUT FOUR 5-OUNCE SERVINGS

2 cups (300 g) raw cashews

½ cup (120 g) water kefir (such as Buchi Lemon Lime Echinacea flavor) or homemade water kefir (see Note on page 53)

¾ cup (100 g) frozen blueberries

¼ cup (90 g) pure maple syrup

Juice from ½ lime

2 probiotic capsules (best if it includes *S. thermophilus*, *L. acidophilus*, *L. casei*, *L. bulgaricus*, and/or *B. lactis*, such as Terranics brand; optional for an even more powerful yogurt)

There was a time when I was obsessed with making my own fermented drinks. I found it truly incredible watching the process of little organisms changing, growing, and producing endless nutrients in just a little bit of sugar water. Of the fermented drinks I made, my favorites were kombucha and—my ultimate favorite but also the most challenging—water kefir. I will tell you, though, that if you have the patience and time to make your own, the taste of a homemade kefir is absolutely unique. So, if you choose to venture into making your own water kefir, you won't regret it. (My favorite flavor combinations were made by mixing in the second fermentation of the kefir with freshly pressed apple juice or passion fruit juice.)

This unconventional yogurt recipe retains all the probiotic benefits of water kefir while adding cashews for creaminess and blueberries for antioxidants. Once you have this recipe down, I encourage you to experiment with other fruits.

SOAK the cashews in a bowl of water at room temperature for at least 8 hours or overnight, covering the bowl with a kitchen towel. Drain, rinse well, and dry lightly with a kitchen or paper towel.

IN a high-powered blender, combine the cashews, kefir, blueberries, maple syrup, and lime juice. If using the probiotic capsules, empty the contents of the capsules into the mix. Blend until smooth and creamy.

REFRIGERATE overnight or for at least 8 hours.

DIVIDE among bowls and serve.

water kefir versus milk kefir

Water kefir and milk kefir are different drinks made with different groups of microorganisms. Milk kefir "grains" are a combination of live bacteria (mainly lactobacilli) and yeasts that exist in a symbiotic matrix on the surface of a complex polysaccharide and feed on lactose generating a double acid-lactic and alcoholic fermentation. These little balls look like small pieces of cauliflower when soaked in milk (cow, goat, or sheep). When the grains are allowed to ferment, they produce a liquid with a texture similar to a liquid yogurt.

Unlike yogurt, in which only lactic fermentation occurs, in kefir, the nodules produce a double fermentation, one carried out by yeasts and the other by bacteria. This transforms not only lactose but also proteins, causing a curdling effect.

On the other hand, water kefir grains, also called tibicos, have a texture similar to a grain of cooked rice—translucent, somewhat gelatinous and hard—and contain a different community of bacteria and yeasts that feed on fructose.

Tibicos cultures are found around the world. No two are identical, but they typically have a mix of bacteria, e.g., *Pediococcus*, *Acetobacter*, *Streptococcus*, *Lactobacillus*, and *Leuconostoc*, as well as yeasts from *Candida*, *Kloeckera*, *Saccharomyces*, and others.

Water kefir is a liquid fermented beverage made with water, sugar, and tibicos. If desired, a second stage of fermentation can be carried out in which fruit juice or herbal infusions are added to this basic kefir to create a delicious flavored drink, which if bottled, will become carbonated. Water kefir is an amazing substitute for sodas and kombucha.

IF YOU WANT TO MAKE YOUR OWN WATER KEFIR: I recommend buying Cultures for Health brand starter grains, which can be found online at CulturesForHealth. com or Amazon.com.

IF YOU WANT TO BUY THE BOTTLED WATER KEFIR: I recommend the brand Buchi, which can be bought at Whole Foods or Sprouts.

quinoa porridge

MAKES 3 SERVINGS

½ cup (95 g) white quinoa (see page 14)

4 thick cinnamon sticks

4 whole cloves

1½ tablespoons (17 g) plantain or green banana flour (see page 8)

1 cup (240 g) Almond Milk (page 304)

Fresh figs, for serving

Raw almond butter, for serving

Raw unfiltered honey and/or a piece of honeycomb, for serving

This creamy and protein-packed porridge is the perfect replacement for oatmeal if you want to try something different for breakfast. Before I got a taste of the art of creating desserts, one recipe that I would prepare occasionally was a divine arroz con leche, which is something like a cinnamon rice pudding. It was made with a lot of condensed and evaporated milk and was cloyingly sweet. It was meant to be eaten in small servings, but the girls died for it and would empty a pot in five minutes.

To re-create that delicious and creamy dessert, but in a less sweet and healthier form that is perfect for breakfast, I swap quinoa for the rice (which provides a lot of protein) and top it with honey. Just glorious! I tested this with the girls, and the verdict was clear—another empty pot.

Remember that the secret to cooking perfect quinoa is in the washing and soaking! Plan ahead—the soaking happens overnight.

THE night before, rinse the quinoa several times and place it in a bowl. Fill it with plenty of water and cover with a kitchen towel. Let it soak overnight.

IN the morning, drain and rinse the quinoa.

PLACE the quinoa, 2 cups (480 g) water, and the cinnamon and cloves in a medium saucepan and bring to a boil over medium heat. Cook, uncovered and without stirring, until most of the water has evaporated, 9 to 10 minutes.

MEANWHILE, in a small bowl, combine the plantain flour and ¼ cup (60 g) water and stir until dissolved.

REMOVE the cinnamon sticks (and cloves, if desired) from the quinoa, add the almond milk, and bring to a boil over medium heat. Reduce the heat to medium-low and add the plantain flour mixture, stirring constantly until thickened, 2 to 3 minutes. It will continue to thicken slightly as it cools.

SERVE in bowls with fresh figs and almond butter and a drizzle of honey on top, perhaps including a small piece of honeycomb!

paleo crepes

MAKES 7 CREPES, TO SERVE 7

2 large eggs

6.7 ounces (190 g) egg whites (measured from about 6 large eggs; use the exact weight; see Note on page 57)

¾ cup (180 g) Almond Milk (page 304)

¼ cup (40 g) arrowroot flour (also known as starch or powder)

3½ tablespoons (35 g) tapioca flour

2 tablespoons (20 g) coconut flour (such as Let's Do Organic brand)

Pinch of salt (see page 15)

Organic extra virgin coconut oil, for cooking the crepes

Who says that healthy food has to be ugly and tasteless, or that eating healthy must be a sacrifice? This recipe is proof that healthy and delicious can go hand in hand. These crepes have the same elasticity you'll find in a conventional crepe, but without the gluten. And with these glorious ingredients, you'll feel much lighter and full of energy than you would after a meal of traditional crepes.

This is one of my daughters' favorite dishes; they even ask for it as a special birthday breakfast. The crepes are so addictive that I love to double the recipe and keep extras in the fridge to satisfy cravings. Every time we prepare these at home, I have the girls practice their crepe-cooking technique—making crepes is like a fun superpower! It gives me great satisfaction to see them assemble their crepes with their favorite fillings and to know that they're eating something both spectacularly delicious and filled with nutrients.

These crepes can be used in both sweet and savory preparations (see the Sweet Crepes that follow on page 62). They are very fast and easy to make.

COMBINE all the ingredients except the coconut oil in a blender and blend until smooth. Let the batter rest for about 15 minutes. (Don't omit this step—patience is very important!)

HEAT a crepe pan over medium heat until you can feel the heat when you place your hand 2 to 3 inches above the pan. Lightly grease the pan with a small amount of coconut oil; you can use a brush or a piece of paper towel to spread the oil over the entire inside surface of your pan. Pour between ⅓ and ½ cup (about 78 g) of batter into the pan, turning your wrist so it spreads it over the entire bottom of the pan, creating a thin layer (the crepe will be about 8½ inches in diameter). (If you don't have a crepe pan, use a large skillet.)

WHEN the edges begin to brown and dry, use a spatula to flip the crepe and cook it on the other side, until light golden. This process will happen very quickly; the first one may not turn out perfectly, but you'll get the hang of it. Transfer the crepe to a plate.

REPEAT to make the rest of the crepes. Depending on your pan, you may only need to add oil for the first crepe.

STORE the crepes in an airtight glass container in the fridge for up to 3 days and keep them on hand for quick meals. You can also freeze them (flat, not folded) for up to 3 months; to thaw them, just leave them overnight in the fridge and then heat them lightly in a pan.

NOTE
For this recipe it is very important to weigh the egg whites and flours precisely; otherwise your crepes could end up with a very eggy flavor or a liquid texture.

crepes with chicken, bacon, mushrooms, and artichokes

MAKES 7 CREPES, TO SERVE 7

I don't think there should be a strict rule about how many times we should eat a day. A doctor I greatly admire once told me that people should eat only when they are "really hungry." I think this is the most natural way to fuel our bodies. Some days the girls wake up and aren't hungry, so I don't make them breakfast. Other days they wake up wanting to eat the whole kitchen, so we do something they call "breakfast-lunch" that keeps them full for many, many hours. This crepe recipe is one of their favorite hearty meals, and if I serve it with a smoothie like Magic Mango (page 260), it's a complete hit!

To bring this recipe (and others containing chicken) together more quickly, it is helpful to always have shredded chicken in the freezer. You can make a large batch and freeze it in portions. For a vegetarian meal, try jackfruit and coconut bacon.

IF you're using pork bacon in the recipe, in a large cast-iron skillet over low heat, cook the bacon until crisp and browned on both sides, 15 to 20 minutes, flipping as needed.

REMOVE the skillet from the heat, but do not discard the fat. Transfer the bacon to a paper towel–lined plate to drain. Crumble the bacon into a medium bowl.

MAKE the crepe batter and let it rest while you make the filling.

ADD the mushrooms to the pan with the bacon fat and cook over high heat until they begin to brown, stirring occasionally. (If you're not using pork bacon, cook the mushrooms in 2 tablespoons of olive oil.)

ADD the spinach and basil, season to taste with salt and pepper, stir, and turn off the heat. The leaves will soften in the heat left in the pan, which prevents them from overcooking and losing their beautiful green color.

8 ounces (227 g) no-sugar uncured pork bacon (such as Applegate or ButcherBox brand) or 2 cups Coconut Bacon (page 61), for a vegetarian option

Paleo Crepes batter (page 56)

8 ounces (227 g) white or baby bella mushrooms, sliced or halved

Extra virgin olive oil, as needed

5 cups (150 g) baby spinach, washed and dried

1 cup (30 g) fresh basil leaves, washed and dried

Salt (see page 15)

Freshly ground black pepper

2 avocados

1 tablespoon fresh lime juice

2 cups (200 g) shredded cooked chicken or 2 cups (300 g) shredded canned jackfruit (such as Native Forest brand, for a vegetarian option)

8 ounces (227 g) jarred grilled artichoke hearts (such as Cara Mia brand), roughly chopped

1 cup microgreens, such as kale, arugula, broccoli, or radish, for serving

Cashew Mayonnaise (page 292), to taste

HALVE, pit, and peel the avocados and place them in a medium bowl. Use a potato masher or fork to mash them roughly. Stir in the lime juice and season to taste with salt and pepper.

PLACE the shredded chicken or jackfruit and the artichokes in separate medium bowls. Place the bowls near the stove, along with the crepe batter and the bowls of bacon, mushrooms and spinach, and avocado.

SET a crepe pan over medium heat and brush it with olive oil. Add ⅓ to ½ cup (approximately 78 g) of the crepe batter and spread it over the entire surface of the pan. (It depends on your crepe pan, but usually the olive oil is necessary only for the first crepe. If you don't have a crepe pan, use a large skillet; the crepes should be about 8½ inches in diameter.)

QUICKLY add some shredded chicken or jackfruit, bacon (if you're using coconut bacon, set it aside as garnish), artichoke hearts, and the mushroom mixture down the center of the crepe. Run a spatula under the outside edges of the crepe. When all the edges are detached, gently fold the sides in to enclose the filling. Let the crepe brown on both sides for a few seconds.

TRANSFER the crepe to a plate, top with the avocado mixture and some microgreens (and some coconut bacon, if using), and drizzle with Cashew Mayonnaise.

REPEAT to make the remaining crepes. Serve immediately.

coconut bacon

MAKES 4½ CUPS

Not only does this recipe serve as a vegan replacement for ba-con in sandwiches, salads, wraps, and tacos, it's also an addictive snack. Try leaving the jar open on the table and you will see that no one will be able to stop eating it. Double the recipe, fill mason jars and put a nice bow on them, and give them to friends and family—they will be delighted!

Remember that not all liquid smoke is the same; avoid those that have flavorings and dyes.

PREHEAT the oven to 300°F (or if using a dehydrator, turn it to 115°F). Line a sheet pan with a silicone mat or parchment paper.

IN a medium bowl, combine the tamari, liquid smoke, maple syrup, paprika, and olive oil. Add the coconut flakes and gently mix to completely coat the coconut.

SPREAD the coconut flakes evenly onto the prepared sheet pan and bake for 10 minutes. Remove the pan from the oven, stir well, and bake until slightly crispy and golden brown, about 10 more minutes. (If you are using a dehydrator, dehydrate until crispy, 10 to 12 hours.)

TRANSFER the coconut bacon to a wire rack to cool completely. It will crisp up more as it cools. Store in a jar at room temperature for up to 1 month.

3 tablespoons (45 g) gluten-free tamari or coconut aminos

¾ teaspoon hickory liquid smoke (such as Lazy Kettle brand)

2 tablespoons (50 g) pure maple syrup

1½ teaspoons smoked paprika (such as sweet Pimentón de la Vera)

1 tablespoon extra virgin olive oil

4½ cups (7 ounces/250 g) unsweetened coconut flakes (not shredded coconut; such as Let's Do Organic brand)

special equipment needed
dehydrator (optional)

sweet crepes

MAKES 7 SERVINGS

7 fully cooked crepes from
Paleo Crepes (page 56)

Hazelnut-Chocolate
Butter (page 232)

2 cups fresh berries, such
as blackberries, blueberries,
and raspberries

AIP Dulce de Leche, at room
temperature (page 302)

Breakfast or dessert? You decide. In my house we love these crepes at any time of the day, and they're even an excellent addition to a school lunch box. I recommend pairing them with unsweetened Fruity Black Tea (page 272), which is great served outside on a hot and sunny day.

SPREAD a crepe with about 1 tablespoon hazelnut-chocolate butter and add some fresh berries. Fold the crepe over the fillings. Transfer the crepe to a plate and drizzle with a little dulce de leche.

REPEAT with the remaining crepes and serve immediately.

smoked salmon and avocado toast

MAKES 2 SERVINGS

When we realized that Camila needed to follow an AIP diet (see page 19), I started experimenting in the kitchen to create the perfect bread for her. I spent a lot of time thinking about the ingredients I should use, their characteristics and interactions. And I always, always held an image in my mind of Camila enjoying a delicious and powerfully healthful sandwich.

Smoked salmon and avocado toast is one of her favorite breakfasts, and as a mom, nothing makes me happier than being able to include an incredible variety of nutrients in a meal that she enjoys so much. These open-faced sandwiches contain resistant starch in the bread, dietary fiber and great monounsaturated fatty acids in the avocado, protein and omega-3 in the salmon, probiotics in the sauerkraut, and a high content of carotenoids and chlorophylls in the microgreens. A complete and nutrition-filled breakfast, made with her favorite bread: mission accomplished!

Four ½-inch slices AIP Sandwich Bread (page 188)

2 avocados, thinly sliced

Pinch of salt (see page 15)

4 slices smoked wild-caught salmon

2 teaspoons dried dill

4 tablespoons sauerkraut (see page 15), drained

Broccoli microgreens, for serving

TOAST the bread slices.

TOP each piece of bread with the avocado slices, a pinch of salt, and a slice of salmon. Sprinkle each with ½ teaspoon of dried dill, then add 1 tablespoon of sauerkraut and a pinch of microgreens.

SERVE immediately with a smile—and enjoy this delicious nutrient bomb.

BREAKFAST

65

baked frittata with caramelized onions and greens

MAKES 6 SERVINGS

8 ounces (226 g) no-sugar uncured bacon (such as Applegate or ButcherBox brand), cut into ½-inch pieces

4 large yellow onions (700 g), thinly sliced

Salt (see page 15)

12 large eggs, at room temperature

1 teaspoon smoked paprika (such as sweet Pimentón de la Vera)

¼ teaspoon chili powder

¼ teaspoon onion powder

½ teaspoon dried oregano

½ teaspoon garlic powder

⅛ teaspoon freshly ground black pepper, plus more as needed

2 cups (100 g) roughly chopped kale, washed and dried

2 cups (60 g) baby spinach, washed and dried

When I was twelve years old, my family and I moved to Bariloche, Argentina, a beautiful city with incredible forests. The whole town had a certain magic and even had its own myth of a great monster that lives under Nahuel Huapi Lake. We spent a wonderful couple of years there.

My dad had a rotisería, a very Argentinian word to describe a store that makes prepared meals to take away. We sold empanadas, pizzas, sandwiches, frittatas, and some groceries.

My mom used to cook some really spectacular frittatas there, and the technique of flipping the frittata, which was done in a large pan with the help of a big lid, was one that I managed to learn with a lot of practice. Once I discovered how wonderful and versatile cast-iron pans were, I realized that cooking the frittata in the oven was an easier technique that produced an equally perfect and delicious result.

At home we love eating organic and pasture-raised eggs, though my girls all have different preferences on how they like their eggs prepared. I'm always inventing new recipes to make sure that everyone is happy. But the one recipe that they can all agree on is a good and tasty tortilla like this one. When I decided to add this recipe to the book, I wondered whether it was too simple but wanted to include it anyway because, really, there is nothing more comforting than a well-made frittata.

The secret to this recipe is the patience, love, and care that is put into the caramelized onions. They will turn a simple frittata into a gourmet breakfast.

PREHEAT the oven to 350°F.

IN a 12-inch cast-iron skillet or large oven-safe skillet over medium-low heat, cook the bacon until the fat has rendered, 15 to 20 minutes, turning the bacon as needed.

ADD the onions and a big pinch of salt and cook, stirring occasionally, over medium-low heat until the onions are softened, browned, and caramelized. This process takes between 35 and 45 minutes to produce perfectly caramelized and sweet onions. Remember to cook on medium-low heat—if the temperature is too high, the onions will burn instead of caramelizing. If you're running short on time, you can prepare the onions faster by cooking on medium heat for 25 minutes, but keep a very close eye on the onions to prevent burning.

A couple of minutes before the onions are ready, break the eggs into a medium bowl and season them with salt, paprika, chili powder, onion powder, oregano, garlic powder, and pepper. Beat them with a wire whisk until well mixed.

WHEN the onions are caramelized, add the kale and spinach and salt and pepper to taste. Turn off the heat, stir, and let the kale and spinach soften.

POUR the egg mixture evenly over the ingredients in the skillet and place the skillet in the oven.

BAKE for about 25 minutes, or until the frittata is puffed, golden brown in parts, and cooked through.

LET rest about 5 minutes, then cut into wedges and serve. The frittata will keep in the refrigerator for about 2 days.

See the photo on page 68.

naan, eggs, and dukkah

MAKES 1 SERVING

dukkah
¼ cup (35 g) raw
unsalted hazelnuts

⅓ cup (40 g) raw unsalted
shelled pistachios

¼ cup (30 g) raw
unsalted cashews

⅓ cup (45 g) unsalted unhulled
raw white sesame seeds

¼ cup plus 1 teaspoon (35 g)
whole cumin seeds

3 tablespoons (15 g)
whole coriander seeds

1½ teaspoons whole
fennel seeds

¾ teaspoon salt (see page 15)

2 pinches freshly
ground black pepper

assembly
1 tablespoon extra
virgin olive oil

1 large egg

Salt, to taste

½ avocado, thinly sliced

Bunch of microgreens (about
15 g), such as broccoli,
kale, radish, or arugula

2 radishes, trimmed
and thinly sliced

2 tablespoons (25 g)
sauerkraut (see page 15),
drained

1 piece Naan (page 192)

I've always found Middle Eastern cuisine fascinating, with its amazing spice blends and exotic recipes. I would love to visit enigmatic Egypt, with its fascinating history, mysterious pyramids, and incredible hieroglyphics—although I think a visit to the local food market would be one of my most enjoyable adventures. One of my favorite recipes is dukkah, an Egyptian condiment made of nuts and spices that are typically crushed using a mortar and pestle (the word *dukkah* derives from the Arabic word for "to pound"). There are many variations of dukkah but the recipe consistently includes hazelnuts, sesame seeds, coriander, cumin, salt, and pepper.

I find that dukkah goes well with a lot of different foods, and my family loves it on top of eggs, with vegetables, or with bread and olive oil, as in this recipe. I'm sure you'll fall in love, too, especially when the smells from roasting and grinding the seeds and nuts begin wafting through your kitchen and blending with incredible family memories.

FOR THE DUKKAH: Heat a medium skillet over medium heat (don't use any fat or oil). Add the hazelnuts, pistachios, and cashews to the skillet and cook, stirring constantly, until fragrant and lightly toasted, about 6 minutes. Transfer to a food processor.

ADD the sesame seeds to the same skillet and cook, stirring constantly, until lightly toasted, about 2 minutes. Transfer to the food processor with the nuts.

ADD the cumin seeds, coriander seeds, and fennel seeds to the same skillet and cook, stirring constantly, until fragrant and lightly toasted, about 4 minutes. Transfer to the food processor with the other ingredients, add the salt and pepper, and pulse until coarsely ground.

TRANSFER the mixture to a jar and let it cool before closing. Store in a cool, dry place for several weeks.

TO ASSEMBLE: Heat the olive oil in a small skillet over low heat. Crack the egg into the skillet and sprinkle with salt. Let it cook slowly.

WHEN the egg white has become opaque, use a spatula to flip it over carefully, trying not to break the yolk. Or spoon hot oil on top to cook the top side. Cook for another 10 seconds or so, long enough to cook the outside but keep the yolk liquid.

TRANSFER the fried egg to a plate. Serve with the sliced avocado on the side and sprinkle both all over with the dukkah. Garnish with microgreens, radishes, and sauerkraut and serve with warm naan for dipping. Serve immediately and enjoy this heavenly egg.

See the photo on page 69.

toasted apple bread

MAKES 12 SERVINGS

bread

1 large (269 g) Granny Smith apple

3 large eggs, at room temperature

Pinch of salt (see page 15)

3 tablespoons (46 g) coconut sugar (see page 7)

5 tablespoons (50 g) flaxseed meal

1 teaspoon ground cinnamon

1 cup (120 g) superfine blanched almond flour (such as Bob's Red Mill brand)

for serving

Cashew butter

1 Granny Smith apple, sliced

Raw unfiltered honey

Ground cinnamon

This recipe is something I dreamed up—literally.

I think about food all the time, and my mind is always trying to find new ways to combine ingredients and formulate recipes. It's common for me to go to bed thinking about a problematic recipe that needs to be worked out and wake up with a potential solution, which I tackle that day.

One night, I went to bed thinking about the aromas of an apple pie, the texture of sweet French toast, the smell of cinnamon, and the sweetness of honey. At 4:00 a.m. I awoke with a vision for a new breakfast recipe that combined all these elements, jumped up to get a pencil and paper, and wrote it all down. The recipe below—which quickly became a family favorite—was indeed a dream come true!

PREHEAT the oven to 350°F. Line a 9 × 13-inch (quarter) sheet pan on the bottom and up the sides with parchment paper.

GRATE the apple, including the peel, over a bowl, using the large holes of a grater. Don't discard any liquid. Discard the core, seeds, and stem.

CRACK the eggs into a bowl and whisk them lightly, then add the grated apple and any juices, salt, coconut sugar, flaxseed meal, and cinnamon. Mix well and let rest for 15 minutes.

ADD the almond flour and mix until smooth.

POUR the batter into the prepared pan and use a spatula to spread it evenly over the bottom of the pan.

BAKE for 20 minutes, until a toothpick inserted into the center comes out clean. This is a flatbread—it won't rise very much and will fit easily in a toaster! Set the pan aside to let the bread cool completely.

CUT the bread into rectangles or squares, or whatever shape you wish! You can be creative with this dream bread.

TOAST the bread and serve topped with cashew butter, apple slices, honey, and ground cinnamon.

appetizers, soups, and sides

sweet potato "cheese"

MAKES ONE 4- TO 5-INCH CHEESE MOLD, OR 6 TO 8 SERVINGS

1 sweet potato (my favorite is the Japanese sweet potato)

1½ cups (185 g) peeled and small-diced zucchini

¼ cup plus 1 tablespoon (88 g) Coconut Yogurt (page 50)

2 tablespoons plus 1 teaspoon (22 g) tapioca flour

2 tablespoons plus 2 teaspoons (35 g) coconut oil with a neutral flavor (such as BetterBody Foods brand)

1 tablespoon plus 1 teaspoon (18 g) coconut butter (such as Nutiva brand)

2 tablespoons (15 g) agar agar powder (see page 3)

1 teaspoon raw unfiltered honey

2½ tablespoons (15 g) nutritional yeast

1 teaspoon salt (see page 15)

1 teaspoon fresh lime juice

This vegan "cheese" is creamy, flavorful, allergen-free, and super easy to make. I love making vegan cheeses; they are full of protein but also full of life thanks to the probiotics they contain! I usually make them with nuts and seeds, but when it comes to the AIP diet, it is very difficult to create a suitable cheese recipe. Cami has never really liked cheese spreads, so this hard version is perfect for her and has become one of her favorite snacks. She likes to eat it with AIP Sandwich Bread (page 188) or Yuca Crackers (page 198). She also likes to cut it into cubes and add them to salads. Of course, you don't have to follow the AIP diet to love this gorgeous cheese!

ROAST the sweet potato in a baking dish in a 400°F oven for about 1 hour, or until you can easily pierce it with a toothpick. Let it cool, then peel it and cut it into small chunks. Measure out ¾ cup (125 g) of sweet potato and reserve the rest for another use.

LINE a 4- to-5-inch round springform pan (preferably with a detachable collar) or medium glass bowl with plastic wrap or cheesecloth, leaving a 2-inch overhang (this will help you to unmold your cheese later).

IN a high-powered blender, combine the sweet potato, zucchini, coconut yogurt, tapioca flour, coconut oil, coconut butter, agar agar, honey, nutritional yeast, salt, lime juice, and ⅓ cup plus 2 tablespoons (110 g) water. Blend until very smooth, about 1 minute.

TRANSFER the mixture to a medium saucepan and cook over medium-high heat until it begins to thicken and comes to a boil, stirring constantly. When it starts to boil, set the timer for 5 minutes (stirring as fast as you can so it doesn't burn or stick to the pot). Remove from the heat.

POUR the mixture into the prepared mold and smooth the surface with a spatula. Let it cool to room temperature, about 1 hour, then cover completely with plastic wrap. Refrigerate for 8 hours or overnight.

UNMOLD the "cheese" onto a plate and return it, uncovered, to the refrigerator for 2 to 3 hours to remove some of the moisture and allow it to firm up. Serve immediately, sliced or cut into cubes, or refrigerate in an airtight container for up to 4 days.

NOTE
This is not a "melty" cheese and is not suitable for use where melting is desired.

wild mushroom pâté

MAKES 2 CUPS

As much as I love the classic chicken liver pâté with truffle oil and cognac, I'm also fascinated by vegan versions. Mushrooms are one of my favorite ingredients to use when crafting a vegan plate; that deep, earthy flavor connects me with nature. The touch of apple cider vinegar here simply enhances all the flavors, bringing them together. This mushroom pâté is incredible when spread on Yuca Crackers (page 198).

PLACE the sunflower seeds in a medium bowl and add enough water to cover them completely. Let sit until softened slightly, about 2 hours. Drain and set aside.

MEANWHILE, place the porcini, chanterelle, and maitake mushrooms in a large bowl and cover completely with the boiling water. Cover with a plate or lid (to hold in the steam) and let sit until they are reconstituted and soft, about 30 minutes.

SET a fine-mesh strainer over a medium bowl and strain the liquid from the mushrooms into the bowl. Squeeze any extra liquid from the mushrooms into the bowl and reserve the liquid.

IN a high-powered blender, combine the sunflower seeds, mushrooms, coconut oil, nutritional yeast, garlic powder, onion powder, vinegar, salt, and pepper. Add 1 cup of the reserved mushroom liquid. Blend until smooth, 3 to 4 minutes. If you have a tamper, use it. The mixture will be very thick. If necessary, turn off the blender periodically and scrape the edges before blending again.

WHEN the mixture is smooth, add salt and pepper to taste. Add the parsley and pulse just to combine. You want to see small parsley pieces distributed throughout the mixture, but don't overblend.

PLACE the pâté in an airtight container and refrigerate for 8 hours or overnight. Serve immediately or within 3 days.

1½ cups (210 g) unsalted hulled raw sunflower seeds

0.7 ounce (20 g) dried porcini mushrooms (about ¾ cup)

0.35 ounce (10 g) dried chanterelle mushrooms (about ½ cup)

0.35 ounce (10 g) dried maitake mushrooms (about ½ cup)

2 cups (480 g) boiling water

2 tablespoons (26g) coconut oil with a neutral flavor (such as BetterBody Foods brand)

1½ tablespoons (9 g) nutritional yeast

½ teaspoon garlic powder

½ teaspoon onion powder

2 teaspoons apple cider vinegar (see page 3)

1 teaspoon salt (see page 15), plus more to taste

½ teaspoon freshly ground black pepper, plus more to taste

2 tablespoons (10 g) minced fresh parsley

appetizer platter

MAKES 1 FAMILY TRAY, OR 6 TO 8 SERVINGS

avocado dip

2 large avocados, halved

Salt (see page 15), to taste

Freshly ground black pepper, to taste

Fresh lime juice, to taste

2 teaspoons extra virgin olive oil

1 tablespoon chopped fresh cilantro

½ cup (90 g) pomegranate arils

for serving

Sweet Potato "Cheese" (page 76)

Wild Mushroom Pâté (page 79)

Yuca Crackers (page 198)

Baby carrots

Celery sticks

Broccoli florets, lightly steamed

Radishes

Cherry tomatoes or any small tomatoes

Sugar snap peas, julienned

Mini sweet peppers

Nuts

Grapes

AIP MODIFICATIONS
Omit the black pepper, mushroom pâté, tomatoes, peas, sweet peppers, and nuts.

This tray of snacks is a hit for entertaining or going to a potluck. It's both beautiful to look at and a pleasure to eat, with a delightful variety of colors, flavors, and textures. My family loves to get creative and have fun decorating their own plates. We even like eating this as breakfast in bed on Sunday morning, with a large serving tray plus individual serving plates so everyone can choose what they want. It is super fresh and light, and there's something for everyone, including those on the AIP diet.

FOR THE AVOCADO DIP: In a medium bowl, use a fork to mash the avocados until almost smooth. Add salt and pepper, lime juice, the olive oil, and the cilantro and mix well. Transfer to a serving bowl and top with the pomegranate arils.

TO SERVE: On a nice large board or platter (or even directly on a wood table), place a bowl of the wild mushroom pâté, the bowl of avocado dip, and the sweet potato "cheese." Arrange the yuca crackers along with the veggies, nuts, and grapes around the outside edge. Serve immediately or within a few hours.

stuffed avocado

MAKES 1 SERVING

One 4.4-ounce can wild-caught sardines (or anchovies) in extra virgin olive oil (such as Wild Planet or Season brand)

2 tablespoons (33 g) Cashew Mayonnaise (page 292) or store-bought paleo mayonnaise (for an AIP diet, use Dill Coconut Yogurt Dressing, page 284)

1 teaspoon Roasted Garlic Paste (page 294)

½ cup (80 g) sauerkraut (see page 15), drained

1 teaspoon apple cider vinegar with manuka honey (such as Wedderspoon brand)

Salt (see page 15)

1 large avocado, halved

Microgreens, such as broccoli, radish, arugula, or mustard

This is one of my daughter Hebe's favorite breakfast dishes. She can easily eat two stuffed avocado halves, which is a lot for a little girl. Watching her gobble this down makes me so happy because I know she's starting her day with a perfectly balanced meal packed with nutrients, flavors, and textures.

IN a small bowl, combine the sardines, mayonnaise, garlic paste, sauerkraut, and vinegar mixture until the sardines are broken up but not entirely crushed.

SPRINKLE salt to taste over each avocado half and divide the filling between the avocado halves.

DECORATE the top of each half with a handful of microgreens. Serve immediately.

black garlic toast

MAKES 1 SERVING

It might look and sound a bit unusual, but if you haven't tried black garlic yet, you're in for a treat. It's garlic that has been specially aged (fermented) until the cloves turn black and become soft and sticky, and it has many health benefits, including cardiovascular and liver protection and anticancer and antibacterial properties. You can find it at gourmet and specialty markets and online. The spiciness of the garlic mellows, and rich umami notes become prominent. I find the flavor to be highly addictive. So, if you're like me, feel free to add additional black garlic cloves to your toast. Besides black garlic, this toast also features fresh avocado, sun-dried tomatoes, fresh basil, and a bit of heat from cayenne pepper, which contains the health-protective benefits of capsaicin. Don't be shy with the amount of cayenne you add—it's up to you!

I like this toast just about any time of day, as a snack, lunch, or breakfast.

2 slices Sun-dried Tomato and Basil Paleo Bread (page 186), toasted

1 avocado, sliced

Salt (see page 15)

Cayenne

2 black garlic cloves, peeled and thinly sliced, plus more if desired

2 organic sun-dried tomatoes, packed in extra virgin olive oil, julienned

Fresh basil leaves

COVER the toast with avocado slices, add salt and cayenne pepper to taste, then the black garlic slices and sun-dried tomatoes. Decorate with fresh basil leaves and serve immediately.

See the photo on page 84.

mango ceviche with shrimp

MAKES 2 SERVINGS

chile salsa

2 habanero peppers

4 jalapeño peppers

4 serrano peppers

1 red onion, finely diced

½ bunch fresh cilantro, finely chopped

Maras salt or sea salt, to taste

Freshly ground black pepper, to taste

¼ cup (60 g) fresh lime juice (from 2 limes)

3 tablespoons (60 g) balsamic vinegar of Modena

Extra virgin olive oil

Apple cider vinegar (see page 3)

special equipment needed

32-ounce mason jar with a lid

Ceviche is basically the Peruvian national dish. The name comes from the Quechua word *siwichi*, which means "fresh or tender fish." It is believed that between the second and fifth centuries, on the Peruvian coast, the Mochica culture prepared a dish based on fresh fish, which was lightly cooked with the juice of a local fruit called tumbo. (By the way, if you come across this fruit, you have to try it—it's one of my favorites! Tumbo is a relative of the passion fruit and has high amounts of vitamin C, a spectacular sweet-and-sour taste, and soft, velvety-smooth skin that turns yellowish when ripe. The juice is a delicacy. When I was a child, I ate tumbo just by splitting it in two and sprinkling a little sugar on it.) After the conquest, the Spanish incorporated lime to give the ceviche more of a cooked texture.

Recipes for ceviche have evolved over time. When I was a child, as was the tradition, my dad left the fish "cooking" in lime juice for a long, long time. Today, that is considered a travesty; modern ceviche must be served and eaten instantly—fresh, practically raw, and very cold. Ceviche has become an emblematic dish and as diverse and fresh as the ingredients are in Peru. Personally, I like all versions of ceviche: fish, mushroom, mango, octopus, shrimp, and ceviche mixto (a seafood mixture). And if you can find Peruvian giant corn to accompany it, you'll have a luxurious dish.

FOR THE SALSA: Cut the chile peppers into small dice, removing the seeds and veins according to how spicy you want the salsa. Mix the peppers, onion, and cilantro well in a bowl, adding salt and pepper.

TRANSFER the mixture to a 32-ounce mason jar and add the lime juice and balsamic vinegar. Eyeball the jar and check where the chiles would be half-covered. Fill the jar with olive oil to that level, then pour in apple cider vinegar until the chiles are completely covered. Seal with the lid and shake well. The salsa can be eaten immediately or refrigerated for up to 2 weeks.

FOR THE CEVICHE: Fill a large bowl with ice water and place the julienned onion in it to keep it crisp until use.

FOR the mango you can choose one of two ways: unpeeled (believe me, it's very good) or peeled. Either way, cut it into thin slices.

PLACE the shrimp in a large bowl. Stir in the lime juice, salt, and pepper and let it rest for about 2 minutes. Add the mango, peach, and cilantro and toss well to combine.

TO serve, place the ceviche on a plate and top with onions and salsa to taste. Serve immediately with some room-temperature sweet potato slices.

See the photo on page 85.

ceviche

1 medium red onion
(315 g), julienned

1 unripe (green-skinned)
mango (442 g)

¾ pound (400 g) medium
(41/50) or large (31/35) raw
wild-caught shrimp, fresh or
frozen (and thawed), peeled,
deveined, and tails removed

½ to ¾ cup (120 to 180 g)
fresh lime juice

Sea salt, to taste

Freshly ground black
pepper, to taste

1 firm peach (182 g),
thinly sliced

¼ cup (25 g) chopped cilantro

2 medium sweet potatoes,
baked, peeled, and sliced into
rounds, for serving (see Sweet
Potato "Cheese," page 76)

AIP MODIFICATIONS
Omit the chile salsa
and black pepper.

VEGAN MODIFICATIONS
Omit the shrimp.

anti-inflammatory chicken soup

MAKES 6 SERVINGS

Bone broth is already powerful, but this healing soup with turmeric and ginger packs an added punch. It's full of anti-inflammatory nutrients that will help your body reestablish the balance it needs. This recipe is very comforting on a winter night or when you feel like you need a boost, so eat it slowly, enjoy every spoonful, and feel grateful for life.

This is a great soup if you are following the AIP diet, but if not, I recommend cracking an egg per serving into the soup and letting it cook without stirring, right before you add the coconut cream. Your call on how long to let the egg cook in the soup; at home we like the white well cooked and the yolk cooked but soft. The egg adds extra protein as well as a delicious surprise.

HEAT the olive oil in a large soup pot over medium-high heat. Add the ginger and sauté lightly, then add the onion and garlic and cook, stirring occasionally, until the onion is translucent, 3 to 5 minutes.

ADD the celery, leek, carrots, mushrooms, and cauliflower and cook, stirring often, until the vegetables begin to brown, 6 to 8 minutes. Stir in the turmeric, salt, and pepper.

ADD the chicken and the broth and bring to a boil. Lower the heat and simmer until the chicken is fully cooked through and tender, 30 to 45 minutes.

STIR in the coconut cream and cook until incorporated and melted, about 1 minute. Turn off the heat and stir in the spinach until it is softened but still bright green.

SERVE immediately or refrigerate and serve within a day or two.

2 tablespoons (30 g) extra virgin olive oil

1 tablespoon minced fresh ginger

1 medium yellow onion (280 g), finely chopped

2 garlic cloves, minced (or 1 teaspoon Roasted Garlic Paste, page 294)

¾ cup (100 g) small-diced celery

¾ cup (100 g) leek, sliced lengthwise, washed, and sliced thinly crosswise (use all but the darkest green end)

1½ cups (200 g) peeled and small-diced tricolor or regular carrots

2 cups (150 g) thinly sliced fresh baby bella mushrooms

8 ounces (250 g) 2-inch cauliflower florets (about 2½ cups)

1½ teaspoons ground turmeric (see page 16)

Salt, to taste (see page 15)

¼ teaspoon freshly ground black pepper

1 pound (500 g) boneless, skinless chicken breasts, each cut into 4 slices

10 cups (2½ quarts/2.5 L) Homemade Chicken Bone Broth (page 90)

One 13.5-ounce can (398 g) coconut cream without guar gum (such as Let's Do Organic; see page 28)

5 ounces (150 g) baby spinach (about 5 cups)

homemade chicken bone broth

MAKES 3 QUARTS (3 L) OR TWELVE 1-CUP SERVINGS

1 leek, cut into 4 pieces and rinsed well between the layers, one long green leaf reserved

Bouquet garni (including a combo of fresh parsley, thyme, basil, rosemary, bay leaves, and tarragon, as desired; see below)

One 4- to 5-pound (1.8 to 2.2 kg) whole chicken (if the chicken still has feet, all the better; you can also find chicken feet sold separately)

2 tablespoons (30 g) extra virgin olive oil

2 large carrots, unpeeled, cut into 2-inch pieces

½ bunch celery (including the leaves) cut into 2-inch pieces

1 yellow onion, washed and unpeeled, cut into 4 pieces

4 garlic cloves, washed and unpeeled

1-inch fresh ginger knob, unpeeled

½ pound (226 grams) daikon radish, cut into 3 pieces

3½ ounces (100 g) baby bella mushrooms

Salt (see page 15)

2 tablespoons (30 g) apple cider vinegar (see page 3)

There's nothing like a delicious, well-made chicken broth, and if you include chicken feet, the nutritional value (and the flavor of your broth) will increase dramatically, starting with the calcium content. The cooking process triggers the release of healing compounds found within animal tissue, such as collagen (and its amino acids), glucosamine, and hyaluronic acid, which help reduce inflammation throughout the body, including the digestive tract (by helping beneficial bacteria grow), and relieve pain in connective tissues for conditions such as arthritis. A good bone broth also contains vital minerals such as calcium, magnesium, phosphorus, and sulfur and can protect against migraine headaches.

So, if you get sick, your mom will give you chicken soup. Maternal wisdom.

Creating delicious homemade food is not difficult; it's just a matter of organizing and making several batches at the same time. I often make several pots of broth at once and freeze them in glass containers to always have a tasty and super-healthy broth on hand, whether it's to incorporate into soup or to warm the soul with a simple cup of hot broth.

PREHEAT the oven to 350°F.

TO make the bouquet garni, lay out the long green leek leaf and set the fresh herbs inside. Wrap up the leaf and tie it like a package using kitchen string.

CUT the chicken into 4 pieces and remove and discard the skin and fat. Remove all the meat (you can cook or freeze it for other preparations).

PLACE all the bones on a sheet pan and roast for 25 minutes.

HEAT the olive oil in a large pot with high sides over medium-high heat. Add the carrots, celery, onion, garlic cloves, ginger, radish, and mushrooms and sauté for 5 minutes, stirring constantly. Add salt, the bouquet garni, and the roasted chicken bones. Pour in 3 quarts (3 L) water and the vinegar.

BRING to a boil, lower the heat to a simmer, and cook for about 6 hours (or 12 hours in a slow cooker on the low setting). If a lot of liquid evaporates (which could happen if it's simmering on the stove), add a bit of water to the pot from time to time so that you have a good amount of broth.

LET the broth cool, strain it, and store in the refrigerator or freezer.

pear, spinach, and fennel soup
with chicken, avocado, and cashew parmesan

MAKES 4 SERVINGS

½ cup (70 g) raw unsalted cashews

2 tablespoons (30 g) extra virgin olive oil

2 large (750 g) yellow onions, julienned

Salt (see page 15)

1 medium (225 g) fennel bulb, trimmed and julienned

1 (200 g) pear, unpeeled, cored and cut into medium dice

4 cups (1 L) Homemade Chicken Bone Broth (page 90) or vegetable broth

2 cups (60 g) baby spinach

1¼ cups (38 g) roughly chopped kale

½ cup (50 g) cooked shredded chicken, for serving

2 avocados, sliced, for serving

Cashew Parmesan (page 301), for serving

Crushed red pepper flakes, for serving (optional)

At home we have a dilemma. Some of my daughters love a light, brothy soup, but others crave a thicker, well-blended cream soup. So, I've had to get creative and come up with a soup that suits all their preferences, and this one does the trick. It's great to keep frozen shredded chicken on hand in case any enthusiastic diner asks for extra (as my girls do).

Soaking cashews for about 8 hours helps to eliminate enzyme inhibitors and activates their nutrients, making them easier to digest.

SOAK the cashews in a bowl of water at room temperature for at least 8 hours or overnight, covering the bowl with a kitchen towel. Drain and rinse well. Set aside.

HEAT the olive oil in a large pot over medium heat. Add the onions and cook, stirring occasionally to prevent burning, until they are very soft, golden brown, and lightly sweet, about 15 minutes. Add salt to taste and continue cooking, stirring constantly so that the onions do not stick or burn. When the onions have reduced to a soft, golden, and well-caramelized consistency, about 10 more minutes, add the fennel and continue cooking until the fennel becomes soft, about 5 minutes.

ADD the pear, cashews, broth, and salt to taste if necessary. Bring the broth to a simmer, then turn off the heat, allowing the flavors to integrate.

WHEN the mixture is cool enough to blend, transfer it to a blender, add the spinach and kale, and blend until the texture is silky and creamy.

SERVE hot immediately in bowls with some shredded chicken, a few slices of avocado, some cashew parmesan, and crushed red pepper flakes (if using). You can refrigerate for up to 3 days (without the chicken, avocado, and cashew parmesan).

olive, raisin, and rosemary cauliflower rice

MAKES 4 SERVINGS

2 tablespoons (30 g) extra virgin olive oil

½ red onion, cut into small dice

1 teaspoon Roasted Garlic Paste (page 294) or minced fresh garlic

1 pound (500 g) cauliflower rice, fresh if possible

1 teaspoon ground rosemary

1 cup (150 g) finely chopped pitted kalamata or Peruvian botija olives (see page 13)

⅓ cup (35 g) roughly chopped raisins

Salt (see page 15)

1 cup (120 g) raw pecan halves (optional; omit for the AIP diet)

For Christmas, my mom used to prepare some dishes worth remembering. Among them were rice with olives and raisins, baked sweet potatoes with orange juice and spices, rice salad with apples and bacon, and the main event, roasted turkey or chicken with pisco, which was truly spectacular. She loves rice and likes to use it as a side dish for everything. I'm not a big fan of it, but I die for those flavors from my childhood, and one of my favorites is her rice with olives and raisins.

This is my version, made with cauliflower rice. The mixture of raisins, olives, and rosemary is absolutely delicious, and it's a perfect side to accompany Roasted Garlic Chicken (page 174) or a roasted turkey. When making this recipe, I cook my cauliflower rice until just al dente. I personally love that slightly underdone texture, but feel free to cook it longer if you like a softer feel.

HEAT the olive oil in a large pan over medium-high heat. Add the onion and cook, stirring occasionally, until soft and translucent, 4 to 6 minutes. Add the garlic paste and cook until fragrant, stirring often. Add the cauliflower rice, rosemary, olives, and raisins and season with salt. Stirring constantly, cook until the rice is al dente, about 3 minutes, or until cooked to your preference.

IF you're using the pecans, bake on a sheet pan in a 350°F oven for about 10 minutes, until lightly toasted. Chop them roughly and use them to top the cauliflower rice just before serving, to keep them crisp.

See the photo on page 96.

roasted kabocha squash with onions and olives

MAKES 4 SERVINGS

Olives are one of those ingredients that people tend to love or hate. I'm an olive lover, maybe because I grew up in Tacna, a city famous for its giant, juicy, and flavorful botija olives, and the wonderful olive oil made with them. It is very common to eat bread with olives for breakfast or as a snack. So I may be biased, but I tend to think that people who don't like olives simply haven't yet found the right quality and type to enjoy.

I remember going to my grandfather's farm and climbing olive trees when I was a child. I think they have the most beautiful wood in existence, so much so that my father cut and varnished two trees from the farm, and the wood was used in lamp bases and other items in our house.

This recipe makes the most out of a few quality ingredients, so enjoy the simplicity and the amazing flavors. A good kabocha roasted to perfection and the richest olives you can find are a glorious combination.

One 3- to 4-pound (1.3 to 1.8 kg) kabocha squash

2 medium red onions (460 g), thinly sliced

2 teaspoons salt, plus more to taste (see page 15)

1 cup (150 g) pitted and halved Peruvian botija or Kalamata olives (see page 13)

¼ cup (60 g) fresh lime juice (from about 2 limes)

2 tablespoons (12 g) chopped fresh cilantro

2 tablespoons (30 g) extra virgin olive oil

PREHEAT the oven to 400°F.

CUT the kabocha squash in half through the stem. Use a spoon to scrape out all the seeds. Place the squash flesh side down in a 9 × 13-inch baking dish. Roast until the squash is soft when pierced with a knife or skewer, 45 to 60 minutes. Transfer the squash to a cutting board and cut each half into 2 wedges.

WHILE the squash is roasting, place the onions in a medium bowl and add enough water to cover. Add the salt, stir, and let the onions sit for about 3 minutes, to help soften the onion's strong flavor. Drain the onions and plunge them into a large bowl filled with ice water. Let sit about 10 minutes. Drain again and place them in a large bowl. Add the olives, lime juice, cilantro, olive oil, and salt to taste and stir well to combine.

TRANSFER the kabocha slices to a serving platter and place a generous portion of onion salad on top and on the side.

See the photo on page 97.

salads

sirloin and blackberry salad with goldenberry dressing

MAKES 2 SERVINGS

½ cup (55 g) dried white mulberries (see page 12)

1 tablespoon extra virgin olive oil

Two 8-ounce (250 g) sirloin steaks, 1½ inches thick

Salt (see page 15), to taste

Freshly ground black pepper, to taste (omit for the AIP diet)

5 cups (150 g) baby spinach

1 cup (140 g) fresh blackberries

2.5 ounces (70 g) fresh goldenberries, cut in half (about ½ cup; omit for the AIP diet)

1 large avocado, cut into ¾-inch dice

Goldenberry Dressing (page 289) or AIP Turmeric Dressing (page 287)

1 cup (20 g) broccoli or radish microgreens

Eating raw vegetables is just as important as eating them cooked; like everything in life, there must be a balance. That's why I like to include plenty of salads in my family's diet, which inspires me to continually think up new ways of combining ingredients. One pairing we love is fruit plus some crunchy element. Dried mulberries, in addition to being delicious and providing a great diversity of nutritional compounds, give that essential crunchy element to Camila's salads, since she cannot eat nuts or seeds. But they're a delicacy the whole family enjoys.

You can make a big batch of toasted mulberries not just for this salad but to add to yogurts, smoothie bowls, wraps—they're just so versatile and amazing. Store them in a glass jar for up to two months, depending on the humidity level where you live.

PREHEAT the oven to 325°F.

SPREAD the dried mulberries evenly in a sheet pan and bake until lightly golden, about 8 minutes. Set aside to cool; they will become crispy as they cool. Store them in a glass jar at room temperature.

HEAT the olive oil in a large pan or grill over high heat. Add the steak, season with salt and pepper, and cook without moving until seared, 3 to 6 minutes. Flip the steak and continue to cook to your desired level of doneness. Transfer the steak to a cutting board to rest for about 10 minutes, then slice it into thin strips.

DIVIDE the spinach, blackberries, goldenberries, and avocado between 2 plates. Top with the steak strips. Drizzle with the dressing of your choice and sprinkle the toasted mulberries and micro-greens on top. Serve immediately.

"maki" salad with smoked salmon, quinoa, avocado, nori, and salsa acevichada

salsa acevichada

⅔ cup (150 g) store-bought avocado oil mayonnaise

¼ cup (50 g) Leche de Tigre (recipe follows)

salad

½ pound (250 g) smoked wild-caught salmon

2 cups (260 g) cooked quinoa (see how to cook quinoa on page 168), cooled

8 baby cucumbers (560 g), cut into ½-inch sticks

2 large avocados, cut into ½-inch slices

2 cups (65 g) fresh cilantro leaves

Smoked paprika (such as sweet or spicy Pimentón de la Vera)

8 sheets toasted nori

When you have maki sushi rolls in Lima, the maki par excellence is the acevichado. This sauce is basically a mayonnaise flavored with leche de tigre, that is poured on top of the makis.

These rolls are my daughters' favorite, but making makis at home takes forever, given how much they eat, so I thought of a way to include all those wonderful flavors in one easy bowl that doesn't take as long to prepare.

This recipe uses quinoa instead of rice, which provides protein and gives the maki a unique touch, and we use the remaining leche de tigre to serve in a traditional way.

FOR THE SALSA ACEVICHADA: In a small bowl, combine the mayonnaise with the leche de tigre and mix until smooth. Refrigerate until ready to serve.

FOR THE SALAD: Slice the salmon into 1-inch strips and roll each one up. Set aside.

PLACE ½ cup quinoa on each of four plates. Top each with cucumber sticks, avocado slices, rolled salmon, and cilantro leaves. Drizzle the salsa acevichada on top and sprinkle with smoked paprika.

CUT the nori into strips and top the salad with them. (If your nori sheets are not roasted and crunchy, you can put them directly on the flame of your stove's burner for a couple of seconds, moving it across the surface so that it roasts evenly, or heat them in a pan.) Serve immediately.

leche de tigre

MAKES 4¼ CUPS (1.15 KG)

4 ounces (112 g) flounder, cod, mahi-mahi, or corvina, skin and bones removed

1 yellow onion (about 175 g, peeled), cut into 8 wedges

8 cilantro stems (no leaves)

1 (40 g) celery stalk, cut into ½-inch slices

1 tablespoon minced fresh ginger

2 garlic cloves, peeled

1½ cups (380 g) fresh lime juice

1 teaspoon fish sauce (such as Red Boat brand)

Salt (see page 15), to taste

Freshly ground black pepper, to taste

1 habanero pepper (10 g), or to taste, roughly chopped

Leche de Tigre is the "cooking" liquid of a ceviche blended with a little piece of fish to give it more consistency and flavor. The best fish for ceviche are corvina and flounder, but you can use any white fish, such as mackerel, cod, mahi-mahi, or halibut.

The traditional way of serving it is in a glass with pieces of fish (and sometimes shellfish), a little red onion, julienned chile, and fresh cilantro on top. You can also add some Peruvian giant corn kernels and toasted cancha serrana, another type of Peruvian dried corn (called chulpe) that is soaked in water for 30 minutes to 1 hour and roasted with a bit of extra virgin olive oil.

These two types of corn can be found in Latin markets, and if you can't find them, you can use plantain chips instead. Some people add a splash of evaporated cow's milk, which of course could be replaced with a splash of coconut cream if desired.

IN a blender, combine the fish, onion, cilantro stems, celery, ginger, garlic, lime juice, fish sauce, salt and pepper, and habanero and blend until very smooth. If you are not using a high-power blender, you can strain the preparation to remove any lumps. Refrigerate until ready to use; it should be very cold. Use within 24 hours.

traditional leche de tigre cups

MAKES 4 SERVINGS

PLACE the onion in a bowl of ice water. This helps mellow it out and keeps it fresh and crunchy.

CUT the fish into 1-inch cubes and season with salt and pepper.

DIVIDE the fish among four glass cups. Add a couple of tablespoons of cooked giant corn (if using) to each cup. Pour 1 cup of the leche de tigre into each of the glasses.

TOP each serving with julienned onions, cilantro, habanero slices to taste, and toasted chulpe corn (if using). Serve with more giant corn and some plantain chips (if using) on the side.

½ red onion, julienned

1 pound (460 g) white fish, such as flounder, cod, or mahi-mahi

Salt (see page 15), to taste

Freshly ground black pepper, to taste

1 cup (150 grams/5.3 ounces) Peruvian giant corn (frozen or canned, such as Belmont brand), cooked (if frozen) and cooled (optional; omit for Paleo)

4 cups (1 L) Leche de Tigre (see page 104)

Chopped cilantro, to taste

1 habanero pepper, julienned

1 cup (150 grams/5.3 ounces) salty toasted chulpe corn (such as Inca's Food or Del Campo brand; optional; omit for Paleo)

Plantain chips, for serving (optional)

rainbow salad with dried goldenberries and hibiscus dressing

MAKES 2 SERVINGS

Surely you've heard the saying "Eat the rainbow." Beyond that lovely phrase is real science on the nutrient content signaled by the colors of our fresh fruits and vegetables. I trust that nature creates all these colors to show us that there is no one magic ingredient that is the secret to great health; a combination of all these colors in their most perfect and natural states can show you the way. But most important, a plate full of colors stimulates your senses, satisfies your hunger, makes you vibrate, and fills your soul with joy—the ultimate in mindful eating.

This salad can be a side dish to share or a complete meal in itself. Crunchy, salty, sweet, and sour—all the textures and flavors merge in a salad that fills you with energy and satisfaction.

1½ cups (80 g) hand-ripped curly kale, tough stems removed

2 cups (40 g) baby arugula

1 cup (80 g) julienned raw beet

1½ cups (100 g) julienned red cabbage

½ cup (40 g) peeled and julienned rainbow carrots

2 avocados, cut into ¼-inch slices

½ cup (10 g) fresh cilantro leaves

¼ cup (40 g) dried goldenberries

3 tablespoons (30 g) roasted shelled pistachios

Hibiscus Dressing (page 283)

DIVIDE the kale, arugula, beets, cabbage, carrots, and avocados equally between two serving bowls, making a little pile of each so you can see the glorious colors. Top with the cilantro, dried goldenberries, and pistachios. Drizzle with a little of the hibiscus dressing. Serve immediately.

kabocha squash and dried fig salad

MAKES 4 SERVINGS

roasted kabocha

One 3-pound (1.3 kg) kabocha squash, unpeeled, halved, seeded, and cut into 1½-inch slices

¼ cup (50 g) extra virgin olive oil

1 to 2 tablespoons pure maple syrup

1 teaspoon ras el hanout

Salt (see page 15)

salad

9 cups (220 g) baby arugula

3 cups (60 g) microgreens, such as arugula, broccoli, radish, kale, mustard, cilantro

¾ cup (108 g) ½-inch-diced dried figs

¾ cup (80 g) toasted walnuts (see page 109)

2 large avocados, cut into 1-inch cubes

Chia Balsamic Dressing (page 282)

Ras el hanout is a Moroccan spice mix. The name translates to "head of the store," which implies a mixture of the best spices that the seller can offer you from their shop. Like all spice mixes, the composition depends on the individual who makes it, as these recipes are typically passed from generation to generation, like Mama's apple pie recipe. Commonly used ingredients include cardamom, cumin, clove, cinnamon, nutmeg, mace, allspice, ginger, chile pepper, coriander seed, peppercorn, sweet and hot paprika, fenugreek, and turmeric. Today you can often find ras el hanout made from organic ingredients.

PREHEAT the oven to 400°F. Line a sheet pan with parchment paper.

FOR THE ROASTED KABOCHA: In a large bowl, combine the kabocha slices, olive oil, maple syrup, ras el hanout, and salt to taste. Use your hands to mix all the ingredients well, so the squash is completely covered in the seasoning. Spread the squash out on the prepared sheet pan and roast until cooked through and caramelized in parts, about 1 hour.

FOR THE SALAD: Divide the arugula, microgreens, dried figs, walnuts, and avocado evenly among 4 plates. Top each with some of the kabocha squash slices and drizzle with the dressing. Serve immediately.

toasting walnuts

HEAT A SMALL SKILLET OVER MEDIUM-LOW HEAT. Add the walnuts and cook, stirring constantly, until they are golden brown in parts and toasted, 3 to 6 minutes. Transfer the walnuts to a small bowl and set aside. (You can also toast walnuts for about 10 minutes in a 350°F oven.)

smoked salmon bowls with crisp air-fried yuca sticks

MAKES 2 SERVINGS

6 ounces (170 g) fresh or frozen yuca, peeled, deveined, and cut into 3 × ½-inch sticks

Extra virgin olive oil, as needed

Salt (see page 15), to taste

3 cups mixed greens, such as chopped or baby spinach, kale, lettuce, and arugula

2 cups (120 g) packaged coleslaw mix

3 cups (170 g) coarsely shredded carrots

½ cup (50 g) thinly sliced radishes

1 cup (20 g) microgreens, such as arugula, kale, radish, broccoli, or mustard

1 large avocado, cut into ¼-inch slices

5½ ounces (150 g) smoked wild-caught salmon

Dill Coconut Yogurt Dressing (page 284)

Bowls can be made in multiple ways with a wide variety of ingredients—cold, hot, cooked, raw, creamy, crunchy—and it's incredibly fun to build them with different colors and textures. I love to lay out all the ingredients in separate containers, creating a buffet where the girls can choose their own unique combinations of vegetables. This also promotes conversation about the flavors, textures, and benefits of each vegetable.

I love including microgreens because they are believed to contain a higher concentration of nutrients than their fully grown, mature counterparts. They are an uberconcentrated superfood.

OPTIONAL: Place the yuca in a large bowl and cover with water. Let soak for a couple of hours (see page 17), then drain and rinse under cold water.

PLACE the yuca sticks in a medium saucepan and cover completely with cold water. Bring to a boil over high heat and simmer just until soft when poked with a fork, about 5 minutes. Be careful not to overcook them.

DRAIN the yuca sticks, then spread them out on a cutting board and pat them dry with a paper towel.

PLACE the yuca in a medium bowl and drizzle with a little olive oil. Season with salt and mix gently with your hands until the yuca sticks are evenly coated in the oil and salt.

TRANSFER the yuca sticks to the air fryer and fry for about 15 minutes. Flip them over and fry until crisp, about another 8 minutes.

MEANWHILE, in two bowls, arrange the mixed greens, coleslaw mix, carrots, radishes, microgreens, avocado slices, and salmon one next to the other. Place the air-fried yuca sticks on the side in the bowl and drizzle everything with the dill coconut yogurt dressing. Serve immediately.

roasted beet, endive, pistachio, and orange salad

MAKES 2 SERVINGS

Have you ever been to a fancy restaurant and been served a dish that the chef executed like a beautiful painting? Well, now it's our turn to create an elegant dish at home using healthy and organic ingredients. The trick here is cooking the beets to sweet, caramelized perfection—they're beautiful paired with a magnificent crisp, fresh endive. This is a lovely dish to look at, worthy of a five-star restaurant. Prepare it as a starter for a romantic meal at home, and pair with your best bottle of wine.

PREHEAT the oven to 350°F. Line a sheet pan with parchment paper.

PLACE the beets on the prepared sheet pan. Drizzle them with the olive oil and season them with salt. Toss to combine, then crumple a second piece of parchment paper and wrap it around the beets (this is a way to avoid using aluminum foil). Roast for 40 minutes, then remove the parchment wrap and roast for 40 more minutes, until the beets are soft and caramelized.

ARRANGE 4 of the beet wedges on each plate, then decorate with the endive leaves. Scatter the supreme orange segments across the plates and sprinkle the microgreens and pistachios on top. Top with the dressing and serve immediately.

2 medium beets (340 g), unpeeled, trimmed, and quartered

2 tablespoons (30 g) extra virgin olive oil

Salt (see page 15), to taste

2 medium to large endive heads, leaves washed and separated (use the hearts as well; they are very tasty)

1 orange, peeled and cut into supremes (see Note)

4 tablespoons (10 g) mustard (or other) microgreens

¼ cup (35 g) roasted shelled pistachios

Mustard-Orange Vinaigrette (page 286)

NOTE

To supreme citrus, use a sharp knife to carefully cut off all the peel and pith, revealing the pulp, then slide the knife between the pulp and the membranes to release the supreme segments. Reserve in a bowl to preserve the juice!

greens and pear salad

MAKES 2 SERVINGS

Does this ever happen to you? You get to the store and see a beautiful display of bright and colorful radish bunches. And all you want to do is pounce on the cutest one and run home to make a salad!

And what about its leaves? Well, they're completely edible—you can eat the small, tender ones raw, and the big ones can be made into an amazing peppery pesto or sautéed with other veggies. They're delicious and loaded with antioxidants and vitamins.

Another great reason to use the entire vegetable is that it has environmental, social, and economic benefits. According to the United Nations, 811 million people go to bed hungry each night and one-third of food is lost or wasted, for a loss of about $1 trillion annually. So, we as consumers need to do something to avoid wasting food at home.

We can change the world from our kitchen. Let's start by using the whole edible plant.

1 medium shallot, peeled and thinly sliced

Salt (see page 15)

Greens from 2 radish bunches

2 bunches (5 ounces/141 g) fresh mustard greens

2 pears, unpeeled, cored and thinly sliced

2 tablespoons (1 or 2 ounces/ 30 g) whole or chopped roasted mixed nuts

AIP Turmeric Dressing (page 287) or Pomegranate Molasses Dressing (page 290)

TO reduce the shallot's strong taste, put the sliced shallot in a fine-mesh strainer and add 1 teaspoon of salt and a splash of water. With one hand, massage for about 5 seconds, then rinse. To maintain the crunch, place the shallot slices in a bowl of ice water and drain right before serving.

PLACE the radish and mustard greens on a plate and top with the pear slices. Add the shallot and toasted nuts and drizzle all over with the dressing. Serve immediately.

creamy potato and pea salad

MAKES 2 SERVINGS

salad

2 medium russet potatoes
(½ pound/250 g)

½ medium red onion,
cut into small dice

½ cup (100 g) cooked peas

3 cups (65 g) hand-torn
romaine or butter lettuce

mayonnaise dressing

¼ cup (68 g) Horseradish
Quinoa Mayonnaise
(page 293)

½ teaspoon dried dill

Juice of ½ lime

1 tablespoon extra
virgin olive oil

¼ teaspoon pure maple syrup

Salt (see page 15)

This is my variation on a recipe my mom used to make for Christmas. Even with potatoes as the main ingredient, it's super fresh and light. Romaine lettuce is one of our favorites at home (we even eat it alone as a snack), and it provides a crunchy, refreshing, flavorful element to this dish. Of course, my mom's original recipe was made with conventional mayonnaise, but I was excited to try swapping in my quinoa mayonnaise for added protein, and it was a great idea.

Having a huge variety of potatoes to choose from in Peru, our favorite for this recipe was the yellow potato. It's quite different from the yellow potatoes found in America, so if you have the opportunity to try them in Peru, or find them here in any market, don't miss the chance—you'll fall in love! Now, being in America, the potato variety that we really love is the russet, which, as a bonus, is also very easy to peel after cooking.

It's important to note that a freshly cooked potato doesn't have the same health benefits as a potato that has been cooked and then refrigerated. Read about how to convert the starch in potatoes into a resistant starch on page 13—and note that you should cook the potatoes a day ahead to help achieve this!

BOIL the potatoes in a saucepan of water to cover until you can pierce them easily with a toothpick, about 20 minutes. Peel the potatoes and refrigerate them overnight. Cut the potatoes into 1-inch cubes.

FOR THE MAYONNAISE DRESSING: In a small bowl, whisk the quinoa mayonnaise, dill, lime juice, olive oil, maple syrup, salt to taste, and 1 tablespoon water.

IN a large bowl, combine the potato, onion, peas, and lettuce. Add the mayonnaise dressing and toss to combine.

SERVE immediately or refrigerate and serve within a few hours.

fennel and apple salad with candied pecans

MAKES 2 SERVINGS

candied pecans

1 cup (115 g) raw unsalted pecan halves

1 tablespoon pure maple syrup

1½ teaspoons coconut sugar (see page 7)

Pinch of salt (see page 15)

salad

2 large fennel bulbs, trimmed and julienned

1 Granny Smith apple, unpeeled, cored and julienned

¼ cup (5 g) microgreens, such as kale, radish, or arugula

¼ cup (8g) julienned fresh mint leaves

Mustard-Orange Vinaigrette (page 286)

There's always fresh fennel in my house. I love adding it to soups and throwing it on the grill, but this crunchy fennel salad is one of my family's favorite dishes. The fennel's delicate, crisp anise flavor blends marvelously with the fruity sweetness of fresh mint and becomes even more vibrant with the addition of apple. The salad doesn't necessarily need any more sweetness, but after eating it many times, I had a craving to add some caramelized pecans, so I found the perfect balance of maple syrup and coconut sugar to coat the nuts and harmonize with the other ingredients. Do not be tempted to eat all the pecans before you finish making the salad!

PREHEAT the oven to 350°F. Line a sheet pan with a silicone mat or parchment paper.

FOR THE CANDIED PECANS: In a medium bowl, mix the pecans, maple syrup, coconut sugar, and salt until the pecans are evenly coated. Spread the pecans out on the prepared sheet pan, taking care that the pecans don't touch each other. This will help them bake evenly.

BAKE the pecans about 15 minutes, or until golden brown. Set them aside on the sheet pan until cooled completely. They will crisp up and harden as they cool.

FOR THE SALAD: Arrange the fennel, apple, microgreens, mint, and pecans on a plate and drizzle the dressing on top. Serve immediately.

supergreens, brussels sprout, fresh fig, and walnut salad

MAKES 2 SERVINGS

Fresh figs are like treasures—so very delicate and as perfect on the inside as nature itself. While living in Lima, we used to take trips to the beach, and on the drive there, we would pass many farms along the highway that produced figs. The farmers used to set up tables made of several wooden boxes on the side of the road and cover them with freshly harvested figs. Waving sticks and plastic bags, the farmers would try to get the attention of people driving by. At the beach we loved adding figs to salads or eating them alone as a snack, and if I had time, I would make jam from them. Camila, who is the number one fig fan at home, likes to eat them with raspberries and coconut nectar as a special snack.

At our new house in Georgia (for which we feel infinite gratitude every day), we grow many things, but the first thing I thought of when we moved in was, *We need a fig tree!* The tree is still young, so while I look forward to the day it bears a harvest, I enjoy the beautiful figs from the local farmers' markets and make the freshest salads, honoring the perfection of figs.

½ medium shallot (30 g), julienned

3 cups (90 g) seasonal baby greens (such as sweet pea leaves, baby kale, baby spinach, baby bok choy, baby chard, and/or any other baby greens in season)

3 Brussels sprouts (40 g), thinly sliced

20 fresh basil leaves

8 (100 g) fresh purple or green figs, quartered

½ cup (30 g) toasted walnuts (see page 109)

Chia Balsamic Dressing (page 282)

PLACE the shallot in a bowl with ice water for 5 minutes to help mellow out the flavor. Drain.

IN a large bowl, combine the baby greens, Brussels sprouts, basil, figs, shallot, and walnuts. Serve with the dressing.

grilled salmon salad with vegetables and tahini sauce

MAKES 2 SERVINGS

tahini sauce

2 teaspoons cumin seeds

2 teaspoons coriander seeds

¼ cup plus 2 tablespoons (100 g) tahini

Juice of 1 lime

2 tablespoons (30 g) extra virgin olive oil

1 teaspoon smoked paprika (such as sweet Pimentón de la Vera)

Sea salt or other salt (see page 15), to taste

Freshly ground black pepper, to taste

salmon

Two 5-ounce (141 g) salmon fillets

1 tablespoon extra virgin olive oil

Salt (see page 15)

salad

4 (about 280 g) baby cucumbers, cut into ½-inch-thick sticks

6 ounces (160 g) sugar snap peas, julienned

¼ cup (8 g) julienned fresh mint leaves

1 cup (3.5 ounces/100 g) halved seedless grapes

2 large avocados, cut into ½-inch dice

½ fresh jalapeño, julienned

1½ cups (30 g) cilantro leaves

¼ cup (45 g) pomegranate arils

Dukkah (page 70), to taste

Grilled salmon makes almost everyone happy, and tahini's unique taste is addictive. Part of my heart is in the Middle East. I have never been there, but it is a dream of mine to be able to take a trip there one day. When I was a child, I loved sitting at the kitchen table reading my mom's cookbooks while I watched her cook. She also collected some cooking magazines with recipes from all over the world, but the ones that most caught my attention were recipes from Israel, Turkey, Lebanon, and Egypt. I am fascinated by these cuisines; the aromas, textures, and the endless combination of spices are really a caress to the soul.

Tahini is one of those ingredients that appears to be very simple—it's basically just a sesame butter. But its flavor is incredibly delightful. It can turn any dish into something marvelous, and it's abundant in nutrients, including calcium.

You can find infinite variety in the depth of flavor, depending on the origin of the sesame, the level of toasting, how it's processed, and so on. Try whatever different brands you can find, focusing on those that are organic and come from Israel, Lebanon, or Palestine. You'll eventually find your favorite among the rainbow of flavors.

FOR THE TAHINI SAUCE: In a small cast-iron pan without any oil, toast the cumin and coriander seeds over medium heat. When they begin to release their aroma, transfer them to a mortar or spice grinder and grind them as finely as possible.

IN a medium bowl, whisk the tahini and lime juice until combined. While continuing to whisk, slowly pour in ¼ cup plus 2 tablespoons (90 g) water and the olive oil until the mixture is smooth. Add ½ teaspoon of the ground cumin and coriander mixture and the smoked paprika and season with salt and pepper. (Reserve the rest of the cumin-coriander mixture for seasoning potatoes or grilling chicken.)

FOR THE SALMON: Preheat a grill or grill pan to medium-high and oil the grates of the grill.

COAT the salmon all over with the olive oil and sprinkle with salt. Grill the salmon until cooked through, 3 to 4 minutes per side. Set aside to rest.

FOR THE SALAD: On one-half of each plate, arrange the cucumber sticks, snap peas, mint leaves, grapes, avocado, jalapeño, and cilantro. Drizzle the tahini sauce over the salad and sprinkle with the pomegranate arils and dukkah. Serve immediately with the salmon on the side.

main courses

yuca cakes

MAKES 8 SERVINGS

These tasty yuca cakes can be eaten alone as an appetizer or snack or turned into a full meal. Easy to transport, they're perfect for school and work lunch boxes or in a picnic basket for a day in the park. When I begin frying these cakes at home, the girls immediately notice the incredible smell and buzz to the kitchen one by one like flies to hover around the plate, impatient for me to finish cooking. I top the plate of cakes with a generous portion of spicy onion salad, and everyone is ready to eat. This dish is in constant rotation at our house!

Don't like pork? You can substitute your filling of choice—such as ground beef, or jackfruit for a vegan option.

Also, note that this recipe requires time to soak the yuca and to refrigerate the yuca cakes, so be sure to read the recipe carefully and plan ahead.

FOR THE YUCA DOUGH: Optional: Place the yuca in a large bowl or pot and cover with water. Let soak for about 2 hours (see page 17), then drain and rinse the yuca.

PLACE the yuca in a pot and cover with water. Bring to a boil over medium-high heat and simmer until the yuca is fork-tender, very soft but firm, about 5 minutes. Do not overcook the yuca or your dough will be very sticky and difficult to handle. Transfer the yuca to a colander and drain well.

WHILE still very hot, carefully puree the yuca by pushing it through a potato ricer, processing it in a food processor, or mashing it with a fork in a large bowl until smooth. Add the ají amarillo paste, garlic-herb or roasted garlic paste, and salt.

WHILE the yuca is still hot (if possible), knead the ingredients into the dough using your hands (you can wait a few minutes for it to cool down if need be). When you have a homogeneous dough, transfer it to a clean bowl, cover it with plastic wrap, and refrigerate until very cold, 2 to 3 hours or overnight (recommended). This

yuca dough

2½ pounds (1.13 kg) fresh or frozen yuca, peeled and deveined, or frozen yuca sticks (3 × 1 inch)

1 tablespoon ají amarillo (yellow pepper) paste or ají panca paste (such as Zócalo brand, found in Latin markets or online)

1 tablespoon Garlic-Herb Paste (page 294) or Roasted Garlic Paste (page 294)

Salt (see page 15), to taste

Avocado oil or organic extra virgin coconut oil, for frying

filling

2 tablespoons (30 g) lard or beef tallow (or shortening or olive oil, for a vegan option)

1 medium yellow onion (320 g), cut into small dice

4 garlic cloves, minced

1 pound (454 g) ground pork (or ground beef or canned jackfruit, such as Native Forest brand)

¼ teaspoon ground cumin

1 teaspoon sea salt, plus more to taste

¼ teaspoon freshly ground black pepper

2 tablespoons (44 g) ají panca paste

1 teaspoon apple cider vinegar (see page 3)

1 teaspoon coconut
sugar (see page 7)

¼ cup (70 g) tomato puree

⅓ cup (50 g) raisins

16 Peruvian botija or
kalamata olives (see page
13), roughly chopped

1 tablespoon chopped
fresh cilantro

Cassava flour (see page
17), as needed

spicy onion salad

2 medium red onions
(640 g), trimmed, halved,
and thinly sliced

Salt, to taste

1 fresh Peruvian yellow pepper,
julienned (or your favorite
chile, such as habanero,
serrano, or jalapeño)

3 tablespoons (25 g)
chopped fresh cilantro

2 tablespoons (30 g)
extra virgin olive oil

3 to 4 tablespoons (45 to
60 g) fresh lime juice

Freshly ground black
pepper, to taste

4 hard-boiled eggs, for serving

will make it easier to shape the cakes. You can also make the dough one day in advance.

FOR THE FILLING: In a large cast-iron or heavy-bottomed skillet, melt the lard over medium-high heat. Add the onion and garlic and sauté until soft and translucent, 4 to 6 minutes.

ADD the ground pork, cumin, salt, and pepper and cook, stirring constantly, until it is just beginning to brown. Stir in the ají panca paste and cook until the meat is browned, 2 to 4 more minutes. Stir in the vinegar, coconut sugar, tomato puree, and ¾ cup (180 g) water.

COVER the pan with the lid and cook over medium heat, stirring once or twice, until the pork is very soft, about 5 minutes. Stir in the raisins and olives and cook, uncovered, until the raisins are plump and heated through, about 3 minutes.

WHEN the meat is fully cooked and the liquid has been reduced almost completely, remove from the heat and stir in the cilantro. Transfer the mixture to a bowl and let cool to room temperature, then refrigerate until very cold, 2 to 4 hours or overnight. When the fat hardens from the cold, it becomes more manageable to fill the cakes and then melts into a very juicy filling.

FOR THE ONION SALAD: Place the onion in a bowl of ice water with 1 teaspoon salt. Let it rest for 10 minutes (this mellows the onion). Drain the onion and dry it lightly with a paper towel. Right before you fry the yuca cakes, combine the onion in a bowl with the chile, cilantro, olive oil, lime juice, and salt and pepper.

TO ASSEMBLE AND FRY: Generously sprinkle a sheet pan with cassava flour. Place about ¼ cup of cassava flour on a separate large plate.

DIVIDE the dough into 8 equal-size balls. Gently flatten a ball of dough into a circle, as thin as you can. You can do this in your hands or use the floured plate to support your dough and stretch it with your fingers. Place one-eighth of the filling in the center. Use your hands to fold the dough over the filling into an oval shape and seal the edges by pinching with your fingers. Roll the cake in the flour on the plate to coat it with a thin layer of flour (this will help keep it from sticking to the pan when frying). Transfer the cake to the prepared sheet pan. Repeat this process with the remaining dough and filling to make a total of 8 yuca cakes.

FILL a large skillet with a finger (about ⅓ inch) of avocado oil and heat until the oil is hot, about 360°F (though I usually just let my hand hover over the oil to see if it's hot enough). Fry the cakes in batches, flipping them halfway through, until golden brown on all sides, adding more oil as needed. Transfer the cakes to a paper towel–lined plate to drain.

SERVE immediately with the onion salad and some hard-boiled egg wedges.

AIP MODIFICATIONS

in the yuca dough
Omit the ají panca and ají amarillo paste.

in the filling
Omit the ají panca paste, cumin, and black pepper.

Replace the tomato paste with cooked beet and carrot puree.

Add ½ teaspoon ground bay leaf.

in the salad
Omit the chile and black pepper.

VEGAN MODIFICATIONS
Substitute jackfruit for the pork and shortening for the lard.

chicken salad tacos

MAKES 4 SERVINGS (1 LARGE TACO PER SERVING)

paleo pink tortillas (for the AIP diet, use AIP Tortillas, page 194)

½ cup plus 1 tablespoon (65 g) superfine blanched almond flour (such as Bob's Red Mill brand)

1½ teaspoons beet powder

¾ cup (100 g) tapioca flour

¼ teaspoon salt (see page 15)

1 tablespoon avocado oil

Cassava flour (see page 17), for rolling out the dough

chicken salad filling

¾ cup (100 g) diced red onion

¼ cup (65 g) diced fresh peach

1½ cups (150 g) shredded chicken (Tip: use frozen precooked shredded chicken)

⅔ cup (150 g) Cashew Mayonnaise (page 292; for the AIP diet, use Dill Coconut Yogurt Dressing, page 284)

Juice of 1 lime

¾ cup (15 g) chopped fresh cilantro

2 cups (60 g) baby spinach

2 large avocados, cut into ¼-inch slices

Salt (see page 15), to taste

These tacos, in addition to being super nutritious, are hilarious for children. Who wouldn't want to eat a taco or wrap that comes in a fun shade of pink? I like these even more because I know that behind that beautiful color are incredible nutrients for my girls. The tacos are also light and delicious and give them an energy kick. Let the kids assemble their own tacos and have fun messing around in the kitchen. It may take a bit of time to get the hang of making these, but you'll figure it out, just like I did.

FOR THE PALEO PINK TORTILLAS: In a medium bowl, combine the almond flour, beet powder, tapioca flour, and salt. Add the avocado oil and ⅓ cup (80 g) water and stir until completely combined.

LET the mixture sit for 15 minutes, until the tapioca has absorbed some of the liquid and the dough takes on a more manageable consistency. The mixture will seem quite liquidy at first, but give it time.

PLACE some parchment paper on a work surface and sprinkle it with cassava flour. Divide the dough into 4 equal portions.

FLOUR your hand with cassava flour and pick up one portion of dough. Sprinkle a little more flour on top and roll the dough into a ball shape. Place it on the parchment paper and flatten it with your hand. Add a little more flour and place another piece of parchment on top. With a rolling pin, roll it into a 6- to 7-inch circle. If necessary, lift the paper and sprinkle more flour so that it does not stick.

HEAT a cast-iron skillet (without oil) over medium-high heat.

WITH an oversize metal spatula or cake lifter, slowly remove the tortilla from the paper and place it in the pan. Lightly brown the tortilla on both sides, 1 to 1½ minutes per side.

TRANSFER the tortilla to a kitchen towel–lined plate. Cover it with another kitchen towel to keep it warm and moist.

REPEAT to make the other three tortillas.

FOR THE FILLING AND TO SERVE: In a medium bowl, combine the onion, peach, chicken, mayonnaise, lime juice, and cilantro. Mix well.

PLACE ½ cup of spinach (or more if you want) and a few slices of avocado on each tortilla and season lightly with salt. Add the chicken salad filling, fold the tacos, and serve immediately.

yuca gnocchi with carrot greens pesto

MAKES 4 SERVINGS

gnocchi

1½ pounds (680 g) frozen yuca sticks

2 cups (300 g) cassava flour (see page 17)

1 teaspoon salt (see page 15), plus more to taste

3 tablespoons (45 g) extra virgin olive oil, plus more for the pan

3 tablespoons (30 g) nutritional yeast

Cashew Parmesan (page 301; omit for the AIP diet), to serve

carrot greens pesto

3½ ounces (about 1 cup/ 100 g) pecan halves (omit for the AIP diet)

Greens from 1 bunch carrots, thick parts of the stems discarded (55 grams)

1½ tablespoons nutritional yeast

2.3 ounces (65 g) basil (2½ cups, lightly packed; increase to 4 cups/100 g for the AIP diet)

½ cup (120 g) extra virgin olive oil, plus more for storing

½ teaspoon Garlic-Herb Paste (page 294; see Notes)

Salt (see page 15), to taste

Making gnocchi is such a wonderful way to include children in the kitchen! When Cami and Gala were little, it was one of our favorite activities, especially when they had their little friends over for playdates. We made the gnocchi in three colors: yellow (with carrot), green (with spinach), and fuchsia (with beet). It was like playing with Play-Doh. And of course, when children participate in the preparation of their food, they are much more eager to eat it. My heart swells with fondness, remembering those uncomplicated and funny times. How fast our children grow, right?

FOR THE GNOCCHI: Optional: Place the yuca in a large bowl and cover with water. Let soak for a couple of hours (see page 17), then drain and rinse under cold water.

PLACE the yuca in a medium saucepan and cover with cold water. Bring to a boil over high heat. Lower the heat to a simmer and cook until the yuca is soft when poked with a fork, about 5 minutes. Be careful not to overcook it; you don't want it too soggy.

DRAIN the yuca and place it in a food processor while still hot. Process until very smooth.

ADD the cassava flour, salt, olive oil, and nutritional yeast and process until a dough forms that is solid enough to shape with your hands, similar to Play-Doh. If the dough seems watery, add more flour. If too firm, add a bit of water.

DUST a work surface or silicone mat with cassava flour. Transfer the dough to the work surface and knead until smooth and uniform. Divide the dough into 5 equal pieces, set them on a plate, and cover the plate in plastic wrap so that the dough does not dry out.

ROLL one piece of dough into a ball, then roll it into a rope about 30 inches (76 cm) long. Cut the rope into pieces about ¾ inch (2 cm) in diameter.

THE gnocchi can be boiled just like this, or you can pass the dough balls over a gnocchi board to shape them, or you can roll them over the back of a fork. The tines will give the gnocchi their distinctive ridges. (See Notes for instructions on freezing if you prefer.)

FOR THE CARROT GREENS PESTO: Preheat the oven to 350°F. Spread the pecans on a sheet pan and toast them for 8 to 10 minutes, until they begin to release the delicious aroma of toasted pecans. Set aside to cool.

PLACE the carrot greens, toasted pecans, nutritional yeast, basil, olive oil, garlic-herb paste, and salt to taste in a food processor or blender and process to your desired consistency. Some people like a pesto with a coarse texture and others like it very creamy. I love both.

STORE the pesto in the fridge in a glass jar with a splash of olive oil on top to protect the top layer from oxidation. I often double or triple the recipe to keep it on hand to use with pasta, to replace tomato sauce on pizza, as a spread on toast, or as a dip or sauce to accompany a variety of dishes.

TO COOK AND SERVE: To cook the gnocchi, bring a large pot of water to a boil over medium-high heat with a tablespoon of olive oil and a little salt.

WORKING in batches, boil the gnocchi. When they float to the top, give them about 10 seconds more, then transfer them with a slotted spoon to a large skillet lightly coated with olive oil. (Remember that the yuca was already cooked, so it doesn't need much time to cook in the water.) Heat the gnocchi further only if they cool down as you work. Stir in the pesto and season with salt.

SERVE in bowls sprinkled with some cashew parmesan.

See the photo on page 134.

NOTES
You can substitute garlic powder, but if you have a jar of this paste in your fridge, you'll end up using it in everything from stir-fries and stews to rice and mashed potatoes. It's even good just spread on toast!

You can freeze these gnocchi for future use! Shape the gnocchi but don't cook them. Place them in a baking dish with a little cassava flour and freeze them for a couple of hours, until well frozen. Transfer them to a freezer bag and store them in the freezer for up to 4 months.

MAIN COURSES

133

mac and huancaína

MAKES 4 TO 6 SERVINGS

1 cup (150 g) raw cashews

16 ounces (454 g) frozen or jarred Peruvian yellow peppers (look in Latin markets or online)

1 medium yellow onion, halved and cut into 8 pieces

½ cup (100 g) extra virgin olive oil

⅓ cup plus 1 tablespoon (50 g) raw pecans

¼ cup (22 g) nutritional yeast

½ teaspoon garlic powder

2 tablespoons (20 g) tapioca flour

2 teaspoons salt (see page 15)

1 tablespoon coconut sugar (see page 7)

¼ teaspoon ground turmeric (see page 16)

¼ teaspoon freshly ground black pepper

Two 8-ounce (227 g) boxes cassava or gluten-free elbow pasta (such as Jovial brand)

Cashew Parmesan (page 301), for serving

A classic dish in Peru, spaghetti with huancaína sauce is a rough equivalent to an American mac and cheese. But what would happen if we put both cuisines together? Here I fuse them into one delicious yet healthy dish.

The classic recipe for Peruvian huancaína sauce contains yellow chile peppers, milk, and cheese. It is served over boiled potatoes, with a botija olive and some lettuce leaves. It became a popular accompaniment to many dishes, such as baby potatoes—an appetizer we call "cocktail potatoes"—and fried yuca sticks. One of the most favorite uses for this divine sauce, and my daughters' favorite when it comes to traditional food, is pasta with huancaína and anticucho (beef heart skewers with a spicy dressing).

The original version of huancaína sauce is creamy but light. Here, I wanted to make it very gooey, to resemble the traditional melted cheese sauce used in macaroni and cheese.

The spice level of your dish will depend on how much of the veins and seeds you include from the Peruvian peppers. I like my peppers with only a few veins, but Sebas, Gala, and Julieta love spicy food, so I often keep all the veins and most of the seeds.

Remember that we must soak the cashews to activate their nutrients and make them more digestible, so plan to soak them overnight or at least eight hours.

SOAK the cashews in a bowl of water at room temperature for at least 8 hours or overnight, covering the bowl with a kitchen towel. Drain and rinse the cashews, then dry them with a kitchen towel.

MEANWHILE, if you are using frozen peppers, bring a medium saucepan of water to a boil over high heat and boil them until soft. Drain the peppers. Then, whether you are using jarred peppers or cooked, put on a pair of gloves (to protect your hands from the peppers, which can burn) and remove the veins and seeds, according to your taste.

HEAT ¼ cup of the oil in a medium saucepan over medium-high heat. Add the onion and sauté until it is deep golden brown in parts, almost burned, about 8 minutes.

TRANSFER the onion, any olive oil left in the pan, and the remaining ¼ cup of oil to a blender (reserve the saucepan for the next step). Add the cashews, yellow peppers, pecans, nutritional yeast, garlic powder, tapioca flour, salt, coconut sugar, turmeric, black pepper, and 1½ cups (360 g) water to the blender and blend into a creamy, silky huancaína sauce.

TRANSFER the sauce to the saucepan, set it over medium-high heat, and cook, stirring constantly, until the sauce thickens, about 4 minutes.

FILL a large pot with water and bring it to a boil. Add salt and a splash of olive oil. Add the pasta and cook according to the package directions.

DRAIN the pasta and place it in a large bowl with the huancaína sauce. Stir to combine. Serve with cashew parmesan sprinkled on top.

See the photo on page 135.

AIP ravioli with oxtail sauce

MAKES 4 SERVINGS

Ravioli has always been one of my daughter Camila's favorite dishes, but after she began following an AIP diet, it was practically impossible to find a ravioli dish that was suitable for her, as the diet is incredibly restrictive and creating a shapable dough was quite a challenge. I finally discovered the perfect balance of ingredients to create the pasta, which prompted the next exciting question: What do we fill them with?

My mom and grandma used to cook a kind of beef called asado, a cut that I haven't been able to find an equivalent for in America. This cut was cooked for hours with red wine, broth, carrots, onions, and dried plums, then served super tender with mashed potatoes or rice for a truly exceptional dish. It was strong, slightly sweet, deep, intense, and super comforting—a classic mother's dish, with all the warmth of home. Camila always asked her grandma for it; it was a very special dish. So asado was the clear choice for our filling. The love of Mom and Abui (what my girls call my mom) in a ravioli shape.

Since the cut of meat we call asado is hard to find in the United States, I'm substituting oxtail for flavor and sirloin for volume. The combination makes a perfect ravioli filling.

Because this gluten-free ravioli dough is very delicate, it will break easily, and these ravioli are best made by hand, one by one. But it's worth practicing until you master it. I like to double or triple the recipe and freeze my ravioli to have on hand for a quick dinner or lunch. You can freeze the ravioli and sauce separately.

The gluten-free ravioli dough does require the use of a bunch of different specialty flours, but they are important to make the dough stretchy, and the combination of acacia and konjac helps to create that elasticity and also is a source of resistant starch, which has great benefits for your gut bacteria.

meat filling and sauce

¼ ounce (7 g) dried porcini mushrooms

½ cup (120 g) boiling water

2 tablespoons (30 g) extra virgin olive oil

2 pounds (850 g) oxtail, cut into 3- to 4-inch chunks, but left on the bone

9 ounces (250 g) top sirloin, cut into 3- to 4-inch chunks

¾ cup (100 g) ½-inch-diced celery

1 cup (100 g) thinly sliced leek (discard the last ½ inch of the dark green part or use it in broth or stock)

¾ cup (100 g) peeled, small-diced carrots

1 small yellow onion, cut into small dice

½ cup (100 g) pitted whole prunes, plus more finely chopped prunes for the filling (optional)

1 cup (240 g) cabernet sauvignon (even here, always try to buy organic), beef bone broth, water, or a combination

½ teaspoon dried thyme

½ teaspoon dried rosemary

1½ teaspoons salt (see page 15), plus more to taste

FOR THE MEAT FILLING AND SAUCE: Place the porcini and boiling water in a bowl. Cover and let sit until the mushrooms are rehydrated, about 30 minutes.

1 cup plus ⅔ cup (230 g) cassava flour (see page 17), plus more as needed

¾ cup (100 g) tapioca flour

2 tablespoons (18 g) coconut flour (such as Let's Do Organic brand)

1 tablespoon plus 1 teaspoon (10 g) acacia fiber (see page 1)

2 tablespoons plus 2 teaspoons (30 g) glucomannan (konjac root powder; see page 9)

½ teaspoon salt (see page 15)

1⅓ cups (330 ml) warm water, plus more as needed

for serving

Extra virgin olive oil (optional)

Nutritional yeast (or Cashew Parmesan, page 301, if not on the AIP diet)

MEANWHILE, in a large pot or Dutch oven (or an Instant Pot), heat the olive oil over high heat. Working in batches as needed so as not to crowd the pan, add the oxtail and sirloin and brown on all sides, about 5 minutes total. Transfer the meat to a bowl and set aside.

ADD the celery, leek, carrots, onion, and pitted whole prunes to the pot and cook until a bit soft and lightly browned, stirring occasionally, about 5 minutes. Add the wine (and/or water), thyme, rosemary, salt, 1½ cups (360 g) water, and the mushrooms with their soaking liquid.

RETURN the meat to the pot and stir everything to combine. Reduce the heat to medium, cover the pot partially with a lid, and let the stew simmer until the meat is pleasantly tender and pulls easily from the bone, about 2 hours. (If using an Instant Pot, use the pressure cooker option and select 1 hour on high pressure, using the manual release.)

REMOVE the meat from the pot, remove and discard the bones, and place the meat in a food processor (the mixture is easier to process when warm). Pulse gently until you achieve a meat paste. Season to taste with salt and set this filling aside to cool.

MEANWHILE, transfer all the vegetables, prunes, and juices from the pot to a blender and blend into a very smooth, creamy mixture. If necessary, scrape out the pot to release any stuck food. Pour the mixture back into the pot and bring it to a boil over medium-high heat. Lower the heat to medium, cover the pot partially to let some of the steam escape, and let reduce to intensify the flavors, 15 to 20 minutes. (Note that this sauce can be served with any pasta dish.)

SET aside while you make the ravioli, or cool or freeze and reheat if you would like to make it ahead.

FOR THE RAVIOLI DOUGH: In the bowl of a stand mixer fitted with the paddle attachment, mix the cassava flour, tapioca flour, coconut flour, acacia fiber, glucomannan, and salt on low speed until well combined.

ADD the warm water and mix until a thick dough forms. Depending on the absorbency of the flours, you might have to add more. The dough should be manageable, neither too dry nor too wet. If your dough needs more water, add it 1 tablespoon at a time.

REMOVE the dough from the bowl and shape it into a ball with your hands. Wrap the dough with plastic wrap and let it rest for 15 minutes.

AS mentioned above, I recommend making these ravioli by hand, one by one, rather than using a machine. First, choose a ravioli cutter. Mine is 2½ inches in diameter. For this size, cut off a piece of dough that's a bit larger than the cutter in diameter and place it between two pieces of parchment paper, using a bit of cassava flour to prevent sticking only if necessary. Roll the dough out into a circle that's about ⅙- to ⅛-inch thick. Cut off a second piece of dough and roll it out the same way. These are the bottom and top of your ravioli.

MAKE a ball with the meat paste. For the 2½-inch cutter size, I use a 1 to 1½ teaspoons of meat. For a bit more sweetness in the filling, include a couple of finely chopped pieces of prune inside each ball. (I love this step, but it's completely optional.)

LAY out the bottom piece of ravioli dough and set the ball of meat paste on top. Carefully set the top piece of ravioli dough over the meat, lining it up with the bottom dough. Use your fingers to flatten the dough around the edges of each ball, taking care not to rip the dough. If needed, use your finger to wipe a bit of water on the bottom edge of the ravioli to help seal it.

USE a ravioli cutter to shape the ravioli into a circle (or use a knife to shape it into a circle or square). Return any excess dough to the main ball of dough to reuse it.

REPEAT to make the rest of your ravioli, placing them in a single layer on parchment paper as you finish them and covering them with plastic wrap (or another layer of parchment and a towel). At this stage you can also freeze them for later (see Note).

BRING a large pot of salted water to a boil over medium-high heat. Add a dash of olive oil.

TO COOK AND SERVE: Cook the ravioli in the boiling water until they float to the surface, about 15 seconds (the boiling water is important to help them firm up and cook quickly). Use a slotted spoon to remove them quickly to a plate or platter. You can drizzle a little olive oil on top if you like.

SERVE the ravioli with warm sauce on top. Sprinkle with a little bit of nutritional yeast (or cashew parmesan, page 301).

NOTE
These ravioli should be cooked and eaten right away unless you freeze them. To freeze the ravioli, place them in a dish with a silicone mat and freeze until they harden, then transfer them to a freezer bag or freezer-safe container. To cook from frozen, bring water to a boil and cook for 10 minutes.

zucchini noodles with coffee-rubbed shrimp and chimichurri

MAKES 4 SERVINGS

coffee-rubbed shrimp

2 teaspoons smoked paprika (such as sweet Pimentón de la Vera)

2 teaspoons onion powder

2 teaspoons garlic powder

1½ tablespoons (19 g) coconut sugar (see page 7)

4 teaspoons (8 g) ground coffee (freshly ground if possible)

1 teaspoon salt (see page 15)

⅛ teaspoon cayenne

1⅔ pounds (750 g) medium (41/50) or large (31/35) raw wild-caught shrimp, peeled

chimichurri

1 bunch (55 g) parsley, finely minced

1 garlic clove, finely minced

½ teaspoon finely minced fresh oregano (or dried oregano)

¼ cup (60 g) avocado oil

1 tablespoon extra virgin olive oil

½ teaspoon apple cider vinegar (see page 3)

½ teaspoon crushed red pepper (optional)

Salt (see page 15), to taste

Freshly ground black pepper, to taste

assembly

8 ounces (226 g) no-sugar uncured bacon (such as Applegate or ButcherBox brand)

4 zucchini

Many regions (and often individual cooks) have their own version of chimichurri, a tasty, fresh sauce made from parsley and garlic. I love to serve it with a good grass-fed rib eye steak, but it can be paired with a wide variety of dishes, such as roasted potatoes or grilled octopus.

I love crunchy zucchini noodles, or zoodles; I always try to make them right before serving so they stay firm and refreshing. This version of chimichurri with a shrimp and coffee rub is simply delicious and comforting, and I won't deny that a good plate like this can use a little bit of good bacon for utter perfection.

Prepare your chimichurri the day before for an even deeper and more intense flavor.

FOR THE SHRIMP: Combine the smoked paprika, onion powder, garlic powder, coconut sugar, coffee, salt, and cayenne in a jar and shake well to mix (see Note).

PLACE the shrimp in a zip-top bag and add 3½ tablespoons of the rub. Seal the bag and mix well so that the shrimp are completely covered. Refrigerate for at least 1 hour.

FOR THE CHIMICHURRI: In a large bowl, combine the parsley, garlic, oregano, avocado oil, olive oil, vinegar, crushed red pepper (if using), and 1 tablespoon water. Mix very well, then season with salt and pepper. Set aside (or refrigerate for up to 3 days; the chimichurri is even tastier the next day).

TO ASSEMBLE: Slowly cook the bacon strips in a large skillet over low heat. When the bacon has released all its fat and is golden brown, remove it and place it on a paper towel–lined plate to drain. Chop the bacon into small pieces. Reserve 3 tablespoons of the bacon fat and save or discard the rest.

WIPE out the pan. Heat the reserved bacon fat over high heat. Add the shrimp and sauté until pink and cooked through, about 5 minutes.

FOR each of four servings, use a spiralizer to cut a zucchini into noodles and set them on a plate. Add 1 to 1½ tablespoons of chimichurri and mix well (this works best if you use your hands). Add some shrimp and a little crispy bacon on top. Serve immediately.

NOTE
You will have extra rub; I always keep it on hand to use on steaks or pork.

chaufa-style fried cauliflower rice with shrimp and bacon

MAKES 3 OR 4 SERVINGS

3 large eggs

Kelp granules seasoning (such as Maine Coast Sea Vegetables brand), to taste

2 tablespoons (30 g) extra virgin olive oil

4 ounces (125 g) no-sugar uncured bacon (such as Applegate or ButcherBox brand)

8 ounces (226 g) medium (41/50) or large (31/35) raw wild-caught shrimp, peeled, deveined, and tails removed

1 large or 2 small scallions, white and green parts separated and finely chopped

2 tablespoons finely minced ginger

6 garlic cloves, roasted (see page 294)or minced raw

1 red bell pepper, cut into small dice

6 cups (600 g) cauliflower rice (see Note)

Coconut aminos or soy sauce replacement, to taste

Toasted sesame oil, to taste

Salt (see page 15; optional, as other ingredients are providing a salty flavor)

Arroz chaufa is a "chifa"-style dish; chifa is a fusion cuisine that derives from the influx of Chinese immigrants who came to Peru in the late nineteenth and twentieth centuries and mixed their culinary techniques and recipes with typical ingredients from the area. In my opinion, Peruvian chifa is one of the great delicacies of Peruvian cuisine. When we lived in Lima, we loved to order several dishes with different sweet, sour, and salty flavors and set up a buffet at home so that everyone could arrange their own plates with their favorites.

But if we all agreed on something, it was chaufa rice as a principal side dish. This popular fried rice usually consists of a mix of rice (preferably cooked al dente and made the day before to generate resistant starches and a more intense flavor), vegetables, scallions, eggs, and meat (usually chicken, pork, or shrimp), cooked quickly over high heat, often in a wok, with soy sauce and sesame oil. It's different from "American" Chinese fried rice in lots of subtle ways, and it's incredibly tasty!

This is my grain-free, soy-free version, achieved by using cauliflower instead of rice, and a great kelp blend, which is a combination of two brown sea vegetables in granule form. The result is deliciously salty yet low in sodium and is a good source of potassium, magnesium, and other mineral salts.

IN a medium bowl, lightly whisk the eggs and kelp seasoning to taste (start with ¾ teaspoon).

HEAT the olive oil in a large skillet over medium-high heat, then add the eggs. Swirl the pan so that the eggs coat the bottom. Let cook until well cooked, about 4 minutes. Transfer the omelet to a cutting board and cut into ½-inch squares. Set aside.

IN the same pan (or better yet, a wok), cook the bacon over medium-low heat until golden and crisp. Chop the bacon and set it aside. Reserve the fat in the pan.

INCREASE the heat to high, add the shrimp to the bacon fat, and cook for a few seconds, until just pink. Add the white part of the scallion, the ginger, and the garlic and sauté until the scallion is translucent, just a few seconds. Add the bell pepper and cook until somewhat soft but still firm—the vegetables in chaufa should not be overcooked.

ADD the cauliflower rice and cook for a few minutes, stirring frequently. I like mine cooked al dente, but the level of doneness is up to you. The shrimp should be pink and cooked through (but not overcooked).

ADD the bacon and season with more kelp and coconut aminos. Add the scallion greens and toasted sesame oil and remove from the heat. Add the little omelet squares and stir well. Serve immediately.

See the photo on page 146.

See the photo on page 146.

NOTE
For this recipe I purchase fresh cauliflower rice, but you can process fresh cauliflower florets into rice-size pieces in a food processor. I don't recommend frozen cauliflower rice for this dish.

plantain and pineapple curry with shrimp or jackfruit

MAKES 4 SERVINGS

1 small ripe pineapple (about 3¼ pounds/1.5 kg)

2 tablespoons (30 g) avocado oil

2 ripe plantains, peeled and cut into ½-inch slices

2 tablespoons (12 g) finely chopped lemongrass (white part of the stem)

1 tablespoon plus 1 teaspoon (13 g) finely chopped fresh ginger

1½ tablespoons (18 g) finely chopped garlic

2 small bunches scallions, white and green parts separated and thinly sliced

1½ tablespoons (13 g) Homemade Curry Powder (page 150)

¼ teaspoon cayenne

1 teaspoon ground turmeric (see page 16)

Salt (see page 15), to taste

One 13.5-ounce (398 g) can coconut milk without guar gum (such as Native Forest's Simple) or 1⅔ cups (400 g) Coconut Milk (page 307)

1½ pounds (680 g) medium (41/50) raw wild-caught shrimp, peeled, deveined, and tails removed (optional), or two 14-ounce (792 g) cans unflavored jackfruit (such as

The Caribbean is my first choice for a relaxing destination. For our honeymoon, Sebas and I went to Punta Cana in the Dominican Republic, and I still remember the fantastic combination of fresh pineapple, green banana, and of course, my favorite ingredient in the whole world: coconut. These flavors make me want to add yellow curry and seafood—the perfect match.

Full of lively color, this recipe has aromas of ginger, garlic, and lemongrass, which make a perfect symphony when cooked together, and the carefully prepared homemade curry powder is a delicious gift of care and love. You can use shrimp or jackfruit or, if you can't decide, some of both.

CUT off the ends of the pineapple, then place the pineapple upright and slice down the sides of the pineapple to cut off long strips of peel (freeze the peel to make Hibiscus and Pineapple Peel Drink, page 271). Cut the pineapple vertically into 4 wedges and remove the hard core from each wedge (freeze the core pieces with the peel). Cut each wedge vertically into 2 slices and cut the slices into about ½-inch pieces.

HEAT the oil in a cast-iron pan over high heat. Add the plantains and cook until browned on both sides, about 3 minutes per side. Remove them from the pan and set aside.

REDUCE the heat to medium-high and add the lemongrass, ginger, and garlic. Sauté until a little browned, 30 to 40 seconds. Add the scallion whites, pineapple chunks, curry powder, cayenne, and turmeric, return the cooked plantains to the pan, and season with salt.

ADD the coconut milk and reduce the heat to medium. Cover with a lid, bring to a simmer, and let cook for about 10 minutes, until the plantain and pineapple soften a little and infuse their flavor into the sauce. Add the shrimp or jackfruit (or a combo), the sesame oil, scallion greens, cilantro, and lime juice. Cook until the shrimp are just pink and cooked through and/or the jackfruit is warmed through.

DIVIDE the curry among bowls and finish with a few slices of fresh avocado and some cilantro leaves on each serving.

SERVE alone or with cauliflower rice, cassava noodles, konjac noodles, or yuca crackers.

See the photo on page 147.

Native Forest brand)
for a vegan option

1½ teaspoons toasted
sesame oil

1 bunch fresh cilantro, roughly
chopped; include most of
the stems and reserve a
few sprigs for garnish

Juice from 1 lime
(2 tablespoons/30 g)

Sliced avocado, for serving

Cauliflower rice, cassava
noodles, konjac noodles, or
Yuca Crackers (page 198),
for serving (optional)

homemade curry powder

MAKES ½ CUP

3⅛ teaspoons (12 g)
mustard seeds

2¼ teaspoons (3 g)
coriander seeds

7⅛ teaspoons (18 g)
cumin seeds

2¼ teaspoons (6 g)
fennel seeds

1 tablespoon (13.2 g)
fenugreek seeds

1¾ teaspoons (5.2 g)
black peppercorns

8 whole cloves

4 teaspoons (12 g) ground
turmeric (see page 16)

½ teaspoon (1.2 g)
ground ginger

1 teaspoon (4 g) garlic powder

½ plus ⅛ teaspoon (1.28 g)
ground cinnamon

Spices are a very important part of Ayurvedic medicine because they offer benefits to the digestive system, have healing capabilities, support the organs, and mobilize and balance energy—and of course they also enhance the flavors of food.

There are many good organic spice blends on the market, but I find that a good homemade mix, made with freshly roasted and ground seeds, elevates the flavor of any meal in a different way than a commercial mix. I like to have control over my ingredients and decide on the level of roasting and grinding, and the smell that fills the house when I make this mix is absolutely incredible. It is aromatic, powerful, intense, full of flavor, and not spicy, so you can choose the level of spiciness in each recipe by adding the chile of your choice.

I highly recommend using a gram scale to measure your spices.

***

IN a dry medium skillet over medium-high heat, combine the mustard seeds, coriander seeds, cumin seeds, fennel seeds, fenugreek seeds, black peppercorns, and cloves. Toast lightly, stirring constantly to release their aromas, about 5 minutes. Remove the pan from the heat to cool a little.

TRANSFER the spices to a spice grinder or a mortar (note that using a mortar and pestle will take you more time) and grind. When the spices are ground almost to a powder, transfer the mixture to a glass jar and add the turmeric, ginger, garlic powder, and cinnamon. Close the lid and shake to mix all the ingredients.

STORE in a glass jar in a cool, dry place for up to 3 months.

turkey cabbage rolls

MAKES 8 SERVINGS

When I was a child, I didn't eat much cabbage or cauliflower or broccoli. My mom didn't like vegetables from the brassica family; she always complained that they gave her indigestion and gas. Isn't it funny how families tend to base their preferences on what Mom likes (or dislikes) to eat?

When I started focusing on food as medicine, I wanted to understand why these kinds of vegetables cause indigestion and gas. I researched and discovered that when these vegetables make us feel bad, it is because we have an imbalance between the bad and the good bacteria that live in our gut. I also found that they have enormous nutritional benefits (page 5). So rather than stop enjoying them, those who experience these unpleasant issues should consider a visit to a functional medicine practitioner to explore what is going on.

Brassicas are an essential part of my cooking. This recipe is one of my favorites and perhaps one of the most addictive ways to prepare cabbage. You don't even have to accompany these rolls with a side dish; a good plateful is both comforting and satiating.

Note that this recipe requires the overnight soaking of cashews, so plan ahead!

FOR THE CABBAGE: Cut the stem off the cabbage to make it easier to remove the leaves after boiling.

BRING a large pot of water to a boil over high heat. Add the whole cabbage and move it around so that it softens, making it easier to remove the leaves. Remove the cabbage from the water and remove the leaves one by one and reserve them in a bowl. If you need to, return the cabbage to the boiling water to allow you to remove the next leaves (we aren't cooking them yet). (You'll use one leaf per roll, or two leaves if one of them breaks. Leftover cabbage can be chopped and used in sauteed vegetables, soups, and meat stews.)

1 large green cabbage (about 2 pounds/907 g)

tomato sauce
2 tablespoons (30 g) extra virgin olive oil

1 medium yellow onion, cut into small dice

2 garlic cloves, minced

2 pounds (954 g) fresh Roma tomatoes

2 teaspoons coconut sugar (see page 7)

1½ teaspoons balsamic vinegar of Modena

1½ teaspoons dried basil

Salt (see page 15), to taste

filling
1 medium yellow onion, trimmed and quartered

2 garlic cloves, peeled

¼ cup plus 2 tablespoons (30 g) fresh parsley

2⅓ cups (230 g) fresh cauliflower rice

1 tablespoon extra virgin olive oil

Juice of ½ lime (about 1 tablespoon)

1 teaspoon smoked paprika (such as sweet Pimentón de la Vera)

1½ teaspoons salt (see page 15)

1 pound (453 g) ground turkey

2½ tablespoons (25 g) pine nuts

MAIN COURSES

151

FOR THE TOMATO SAUCE: Heat the oil in a Dutch oven over high heat. Add the onion and garlic and sauté until translucent and lightly browned, 4 to 6 minutes.

CUT the tomatoes in half and remove the hard-to-digest seeds (not the flesh) with your hands or with the help of a knife. Place the tomatoes in a blender and blend until smooth. Add them to the pan.

ADD the coconut sugar, balsamic vinegar, basil, and salt and bring the mixture to a boil. Reduce the heat to medium and simmer until the mixture is reduced to a light sauce, 18 to 20 minutes.

FOR THE FILLING: Meanwhile, place the onion, garlic, and parsley in a food processor and pulse until chopped. Add the cauliflower rice, olive oil, lime juice, smoked paprika, and salt and pulse until combined. Add the ground turkey and pulse again to combine.

PLACE the filling in a large bowl, add the pine nuts, and stir well to combine.

FOR THE WHITE SAUCE: Drain and rinse the soaked cashews. Place them in a high-powered blender with the cauliflower, almond milk, garlic powder, nutritional yeast, tapioca flour, and ¼ cup (60 g) water and blend into a very smooth and silky sauce.

TO ASSEMBLE: Preheat the oven to 350°F.

POUR the tomato sauce into a 7 × 11-inch baking dish (or divide it among 8 small individual oven-safe serving dishes).

TO assemble the rolls, take a softened cabbage leaf and place a large spoonful of the filling in the middle. Fold two sides of the leaf over one another on top of the filling, then roll it up like a burrito. Place the cabbage roll seam side down in the tomato sauce. Repeat until you have about 8 rolls.

POUR some white sauce over each roll and sprinkle with a good amount of cashew parmesan.

BAKE for 1 hour, until the rolls are firm and the meat stuffing is cooked through. Serve hot.

white sauce

⅔ cup (100 g) unsalted raw cashews, soaked in water overnight

2½ ounces (75 g) fresh cauliflower florets (about ⅔ cup)

½ cup (120 g) Almond Milk (page 304)

½ teaspoon garlic powder

1 tablespoon nutritional yeast

1½ teaspoons tapioca flour

Cashew Parmesan (page 301)

beef liver and onions

MAKES 4 SERVINGS

2 pounds (900 g) beef liver, cut into 4 × ½-inch strips

3 tablespoons (45 g) chopped garlic

1½ teaspoons apple cider vinegar (see page 3)

1 teaspoon ground cumin

¾ teaspoon freshly ground black pepper

½ teaspoon dried oregano

¼ cup plus 1 tablespoon (67 g) extra virgin olive oil, plus more as necessary

Salt (see page 15), to taste

3 red onions (2.2 pounds/ 1 kg), cut into quarters

3 tablespoons (45 g) balsamic vinegar of Modena

½ teaspoon coconut sugar (see page 7)

1½ pounds (680 g) Roma tomatoes, each cored and cut into 6 or 8 wedges

1 bunch fresh parsley, finely chopped

1 fresh chile, such as a serrano or habanero, julienned (optional)

Cauliflower rice or air-fried yuca sticks (see page 110), for serving

Liver can cause some people to react to it with disgust, but it's likely because they haven't tasted the right recipe. When I was a child, at our house it was very common to eat viscera such as liver, kidneys (my grandmother used to make some kidneys with red wine that were finger-licking good), tripe, heart, and more. Beyond its nutritional benefits, I believe eating organ meat is also a way to honor the death of an animal. We shouldn't waste anything.

Including organ meats in your diet provides enormous health benefits, and believe me, they can be truly scrumptious. Beef liver contains high amounts of valuable protein and several important minerals, including iron, zinc, copper, potassium, phosphorus, and selenium. It also contains significant levels of riboflavin, folic acid, and vitamins A and D, as well as an abundance of vitamin B12, which helps produce brain chemicals like serotonin and dopamine, helping to regulate mood and anxiety levels. Give this recipe a try and enjoy every bite.

PLACE the liver in a large bowl and add 1 tablespoon of the chopped garlic, the apple cider vinegar, ½ teaspoon of the cumin, ¼ teaspoon of the pepper, and the oregano. Mix well, cover, and refrigerate for 1 hour.

HEAT a cast-iron skillet over high heat and add the oil. Add the marinated liver, season with salt to taste, and sauté, stirring constantly, until browned. To gauge the doneness of your liver, remove a piece and slice it to look inside. I like it with a medium sear on the outside, still a little soft to the touch, and juicy and slightly pink on the inside. Overcooked liver is tough. Transfer the liver to a clean bowl and set aside.

ADD a little more olive oil to the skillet, if necessary, then add the onions and remaining 2 tablespoons garlic and sauté until the onions are slightly translucent (we want the onions crisp and al dente, not soft and overcooked). Add the balsamic vinegar, coconut sugar, and remaining ½ teaspoon black pepper and ½ teaspoon cumin. Stir. Add the tomatoes, parsley, chile (if using), and salt (if needed).

RETURN the cooked liver strips to the skillet and cook over high heat, stirring constantly, for a few seconds to integrate all the flavors. The tomatoes should be just warmed through, not cooked and crushed.

SERVE with cauliflower rice or air-fried yuca sticks.

breaded fish and yuca fries with balsamic beans and peppers

MAKES 4 SERVINGS

As I've mentioned, my mother is an expert cook and the best pastry chef I know, but my grandmother, who lived with us, had other talents. In our community, she dedicated her life to helping others and performed many acts of social work, like assisting in a home for orphaned children and teaching sewing classes to low-income women so that they could find work and support their families. She was kind and giving to everyone around her.

Grandma was also the best kitchen helper Mom could ask for. Not only did Mom cook for us at home, but she also made sweet and savory baked goods for Dad to sell in our store in Tacna, our hometown. Grandma was her right hand for this task.

But even though she mostly assisted in the kitchen, she did have a knack for making rice, fried eggs, and this fish recipe. She originally made it with potato starch and wheat flour, but my version uses arrowroot and coconut flour.

Grandma died of breast cancer at age sixty, breaking my heart into a thousand pieces. She was my second mom, and I'm sure that like Mom now, she would have been my right hand in the kitchen, and the happiest great-grandmother in the world. I know you will always be with me, Grandma Tota.

For a lighter meal, try serving cauliflower rice in place of the fried yuca.

yuca
1½ pounds (680 g) frozen yuca sticks

Avocado oil, for frying

Salt (see page 15), to taste

fish
Four 6- to 7-ounce (170 to 200 g) wild-caught flounder or Atlantic cod fillets

2 large eggs

Arrowroot flour (also known as starch or powder), as needed

Coconut flour (such as Let's Do Organic brand), as needed

Salt (see page 15), to taste

Freshly ground black pepper, to taste

Avocado oil, for frying, as needed

FOR THE YUCA: Optional: Place the yuca in a large bowl and cover with water. Let soak for a couple of hours (see page 17), then drain and rinse under cold water.

DRAIN and rinse the yuca sticks and place them in an Instant Pot or Ninja Pot with the steam basket. Add ½ cup (120 g) water and cook on high pressure for 15 minutes, using the manual release. Pour out the water and add a splash of olive oil and a sprinkle of salt. Turn on the air fryer mode and cook for 25 minutes, until the yuca sticks are golden and crisp. (Alternatively, you can cook the

157

1 tablespoon tapioca flour

1 tablespoon arrowroot flour (also known as starch or powder)

2 tablespoons (30 g) avocado oil

2 garlic cloves, minced

1 tablespoon coconut sugar (see page 7)

¼ cup plus 1 teaspoon (70 g) balsamic vinegar of Modena

1¼ pounds (566 g) green beans, cut into 2-inch pieces on a deep bias

1 large red onion, trimmed and sliced into 8 wedges

1 green bell pepper, seeded and cut into ¼-inch strips

1 red bell pepper, seeded and cut into ¼-inch strips

1 yellow bell pepper, seeded and cut into ¼-inch strips

1 or 2 hot chile peppers, such as serrano, jalapeño, habanero, or ají amarillo, cut into ¹⁄₁₆-inch julienne strips (optional)

Salt (see page 15), to taste

1½ cups (360 g) Homemade Chicken Bone Broth (page 90)

yuca in water until soft but firm when pricked with a knife, about 5 minutes. Drain and dry well. Fry the sticks in a skillet with about ¼ inch [½ cm] avocado or coconut oil until golden and crispy, turning them to crisp all sides.)

FOR THE FISH: Pat the fish fillets dry with a paper towel.

IN a medium bowl, whisk the eggs well with a fork. Place the arrowroot flour in a separate medium bowl and the coconut flour in another.

SEASON the fillets with salt and pepper, then dredge them through the arrowroot flour, then the egg, and then the coconut flour. Be sure to press the fish firmly into the coconut flour so that it sticks well to the fillets. Set the coated fillets on a sheet pan as you finish them.

POUR a thin layer of oil into a large skillet and set it over medium-high heat. Fry the fish fillets on both sides until golden brown, about 1 minute on each side for thin flounder fillets or 2 to 4 minutes per side for thicker cod fillets, until opaque. Don't crowd the pan; work in batches as needed and add more oil if necessary.

FOR THE VEGETABLES: Meanwhile, in a small bowl, whisk ¼ cup (60g) water, the tapioca flour, and the arrowroot flour until the flours are dissolved.

HEAT the avocado oil in a large skillet over high heat. Add the garlic and let it cook for a few seconds (don't let it burn), then, while stirring constantly, mix in the coconut sugar and balsamic vinegar. Add the green beans and cook for a couple of minutes, stirring often, until they turn bright green. Add the onion, bell peppers, and chiles (if using), season with salt, and sauté for a couple more minutes, until the veggies are al dente. Don't overcook them.

ADD the broth and the tapioca mixture to the pan and cook, stirring constantly, until thickened into a sauce, 2 to 3 minutes.

FOR SERVING: Serve a fish fillet on each plate, with the vegetables and yuca fries on the side.

pork and beef burgers with pumpkin spice plantains

MAKE 6 SERVINGS

Sometimes the girls ask me, "Mom, why do people eat things that are not healthy, knowing that it's not good for them?" My answer? "Because junk food is delicious! Why else would they eat it?" But that question always leaves me wondering—how can I make my daughters fall so in love with healthy ingredients that they don't need those other delicious "foods"? No matter how hard I try, I won't be able to protect them from junk food forever, but I can teach them to make conscious decisions. First, I teach them to fall so in love with themselves that they only want to give their bodies the best fuel. Second, I try to make such spectacularly delicious meals that other kinds of food don't attract their attention.

When I was thinking up recipes that could be healthier alternatives to junk food, burgers were the first thing that came to my mind. But I wanted my family to enjoy them in their truest form, not hidden in the middle of a bun. Here the burger is served right on the plate, accompanied and enhanced by a range of flavors and textures, including sweet spiced plantains, a bright and crunchy salad, tart and creamy mashed avocado, and a unique homemade mayonnaise. I hope this dish, and the conversations around it, stays with my kids forever.

FOR THE OREGANO AND ROSEMARY MIX: Place the oregano and rosemary in a spice grinder and grind them into a coarse powder.

FOR THE BURGERS: In a large bowl, combine the pork, beef, bacon, shallots, roasted garlic, onion powder, paprika, chili powder, oregano and rosemary mix, salt, and pepper. Knead the mixture with your hands until thoroughly combined. Divide the mixture into 6 portions and shape each into a ¾-inch-thick patty.

HEAT the avocado oil in a large skillet over high heat. Add the burger patties and cook for 5 to 6 minutes, then flip and cook for about 6 more minutes, depending on your desired doneness, flip-

oregano and rosemary mix

1 tablespoon dried oregano

1 tablespoon dried rosemary

burgers

1 pound (454 g) ground pork

1 pound (454 g) ground beef

4 ounces (113 g) no-sugar uncured bacon (such as Applegate or ButcherBox brand), finely chopped

4 shallots (150 g), peeled and cut into small dice

10 garlic cloves, roasted (see page 294)

1 teaspoon onion powder

2 teaspoons paprika (such as sweet Pimentón de la Vera; omit for the AIP diet)

¼ teaspoon chili powder (omit for the AIP diet)

1 teaspoon Oregano and Rosemary Mix (1 tablespoon for the AIP diet)

1 teaspoon salt (see page 15)

¼ teaspoon freshly ground black pepper (omit for the AIP diet)

2 tablespoons (30 g) avocado oil

pumpkin spice plantains

3 ripe plantains (2½ pounds/1.2 kg)

¼ cup (50 g) extra virgin olive oil or avocado oil

4 teaspoons coconut
sugar (see page 7)

2 teaspoons Pumpkin
Spice Mix (page 299; use 2
teaspoons ground cinnamon
plus ⅛ teaspoon ground
cloves for the AIP diet)

mashed avocado with pomegranate

3 avocados, halved

2 tablespoons (16 g)
chopped cilantro

Extra virgin olive oil, to taste

Fresh lime juice, to taste

Salt (see page 15), to taste

Arils from 1 pomegranate
(about 1 cup/8 ounces/226 g)

arugula salad

9 cups (6½ ounces/180 g)
baby arugula

10 ounces (300 g) small
sugar snap peas, julienned
(use baby cucumber
sticks for the AIP diet)

10 medium radishes
(100 g), sliced thin

Chia Balsamic Dressing
(page 282; omit the chia
for the AIP diet)

garlic mayonnaise (omit for the AIP diet)

¼ cup plus 2 tablespoons
(100 g) Cashew
Mayonnaise (page 292)
or Horseradish Quinoa
Mayonnaise (page 293)

1 tablespoon Garlic-Herb
Paste (page 294)

ping halfway through. (You can also cook the patties on a grill using the same timing.) Be sure to cook to an internal temperature of 160°F to 165°F to make sure the meat is safe to eat.

FOR THE PLANTAINS: Peel the plantains very carefully so as not to break them. Cut each plantain in half vertically, then cut each half horizontally.

PLACE the plantains on a sheet pan and brush or drizzle them with 2 tablespoons of the olive oil, just to coat (this helps the sugar and spice to adhere). Sprinkle all sides with the coconut sugar and pumpkin spice mix. Gently mix with your hands so that the plantains are well coated.

HEAT the remaining 2 tablespoons oil in a large skillet over medium-high heat. Add the plantains and fry until golden brown, 3 to 4 minutes per side.

FOR THE MASHED AVOCADO: Place the avocados in a large bowl and mash them rustically (I like to leave some larger chunks to give it a little texture). Add the cilantro, olive oil, lime juice, and salt and mix well. Reserve the pomegranate arils for serving.

FOR THE ARUGULA SALAD: In a large bowl, combine the arugula, sugar snap peas, and radishes. Add the dressing to taste and toss to combine.

FOR THE GARLIC MAYONNAISE: In a bowl, mix the mayonnaise with the garlic-herb paste until combined.

TO SERVE: Place a burger patty on each plate and top with a tablespoon of the garlic mayonnaise. On the side, add a generous serving of salad, a couple of plantains, and mashed avocado to taste, with some pomegranate seeds on top.

chard and egg tart

MAKES ONE 9½-INCH TART, TO SERVE 6

Quiche Crust (page 197)

8 ounces (226 g) no-sugar uncured bacon (such as Applegate or ButcherBox brand; omit for vegetarian)

1 tablespoon extra virgin olive oil

1 pound (453 g) chard leaves, hard part of the stems removed (about 3 bunches)

Salt (see page 15)

7 large eggs

Freshly ground black pepper

⅓ cup Cashew Parmesan (page 301), more to taste

Lime slices, for serving

I get really excited about how we create memories around food, how through smells and flavors we can relive moments of happiness with those we love the most. The kitchen not only unites the family and preserves stories in time but allows us to create rituals and traditions that nourish the soul. As soon as I say, "We're having chard and egg tarts for dinner," the girls smile and ask, "The one that you eat with a squeeze of lime in each bite?" They're remembering fun times around the table and the special ritual with the squeeze of lime.

So, to truly enjoy this dish, you must perform "the ritual." You must eat it hot in generous portions, with a slice of lime for each piece. Before taking the first bite, squeeze the lime over your tart. Without this step, the tart cannot be the delicious dish it is meant to be.

PREHEAT the oven to 350°F.

MAKE the crust recipe using a 9½-inch round quiche pan. Bake the crust for 30 minutes, until light brown.

COOK the bacon in a large skillet over low heat until it's browned and much of the fat has been released. Transfer the bacon to a paper towel–lined plate, then chop it roughly.

HEAT the olive oil in a large pot or Dutch oven over high heat. Add the chard leaves (they don't need to be dry; the water on the leaves will help them cook). Add a sprinkling of salt and cook the chard, stirring often, just until the leaves have softened and their color lightens, 1 to 2 minutes.

TRANSFER the chard to a strainer to drain the excess water, then transfer to a large bowl. Add the bacon and mix well.

SPREAD the chard mixture evenly in the quiche crust. With a spoon or your hand, create 7 holes in the mixture—6 around the outside and 1 in the center. Crack an egg into each one. Season the eggs with salt and pepper, and sprinkle the whole surface of the tart with the cashew parmesan.

BAKE for about 20 minutes, until the cashew parmesan is lightly browned and the eggs are cooked to your liking (I prefer the egg white well cooked and the yolk firm but not overcooked; a slightly runny yolk would also be delicious).

CUT the tart and serve each portion hot or warm with a slice of fresh lime. Squeeze the lime over your tart and enjoy the ritual.

BBQ ribs

MAKES 12 SERVINGS

BBQ sauce

3½ ounces (100 g)
pitted Medjool dates

One 28-ounce (793 g) can
fire-roasted tomatoes (such
as Muir Glen Organic brand)

1 tablespoon pure maple syrup
or yacon syrup (see page 17)

2 tablespoons (50 g) coconut
nectar (see page 7)

⅓ cup plus 1 teaspoon (84 g)
apple cider vinegar (see page 3)

2 teaspoons hickory
liquid smoke (such as
Lazy Kettle brand)

1¼ teaspoons salt (see page 15)

3½ tablespoons (60 g)
Worcestershire sauce

¼ teaspoon cayenne

¼ cup (60 g) bourbon

ribs

9 pounds (4 kg) pork loin
back ribs (baby back ribs)

Salt (see page 15)

¼ cup (50 g) extra
virgin olive oil

Garlic powder, to taste

Dried parsley, to taste

Our family really enjoys a nice Sunday barbecue, especially one with guests. I don't know if it's ancestral, something we carry in our veins and in our roots from the time when food was the most valuable thing that humanity could offer—or maybe we just like to feed people—but we think the best way to honor a guest is to feed them so well that they can't possibly eat any more. So every time we have a barbecue, we make tons of food and don't stop grilling until the sun sets, which is the perfect excuse to spend the maximum amount of time with our friends. And of course, each guest must go home with a container of food as a gift.

These BBQ ribs are a wonderful option for a family Sunday lunch—incredibly juicy and tender enough to fall off the bone. You can make them in the oven or on the grill and serve them with Fennel and Apple Salad with Candied Pecans (page 118), Greens and Pear Salad (page 115), or Olive, Raisin, and Rosemary Cauliflower Rice (page 94). Or you can even take a couple of toasted slices of my AIP Sandwich Bread (page 188) and make a mouthwatering sandwich. Invite some friends over and honor them with a comforting yet healthy BBQ.

FOR THE BBQ SAUCE: Place the dates in a bowl and add boiling water to cover. Let the dates hydrate for about 15 minutes, so that your blender has less work to do. Drain the dates.

PLACE the tomatoes in the blender along with the dates, maple syrup, and coconut nectar. Blend until smooth and lump-free.

TRANSFER the mixture to a Dutch oven or other heavy-bottomed pot. Add the vinegar, liquid smoke, salt, Worcestershire sauce, cayenne, and bourbon. Turn the heat to high, stir well, and bring to a boil, then lower the heat and simmer for 30 minutes. After 30 minutes, cover the pot, leaving the lid slightly askew so steam can escape. Cook until the sauce is thick, stirring occasionally so that the sauce doesn't stick to the pot, 20 more minutes.

SET aside to cool in the pot, then use the BBQ sauce or store it in glass jars in the fridge (or freeze up to 4 months).

FOR THE RIBS: Season the ribs with salt (about ¼ to ½ teaspoon per pound). Place the steamer basket and a couple of fingers of water in an Instant Pot or pressure cooker and add half of the ribs in the basket, making sure the water doesn't touch the ribs. Cook the ribs on high pressure for 45 minutes, until they are super tender, using the manual release. Set aside in a covered bowl (so they don't lose too much heat) and repeat with the remaining ribs. (Alternatively, you can place all the ribs in a large pot and add water to cover three-fourths of the ribs. Cover and bring to a boil over medium-high heat, then lower the heat to medium and simmer until tender, 2½ to 3 hours.)

PREHEAT the oven to 350°F or a grill to 250°F to 300°F (the grill is my favorite way to cook ribs).

PLACE the ribs on a sheet pan and drizzle them with the olive oil. Sprinkle lightly with salt and the garlic powder and parsley.

BAKE or grill for 30 to 45 minutes, until golden brown (for Sebas) or almost burned (for me)—take your pick! And use the time to share some conversation and a glass of wine with your friends and family.

SERVE the ribs with the BBQ sauce, salad, grilled veggies, and/or cauliflower rice (see the headnote for some ideas).

See the photo on page 166.

NOTE
The sauce recipe is great to double and store in the freezer for convenient entertaining!

milky quinoa with shrimp

MAKES 4 SERVINGS

2 cups (400 g) uncooked quinoa (see page 14)

2½ cups (375 g) raw cashews, soaked for 8 hours, drained, and rinsed

¼ cup (22 g) nutritional yeast

Salt (see page 15), to taste

¼ cup plus 2 tablespoons (80 g) extra virgin olive oil

1 pound (500 g) large (31/35) raw wild-caught shrimp, peeled, deveined, and tails removed

Freshly ground black pepper, to taste

2 Vidalia (sweet) or yellow onions, cut into small dice

Poblano Sauce (page 296)

When I was a child, my mother made a classic dish called "quinua con leche," which means "quinoa with milk." She made it with cow's milk, of course (like everything else in those days), and artisanal, unpasteurized fresh white cheese that she bought in Tacna's central market. She liked to serve it with steak.

I created this recipe so my daughters could experience the same flavors I enjoyed in my childhood, at a time when quinoa had less prominence and worldwide popularity, when it was eaten without much seasoning, just alone as the star of the plate. I wanted my daughters to understand how sometimes perfection is found in a dish's simplicity.

So I made my own version without dairy, and as much as I love this recipe with steak, I wanted to include more seafood. I truly believe that a variety of ingredients is the key to a healthy diet—and my kids go crazy for the shrimp. This is the quinoa of my childhood, but my way.

Note that the cashews and quinoa need to soak for 8 hours, in case you want to plan ahead.

WASH the quinoa several times, then soak it in fresh water for 8 hours or overnight. Once it's done soaking, drain and rinse it once more with fresh water.

PLACE the quinoa in a pot along with 6 cups (1.5 L) water. Bring the water to a simmer over medium-high heat, uncovered. You must keep a close eye on the quinoa, as we want it al dente, not mushy. When it starts to cook, you will see a white dot in the center of the quinoa grains. When that dot disappears (about 6 minutes from when the water starts to bubble), remove the pan from the heat and drain immediately, leaving the quinoa to drain in the strainer.

IN a high-powered blender, combine the cashews, nutritional yeast, salt, and 5 cups (1.25 L) water. Blend into a super-smooth cream.

MEANWHILE, make the shrimp. Heat 2 tablespoons of the olive oil in a large skillet over medium-high heat. Add the shrimp and sauté until they turn pink, turning as needed. Season with salt and pepper. Transfer the shrimp to a plate.

IN the same skillet over medium-high heat, heat the remaining ¼ cup olive oil. Add the onions and sauté until they are translucent and begin to brown, 8 to 10 minutes. Add the quinoa and stir well. Pour in the cashew cream and cook, stirring often, until the mixture is well combined and the sauce is thickened, with a very creamy texture, 6 to 8 minutes.

FOR each serving, place a portion of creamy quinoa on a deep plate. Place some shrimp on top and drizzle with 1 tablespoon of the poblano sauce (or to taste). (Reheat refrigerated quinoa in a saucepan over low heat with a little extra water; the cashews will thicken the preparation in the fridge.)

See the photo on page 167.

leek, onion, and bacon quiche

MAKES ONE 9½-INCH QUICHE, TO SERVE 6

Quiche Crust (page 197)

filling

5½ ounces (156 g) no-sugar uncured bacon (such as Applegate or ButcherBox brand), cut into small chunks (omit for vegetarian)

1 medium yellow onion, julienned

Salt (see page 15), to taste

Extra virgin olive oil, as needed

1 large (283 g) leek, julienned (white and light green parts only; save the dark green parts and make Homemade Chicken Bone Broth, page 90)

2 tablespoons minced fresh chives

1 large egg

¼ cup (60 g) Almond Milk (page 304)

⅓ cup Cashew Parmesan (page 301), plus more to taste

When I met Sebas, he was part of the Peruvian national rowing team. He grew up with a group of rowers, and his friends became my friends, too. Of the rowers, Diego and Mapi were our dearest friends; they were with us not only in the good times but the bad, too. They were our chosen family, and I never felt more honored than when Mapi asked me to be the witness to their marriage (somewhat similar to being the maid of honor). Every time Diego and Mapi came over for a meal (which was very frequent), I cooked my leek and onion quiche, and each time they praised it as if it were their first time eating it. We would then stay up very late talking and sharing, and those moments with them filled our hearts with joy during a time when we were suffering a lot. When Sebas and I had the opportunity to buy the bakery in Roswell but didn't have a penny, Diego and Mapi lent us money from their savings and never rushed us to pay them back. They had great faith that everything would work out for us.

Cooking is an act of love, and I hope this quiche reflects even a fraction of the enormous love and gratitude that we feel for them. Thank you, my dear friends, for helping us make this dream come true.

FOR THE CRUST: Preheat the oven to 350°F.

MAKE the crust recipe using a 9½-inch round quiche pan, but bake it for only 25 minutes. Set aside to cool.

FOR THE FILLING: Cook the bacon in a large skillet over medium-low heat until it is golden brown and begins to release its fat, 10 to 15 minutes. Add the onion and salt and sauté over medium heat until the onion is reduced, softened, and light golden in color, 15 minutes. If the pan is a bit dry, add a little olive oil. Add the leek and sauté until the onion and leek are caramelized, stirring constantly, 20 to 25 minutes. Add the chives, stir, and remove from the heat. Transfer the filling to a bowl and let cool slightly.

IN a medium bowl, whisk the egg and almond milk. When the filling has cooled slightly, add the egg mixture and stir to combine.

POUR the filling into the prebaked crust and sprinkle the cashew parmesan evenly over the surface.

BAKE for 25 to 30 minutes, until the filling is well set and the cashew parmesan is golden brown.

CUT into 6 slices and serve hot.

pork chops and roasted veggies with sweet-and-sour mango chutney

MAKES 4 SERVINGS

Pork with a sweet sauce is always a crowd-pleaser. Pork with a sweet *and sour* sauce elevates things to the next level. And when it comes to a side dish (for this or any meal), for me, roasting vegetables is the fastest and easiest way to complement the nutritional content of a dish in an exquisite way. When vegetables are roasted, their flavors are enhanced, even more so with the help of a light sprinkling of spices or seasonings. You can eat them alone, as an accompaniment to meat or eggs, or as a base for another recipe. With roasted veggies, the possibilities are endless, but they're truly divine when paired with a pork chop and my sweet-and-sour chutney.

PREHEAT the oven to 425°F.

CUT the buttercup and delicata squashes in half from top to bottom, seed the halves, and cut the squash into ½-inch slices (do not peel).

FOR THE SQUASH: Line a sheet pan with parchment paper and spread out the squash slices. Add the olive oil, sumac, and salt. Mix well with your hands to distribute the oil and seasonings evenly. Roast for 30 to 45 minutes, until tender and golden brown.

FOR THE BROCCOLI: Line another sheet pan with parchment paper and add the broccoli, olive oil, garlic powder, and salt. Mix well with your hands. Roast for 15 minutes, until the tips are slightly browned.

FOR THE PORK CHOPS: Season each pork chop on both sides with ¼ teaspoon of the cumin, ¼ teaspoon of the salt, and pepper. Heat a large skillet over medium-high heat with a little olive oil. Add the pork chops and cook them until golden brown, about 8 minutes on each side, then lower the heat to medium-low and cook for about 5 minutes on each side. I prefer my pork well done, but follow your personal preference.

FOR SERVING: Serve the pork chops with a little chutney on top. Place the roasted veggies on the side and drizzle with the tahini sauce.

roasted squash

1 buttercup squash, 4 to 7 inches across, or acorn or honeynut squash

1 delicata squash, about 6 inches long

3 tablespoons (45 g) extra virgin olive oil

1 teaspoon ground sumac

Salt (see page 15), to taste

roasted broccoli

1 large broccoli head, cut into 2-inch florets (save the stem for soup or to make broccoli rice

2 tablespoons (30 g) extra virgin olive oil

½ teaspoon garlic powder

Salt (see page 15)

pork chops

Four 10-ounce (300 g) bone-in center-cut pork chops

1 teaspoon ground cumin

1 teaspoon salt (see page 15)

Freshly ground black pepper

Extra virgin olive oil

for serving

Mango Chutney (page 291)

Tahini Sauce (page 122)

roasted garlic chicken

MAKES 4 SERVINGS

12 garlic heads

Extra virgin olive oil

Salt (see page 15)

2 small yellow onions, peeled and halved

1 fresh rosemary sprig

One 5-pound (2.3 kg) whole chicken

5 ounces (125 g) no-sugar uncured bacon (such as Applegate or ButcherBox brand), cut into 2-inch pieces

I have two sisters—I am the oldest, followed by Diana, an amazing artist and journalist, and Daniela, a very talented graphic designer and illustrator. After my family's story was posted on Humans of New York, Diana came to help me for two months. I carry that time we shared in my heart, and I am infinitely grateful to have been able to have her at home with us. I wish Daniela could have come, too, but I hope that we all can be together again soon.

It was during that time that I started to create the recipe list for this cookbook. I brainstormed with Diana, remembering that in Lima she always told me, "An onion turns a baked chicken into a delicacy, moist and soft." (That was her sisterly way of letting me know that my roasted chicken tended to be overcooked and dry.) So I told her, "Let's use your roasted chicken recipe!" However, we included not only the requisite onion but lots of garlic that can be eaten by the spoonful. The result was a tender and juicy chicken that we shared on an incredible summer afternoon and paired with a glass of good bourbon.

PREHEAT the oven to 400°F.

CUT off the top one-third of the garlic heads, so that the garlic cloves are visible from above. Place them cut side up in a 13- to 15-inch roasting pan, drizzle with olive oil, and sprinkle with salt. Add the onions cut side down in a single layer with the garlic. You have made a delicious bed for your roasted chicken.

PLACE the rosemary sprig, about ½ teaspoon of salt, and the bacon in the chicken cavity. Sprinkle the outside of the chicken with a little olive oil and about 1 tablespoon salt, making sure the salt goes all over the skin. Set the chicken on top of the garlic and onions in the pan.

REDUCE the oven temperature to 350°F. Roast the chicken for 1½ hours, until the chicken is cooked, with an internal temperature of 165°F.

CUT the chicken into 4 pieces and serve with the roasted garlic cloves and onions. With a spoon, pour a little of the juice that remains in the pan over the chicken.

stuffed poblanos with lamb

MAKES 4 SERVINGS

I first tried poblano peppers when we arrived in America. I fell in love with them because they are not very spicy, so you can eat them whole and fully enjoy their flavor. They can be adapted to any cooking method—roasting over a flame, long or short cooking in a pot, roasting in the oven—however you want to prepare them, they will never disappoint you. When my dad came to visit us in Roswell, Georgia, he told me that he hadn't eaten lamb in years, so I immediately made these stuffed poblanos with lamb for him. He sat down with his plate and savored every bite, and I sat down to watch him, enjoying every second of his company.

PREHEAT the oven to 400°F.

HEAT the olive oil in a large skillet over medium-high heat. Add the onion and sauté until translucent, about 4 minutes.

ADD the lamb and roasted garlic paste and season with the salt, cumin, pimentón, cinnamon, and pepper. Cook, stirring, until the meat is browned and cooked through, about 8 minutes.

ADD ½ cup (120 g) water, the tamarind paste, raisins, olives, mint, and cilantro. Stir well and cook until heated through, 1 to 2 minutes. Stir in the pine nuts and remove from the heat.

WITHOUT cutting off the end, make a long cut from the stem end to the pointy bottom of the poblano. Carefully open the pepper and use a knife or spoon to remove the seeds and veins. Repeat with the other peppers.

FILL the poblanos with the lamb mixture and place them in a 7 × 11-inch or 9 × 13-inch baking dish (whichever fits the size of your peppers), open side up. Crumple a sheet of parchment paper, open it up again, and cover the peppers with it, tucking it around the sides of the baking dish (or use a parchment baking bag). Roast for 13 minutes. Remove the parchment and roast 7 to 17 more minutes, until the poblanos are cooked through. I love them al dente, but you can cook them until they're soft if preferred.

3 tablespoons (45 g) extra virgin olive oil

1 yellow onion, cut into small dice

1 pound (453 g) ground lamb

1 tablespoon Roasted Garlic Paste (page 294)

¾ teaspoon salt (see page 15)

½ teaspoon ground cumin

¾ teaspoon sweet Pimentón de la Vera or sweet paprika

½ teaspoon ground cinnamon

¼ teaspoon freshly ground black pepper

2 teaspoons tamarind paste

⅓ cup (35 g) raisins

⅓ cup (50 g) chopped Peruvian botija olives (see page 13) or Kalamata olives

1 tablespoon chopped fresh mint

1 tablespoon chopped fresh cilantro

¼ cup (40 g) pine nuts

4 large poblano peppers

peruvian seco, my way

MAKES 4 SERVINGS

Seco (which means "dry") is a typical dish that is part of everyday cuisine in Peru. But there's actually nothing dry about it—it is a very juicy dish. The original recipe is prepared with chicha de jora, a fermented drink made from a type of Peruvian corn called jora. You can use sirloin, beef stew meat, lamb, baby goat, or even ossobuco in this slow-cooking recipe that turns any meat into tender and juicy chunks. But the star of this dish is the cilantro—we use the stems, which provide a ton of flavor.

My dad can be my biggest critic when it comes to food. Whatever I do, he always has a "but." Every time I cook, he walks into the kitchen with his hands behind his back, sniffing and asking what I'm doing. However I respond, he gives me the "I doubt I'll like it" face. And my use of kombucha instead of the traditional chicha de jora really offended his traditional Peruvian palate. But I knew that this recipe would change his dour face in an instant. I served him the dish, and I had to wait only a second for his response—"It's as good as if I made it!" We all laughed, and it was the sweetest compliment he could have given me. That's how my dad is, like the seco—dry in words, but deep down, he has the most tender heart in the world.

TO roast the poblano peppers, place a whole pepper directly on the flame of a gas burner until the skin on the bottom has blackened, then turn it over and blacken the other side. Repeat until the entire poblano skin is completely black. Remove from the heat, wrap in a clean kitchen towel, and let sit for about 10 minutes so that the pepper "sweats." Repeat with the other pepper. (Alternatively, you can broil on high for 5 to 8 minutes, depending on the size of the pepper. Flip and broil another 5 to 8 minutes, until blackened.)

WHEN the peppers are cool enough to handle, peel them under running water. Remove the seeds and veins, reserving ⅓ cup (50 g) of the roasted pepper for the sauce. Cut the rest of the poblanos into strips and set aside.

2 large poblano peppers

3 tablespoons (45 g) extra virgin olive oil

1 yellow onion, cut into small dice

1½ pounds (700 g) sirloin steak (or beef or lamb stew meat), cut into 3-inch chunks

1 tablespoon Roasted Garlic Paste (see page 294) or 1 teaspoon garlic powder

1 teaspoon salt (see page 15)

1 teaspoon freshly ground black pepper

1 teaspoon ground cumin

½ teaspoon dried oregano

2 cups (16 ounces/475 g) unflavored kombucha (such as GT's brand, Original)

1 bunch (95 g) fresh cilantro (with stems)

1 cup plus 2 tablespoons (145 g) small-diced or thinly sliced carrots

¾ cup finely shredded kabocha (or acorn) squash, from about 3.7 ounces (90 g) peeled squash

1 cup (145 g) frozen peas

Cooked yuca and/or cauliflower rice, for serving

Omit the cumin, pepper, poblano pepper, and green peas.

Increase the carrots to 1½ cups (250 g).

Add ¾ cup (90 g) ¾-inch-cubed kabocha squash (in addition to the shredded squash).

Add ¼ teaspoon more garlic powder and ¼ teaspoon more oregano.

HEAT the olive oil in a large skillet over medium-high heat. Add the onion and sauté until translucent, 4 to 6 minutes. Add the meat and garlic paste and brown on all sides, about 4 minutes total. Season with the salt, pepper, cumin, and oregano.

ADD the kombucha and simmer for 10 minutes, still over medium-high heat. (If you're using beef or lamb stew meat, simmer for 20 minutes—these meats take longer to cook than sirloin. If the mixture needs more liquid, you can add water.)

CUT about ½ inch (1 cm) from the end of the cilantro stems. Place the cilantro in a blender with ⅔ cup (160 g) water and the reserved ⅓ cup/50 g of poblano pepper. Blend until very smooth.

ADD the cilantro sauce and carrots to the pan, reduce the heat to medium, cover, and cook until the carrots are tender and the meat is almost done, 15 minutes.

ADD the shredded squash and frozen peas to the pan, reduce the heat to medium-low, cover, and cook until the meat is soft and tender, 15 to 20 minutes.

SERVE with cooked yuca and/or cauliflower rice.

cauliflower rice with chicken

MAKES 6 SERVINGS

At home, when I ask my family what they want to eat, the first to raise his voice is Sebas, and he always says, "Arroz con pollo!" (rice with chicken). He is a huge fan of this classic Peruvian dish, but I don't like rice. It is a Peruvian custom that everything is eaten with rice—even mashed potatoes! I remember when I was young, my mom made rice every day as a side dish for whatever she was cooking. I must admit that the method of cooking rice in Peru is absolutely perfect (we call it "graneado" rice) because it is cooked to a precise level of doneness that is not mushy or crunchy, neither soft nor hard. But even at that level of perfection, I don't like rice at all. So the only way I can make Sebas happy is to make arroz con pollo my way, with cauliflower rice.

This is a comforting dish, but light at the same time; tasty, cozy, and intensely flavored. And although it does not contain rice, it has now become one of Sebas's favorites.

CUT the bottom 1 inch from the cilantro stems (discard the trimmings or save to make Homemade Chicken Bone Broth, page 90). Mince 2 sprigs and reserve for the onion salad. Combine the rest of the cilantro and the kombucha in a blender, blend well, and reserve.

HEAT the olive oil in a large pot or Dutch oven over high heat. Add the chicken pieces, sprinkle with salt, and brown them on all sides, 10 to 12 minutes on the skin side and 8 minutes on the other side (they won't be fully cooked). Transfer them to a plate.

ADD the onion to the same pot and sauté until translucent, 4 to 6 minutes. Add the garlic paste, ají amarillo paste, salt, black pepper, and cumin and cook, stirring, for a few minutes. This is the flavor base of the dish.

RETURN the chicken pieces to the pot and add the cilantro mixture, and the peas and carrots.

1 bunch cilantro (2 sprigs reserved for the onion salad)

2 cups (16 ounces/475 ml) unflavored kombucha (such as GT's brand, Original)

3 tablespoons (45 g) extra virgin olive oil

6 skin-on, bone-in chicken thighs

Salt (see page 15), to taste

1 large yellow onion, cut into small dice

1 tablespoon Garlic-Herb Paste (page 294)

1 tablespoon ají amarillo (yellow pepper) paste (such as Zócalo brand; found in a Latin market or online)

½ teaspoon freshly ground black pepper

½ teaspoon ground cumin

One 10-ounce (283 g) package frozen peas and carrots

10 cups (two 1-pound bags/ 1 kg) fresh cauliflower rice

onion salad

1 red onion, julienned

1 teaspoon salt, plus
more to taste

1 fresh spicy chile pepper
of your choice, such as
serrano, jalapeño, or
habanero, julienned

2 cilantro sprigs, minced

2 tablespoons (30 g)
extra virgin olive oil

Freshly ground black
pepper, to taste

Fresh lime juice, to taste

COVER and cook over medium heat until the chicken is completely cooked, 20 to 30 minutes, with an internal temperature of 165°F.

ADD the cauliflower rice and cook until the flavors are just combined (do not overmix or the cauliflower will get mushy). Al dente cauliflower rice takes about 2 minutes.

FOR THE ONION SALAD: Place the julienned onion in a strainer and add the salt. Rub the onion well with your fingers and rinse it under cold water. Place the onion in a bowl with ice water for a few minutes, then drain and place in a medium bowl (this step takes away the strong spicy flavor of the onion). Add the chile, reserved cilantro, olive oil, salt, pepper, and lime juice and mix well. (I prefer this salad eaten the day it's made, but it can also be refrigerated overnight.)

FOR SERVING: Serve the cauliflower rice with one chicken thigh and some onion salad on top.

baked goods, desserts, and sweets

sun-dried tomato and basil paleo bread

MAKES 1 LOAF, ABOUT 12 SLICES

1½ cups plus 1½ tablespoons (340 g) unhulled raw sesame seeds

2 tablespoons (25 g) chia seeds

¾ cup (75 g) flaxseed meal

4 teaspoons (18 g) Homemade Baking Powder (page 297)

2 teaspoons psyllium powder (such as Anthony's brand)

1½ teaspoons salt (see page 15)

6 large eggs, at room temperature

½ cup (120 g) Almond Milk (page 304)

¾ cup (18 g) chopped fresh basil leaves (cut into chiffonade, then cut crosswise into small pieces)

⅓ cup (50 g) small-diced sun-dried tomatoes packed in extra virgin olive oil

I started reading about the paleo diet, or evolutionary nutrition, many years ago and found it fascinating to think about what life was like thousands of years ago, how our brains have evolved since, and the role that food played in that development. Of course, the paleo recipes of the modern era are our interpretation of what was eaten at the time, but I think it's a clean, pure, nutrient-packed way to give our bodies real food, real fuel. And of course, eating this way can be a delight to our palate as well.

This bread is one of my favorite paleo recipes because it is powerfully nutritious. Sesame seeds contain a ton of calcium and a large number of natural bioactive components with high antioxidant potential. Chia, flaxseeds, and psyllium are excellent sources of fiber, fat, protein, vitamins, and minerals. All these superfoods, combined with sun-dried tomatoes and basil, come together in a scrumptious bread that you can eat any time of the day, and my favorite way to eat it is toasting it first!

PREHEAT the oven to 350°F. Line a 4½ × 8½-inch loaf pan with parchment paper on the bottom and sides, with an overhang on the long sides for easy lifting.

IN a high-powered blender, process the sesame seeds just long enough to turn them into a fine flour (be careful; if you blend for too long, you might make sesame butter).

IN a medium bowl, combine the sesame flour, chia seeds, flaxseed meal, baking powder, psyllium, and salt. Mix well with a spoon.

IN the bowl of a stand mixer fitted with the whisk attachment, beat the eggs until very foamy, starting on low speed and slowly increasing the speed to high. Lower the speed and slowly add the almond milk. Little by little, add the dry ingredients until completely combined. Add the chopped basil and sun-dried tomatoes and mix until combined.

POUR the batter into the prepared pan and smooth the surface with a spatula. Bake for 50 minutes, until a toothpick inserted into the center comes out clean.

TRANSFER to a wire rack and let cool completely. Because this bread can get a bit dry, I slice it right after it's cool and freeze it, two slices to a zip-top bag. To toast a frozen slice, place it directly in the toaster or oven.

AIP sandwich bread

MAKES 1 LOAF, ABOUT 12 SLICES

2½ cups (600 g) warm water

1 tablespoon active dry yeast

1½ teaspoons coconut
sugar (see page 7)

1 cup plus 1 tablespoon (158 g)
cassava flour (see page 17)

1 cup plus 2 tablespoons
(158 g) plantain flour
(see page 8)

1 cup (113 g) sifted tigernut
flour (see page 16)

1½ cups (180 g) arrowroot
flour (also known as
starch or powder)

1 tablespoon glucomannan
(konjac root powder;
see page 9)

1½ teaspoons Homemade
Baking Powder (page 297)

¾ teaspoon baking soda

1½ teaspoons salt
(see page 15)

½ cup (114 g) extra
virgin olive oil

1 tablespoon apple cider
vinegar (see page 3)

This bread is very special to me because our daughter Camila follows the AIP diet, and when she began her journey with this eating regimen, one of the things she missed the most was bread. I know how hard it is for anyone who has dietary restrictions to feel like they are eating "normal" food, as I am often told by our customers how difficult it can be. And bread is one of those "normal" foods that is more difficult to find, especially with a texture you can fully enjoy. I tell our daughters and our customers that instead of feeling limited by these restrictions, let's look at them as an opportunity to evaluate the quality of ingredients we are choosing to eat. Let's think of them as a wake-up call, a way to improve our health through better and more nutritious food.

After many test versions, Camila approved the flavor and texture of this recipe, and I was pleased that I was able to include all the nutrients I wanted in a look-alike "normal" bread that she (and all my family) can fully enjoy.

PREHEAT the oven to 350°F. Line a 5 × 10-inch loaf pan with parchment paper on the bottom and sides, with an overhang on the long sides for easy lifting.

IN a small bowl, combine ¾ cup (180 g) of the warm water, the yeast, and the coconut sugar. Stir well and let rest until the yeast is activated—the mixture should have at least doubled in volume and have lots of bubbles, 20 to 25 minutes (but the volume and bubbliness are more important than the time).

IN the bowl of a stand mixer fitted with the paddle attachment, combine the cassava flour, plantain flour, tigernut flour, arrowroot flour, glucomannan, baking powder, baking soda, and salt and mix on low speed.

SLOWLY add the remaining 1¾ cups (420 g) warm water, the olive oil, vinegar, and the activated yeast mixture. Mix until combined.

POUR the batter into the prepared pan and smooth it out with a spatula or wet hands. Cover it with a clean cloth and let it rise in a warm place until it reaches the top of the pan but is not spilling over, about 1 hour. (Remember, this time depends on the room's temperature.)

BAKE for 55 minutes, until the bread is golden brown and a toothpick inserted into the center comes out clean.

TRANSFER to a wire rack and let cool completely. Cut into slices and serve (Camila's favorite way to eat it is by toasting it first). At home, I always make two or three loaves, slice them, and freeze them two slices at a time.

See the photo on page 190.

naan

2½ cups (600 g) warm water

1 tablespoon active dry yeast

4 teaspoons (14.4 g) coconut sugar (see page 7)

1 cup (186 g) white rice flour, plus more for the work surface

½ cup plus ⅓ cup plus 1 tablespoon (134 g) quinoa flour (see page 14)

⅓ cup (36 g) chickpea flour

½ cup plus 1 tablespoon (84 g) potato starch

1 cup (134 g) arrowroot flour (also known as starch or powder)

2½ tablespoons (26 g) psyllium powder (such as Anthony's brand)

2 tablespoons (22 g) pumpkin seed protein powder (such as Sprout Living brand)

2 teaspoons salt (see page 15)

2 teaspoons Homemade Baking Powder (page 297)

1 teaspoon baking soda

¼ cup (60 g) Coconut Yogurt (page 50) or canned coconut cream without guar gum, (such as Let's Do Organic brand; see page 28), solid part only

The word *naan* means "bread" in old Persian. It is a soft and smooth bread native to west, central, and South Asia, traditionally baked in a clay oven called a tandoor. Like most breads, naan is made of flour, yeast, water, and salt; the big difference is the addition of yogurt, an ingredient that gives it its unique flavor and texture.

This is my gluten-free, dairy-free, and superpowerful version of this bread, which requires some patience (because the pieces of naan are cooked one by one) and a functional kitchen ventilation hood, because the house can sometimes fill with smoke. Josefina is the number one lover of bread at home, and this is one of her favorites. Every time I make it, she patiently waits for her portion. With her little face full of emotion and her sweet voice, she reminds me, whispering: "With fried egg, right, Mama?" (as in Naan, Eggs, and Dukkah, page 70). When I make naan at home, I make a big batch and freeze it. You can reheat it directly in the oven and enjoy it as if it were freshly made.

IN a small bowl, combine the warm water, the yeast, and the coconut sugar. Stir well and let rest until the yeast is activated—the mixture should have at least doubled in volume and have lots of bubbles, 20 to 25 minutes (but the volume and bubbliness are more important than the time).

IN the bowl of a stand mixer fitted with the paddle attachment, combine the rice flour, quinoa flour, chickpea flour, potato starch, arrowroot flour, psyllium powder, pumpkin seed protein powder, salt, baking powder, and baking soda and mix on low speed. Slowly add the activated yeast mixture. Add the yogurt and increase the speed to high, mixing until well combined. The dough may be very sticky and that's okay.

HEAT a large cast-iron skillet over medium-high heat (without any oil).

PLACE a silicone mat or a large piece of parchment paper on a work surface and sprinkle with rice flour. Use floured hands to divide the dough into 12 portions. For each piece of naan, roll a piece of dough into a ball and sprinkle a bit more rice flour on top. Flatten it on the work surface into a circle or slight oval that's 5 to 5½ inches in diameter and about ¼ inch thick. This is a very delicate dough, and your hands work better than a rolling pin.

USING an oversize spatula or a cake lifter, carefully place the bread in the hot skillet and cook until lightly browned or slightly toasted, 1 to 1½ minutes on each side.

TRANSFER the naan to a wire rack and repeat to make the remaining naan. The rice flour on the naan will burn in the pan, so scrape out the pan a little with a spatula to remove any burned flour before making the next naan.

YOU can make a double or triple batch and freeze these, and then heat them from frozen in the oven or toaster.

See the photo on page 191.

AIP tortillas

MAKES SIX 6-INCH TORTILLAS

½ cup (70 g) sifted tigernut
flour (see page 16)

¼ cup plus 1 tablespoon (60 g)
cassava flour (see page 17), plus
more for the work surface

1½ cups (200 g) tapioca flour

½ teaspoon salt (see page 15)

2 tablespoons (30 g)
avocado oil

Wraps are one of my favorite foods. When my house became gluten-free so many years ago, nobody in Peru sold gluten-free tortillas (and I needed my recipe to be corn-free), so I had to figure out how to make my own. I tested about two million different recipe variations but could not for the life of me understand why it wasn't working. That is, until one day when I had a breakthrough. I made the dough and it was very liquid (as had been happening over and over again). I sat down, looking at it, thinking and thinking (like Winnie-the-Pooh) about how to improve it. I spent several minutes lamenting my tortilla failures but decided to go ahead and cook it anyway because I refuse to waste ingredients. So I reached into my bowl of dough and—ta-da!—the batter had the perfect texture. The secret was simple: letting the dough sit long enough. How much wisdom is there in patience, right?

IN a medium bowl, combine the tigernut flour, cassava flour, tapioca flour, salt, avocado oil, and ⅔ cup plus ¼ cup (220 g) water and mix well. Cover with a kitchen towel and let the dough rest for 15 minutes (this is a very important step!).

PLACE a large piece of parchment paper on the work surface and sprinkle it with cassava flour. Divide the dough into 6 portions.

PLACE one piece of dough on the paper. Sprinkle a little flour on the dough and lay another piece of parchment on top. Use a rolling pin to roll out a tortilla as thin as you can.

HEAT a large cast-iron skillet over medium-high heat (without any oil). Slowly and carefully remove the paper on top of your tortilla. Lift the tortilla on the bottom paper and quickly flip it over to lay it in the pan (the paper will now be on top); you can also use a cake lifter to transfer the tortilla to the pan. Slowly remove the paper, starting on one side and taking care not to rip the tortilla. (The secret is using the right amount of flour so that the dough doesn't stick. Too much and the dough will dry out and rip. Practice and you'll figure out the perfect amount.) Cook until brown spots appear, 1 to 1½ minutes on each side.

TRANSFER the tortilla to a clean, dry kitchen towel and place another on top to keep it warm, moist, and flexible. Repeat to make the rest of the tortillas.

YOU can freeze these tortillas flat and heat them in the pan any time you want to use them.

sweet pastry crust

MAKES ONE 9½-INCH PIE OR TART CRUST

Organic extra virgin coconut oil, melted, for the pan

2.54 ounces (75 g) shortening (such as Spectrum organic all-vegetable shortening), frozen until very hard (see Note)

¾ cup (100 g) cassava flour (see page 17)

¾ cup (90 g) superfine blanched almond flour (such as Bob's Red Mill brand)

¼ cup plus ½ tablespoon (35 g) arrowroot flour (also known as starch or powder)

2 tablespoons (20 g) coconut flour (such as Let's Do Organic brand)

1 tablespoon flaxseed meal

3 tablespoons (35 g) coconut sugar (see page 7)

1 teaspoon Homemade Baking Powder (page 297)

1 teaspoon fresh lime juice

¼ cup (60 g) cold water

I've always been intimidated by making tarts and pies, especially compared to my mom, with her brilliant talent and patience. She made the most perfect tarts in the world, with a delicate crust and exquisite fillings, and my daughters loved them. When I started creating my gluten- and dairy-free recipes, my girls made their list of recipes they wanted me to re-create, and of course Abui's tarts topped the list!

I'm not a fan of making complicated doughs that need to be stretched to perfection and decorated with a lot of patience, such as when you arrange strawberries on top slice by slice. But then I'd remember Mom's perfect tarts—I could even taste her strawberry tart or her fabulous grape tart just by thinking about them—so it was worth trying to make a quick-and-easy gluten- and dairy-free dough to re-create those sweet memories. The result is a delicious crust and a reminder that my mother's secret was not only her talent and patience but also the love she put into each recipe she created. Just as I adore seeing my daughters enjoying my food today (with the strawberries sliced and placed in perfect position), Mom enjoyed watching me and my sisters devour her amazing tarts.

This super-easy dough is the base for the paleo version of my mom's Strawberry Tart (page 240) and an incredible Lime Meringue Pie (page 229).

NOTE
Freezing the shortening makes the dough easier to work with. Measure the shortening by weight for best accuracy. Place a small bowl on the scale and add small spoonfuls to the center of the bowl, one by one, until you reach the correct weight. Freeze the shortening in the bowl until hard.

PREHEAT the oven to 350°F. Grease a 9½-inch pie or tart pan with coconut oil.

IN a food processor, combine the shortening, cassava flour, almond flour, arrowroot flour, coconut flour, flaxseed meal, coconut sugar, baking powder, lime juice, and cold water and process just until a soft, sticky dough forms.

PLACE the dough in the prepared pan and spread it out with your fingers to cover the bottom and sides evenly.

BAKE for 30 to 35 minutes, until light golden brown. Set aside to cool, then proceed with your recipe.

quiche crust

MAKES ONE 9½-INCH PIE OR TART CRUST

My Sweet Pastry Crust (page 196) was so good and easy to do that I decided to create a savory version, so my family could enjoy the quiches they'd liked so much before we became a gluten- and dairy-free household. I really enjoy how versatile quiche can be; you can eat it for breakfast, lunch, or dinner and serve it as an appetizer, side, or main dish. It even travels well for a potluck dinner at a friend's house. People won't believe they're eating something so delicious that's also gluten-free, dairy-free, paleo, and super healthy.

This nourishing base is fantastic for any savory tart or quiche. The Leek, Onion, and Bacon Quiche (page 170) and Chard and Egg Tart (page 162) are two of my very favorites.

PREHEAT the oven to 350°F. Grease a 9½-inch pie pan with a little olive oil.

IN a food processor, combine the shortening, cassava flour, almond flour, arrowroot flour, coconut flour, flaxseed meal, nutritional yeast, salt, lime juice, and cold water and process just until a soft, sticky dough forms.

PLACE the dough in the prepared pie pan and spread it out with your fingers to cover the bottom and sides evenly.

BAKE for 30 to 35 minutes, until golden brown. Set aside to cool, then proceed with your recipe.

Extra virgin olive oil, for the pan

2.54 ounces (75 g) shortening (such as Spectrum organic all-vegetable shortening), frozen until very hard (see Note, page 196)

¾ cup (100 g) cassava flour (see page 17)

¾ cup (90 g) superfine blanched almond flour (such as Bob's Red Mill brand)

3½ tablespoons (35 g) arrowroot flour (also known as starch or powder)

2 tablespoons (20 g) coconut flour (such as Let's Do Organic brand)

1 tablespoon flaxseed meal

1 tablespoon nutritional yeast

¾ teaspoon salt (see page 15)

1 teaspoon fresh lime juice

¼ cup (60 g) cold water

yuca crackers

MAKES ABOUT 36 CRACKERS

1.8 pounds (816 g) fresh or frozen 3 × 1-inch yuca sticks (deveined; see page 17)

¼ cup extra virgin olive oil

1 teaspoon salt (see page 15)

½ teaspoon garlic powder

1 teaspoon dried basil

The first few times I made these crackers, I thought, *If I make a giant batch and store them in tightly sealed bags, I won't have to make more for a while.* They were super useful for the girls' lunch boxes and an amazing after-school snack, too. I just had to take out a bag of crackers, some avocado dip, and some cashew cheese and everyone was happy and satisfied. Brilliant idea! But the bags didn't last long at all. The girls loved the crackers and knew where I kept them, and often the bags would just mysteriously disappear. Two pieces of advice: make a really giant batch—and find a better hiding place than I did.

OPTIONAL: Place the yuca in a large bowl and cover with water. Let soak for a couple of hours (see page 17), then drain and rinse under cold water.

PLACE the yuca in a large pot with plenty of water. Bring the water to a boil and cook just until the yuca can be pierced easily with a fork, about 5 minutes after the water comes to a boil. Do not overcook it, as we do not want it soggy. Drain and weigh out 750 grams of the yuca sticks. (Any extras can be fried in an air fryer or in a pan with a bit of avocado oil, or you can add them to a soup, stew, or salad, or freeze to fry later.)

WHILE the yuca is still hot, place it in a food processor, along with the olive oil, salt, garlic powder, and basil. Process into a smooth dough (the timing will vary depending on your machine).

WRAP the dough in plastic wrap and refrigerate it overnight.

PREHEAT the oven to 350°F. Place a silicone baking mat on a work surface.

UNWRAP the dough and place it on the mat. Set a piece of parchment paper on top of the dough. Use a rolling pin to roll out the dough into a very thin rectangle—so thin that you can almost see through it.

WITH a pastry cutter wheel, mark rectangular strips of approximately 2 × 5 inches. (If you don't have a pastry cutter wheel, it's fine to bake as a solid sheet.)

PLACE the silicone mat on a sheet pan and bake for 15 minutes, until the dough can be easily removed from the mat. The cracker will be light golden brown, not changed much in color.

CAREFULLY flip the cracker with your hands and bake another 15 minutes, until dry, crisp, and light brown.

SET the crackers aside to cool completely on the pan. Break the crackers apart with your hands by following the marks you made (or simply break them into rough individual crackers). Store in a sealed bag or a glass jar.

NOTE

The freshly made yuca dough is very sticky and difficult to handle. The secret to making it manageable is to refrigerate it overnight, so plan ahead!

pumpkin bread

MAKES 2 MINI LOAVES

1 tablespoon organic extra virgin coconut oil, melted, plus more for the pans

⅓ cup (50 g) cassava flour (see page 17)

½ cup (50 g) sifted tigernut flour (see page 16)

3 tablespoons (30 g) arrowroot flour (also known as starch or powder)

½ cup (45 g) unsweetened shredded coconut (such as Let's Do Organic brand)

1 teaspoon Homemade Baking Powder (page 297)

2 teaspoons Pumpkin Spice Mix (page 299)

½ teaspoon ground cinnamon

Pinch of salt (see page 15)

2 large eggs, at room temperature

¾ cup plus 1 tablespoon (135 g) coconut sugar (see page 7)

½ cup plus 1 tablespoon plus 1 teaspoon (150 g) pure pumpkin puree (not pumpkin pie filling)

¼ cup (80 g) pure maple syrup

⅓ cup plus 1 tablespoon plus 1 teaspoon (90 g) extra virgin olive oil

We arrived in America on October 16, 2019, and I remember that date clearly, because we'd dreamed of it for a long time. Our friends Santiago and Paige, who live in Georgia, lovingly welcomed us into their home until we could find a house to rent. We are very lucky to have friends with such big hearts; not everyone would accept into their home friends with five daughters and a dog. Not only that, but they showered us with unconditional love, offering us the very best of everything. They served the girls breakfast every day, and even walked our dog, Chia, with their dog, Silvester, while we organized our new life here and took care of paperwork.

It was autumn, and of course pumpkins were everywhere. In Peru you might see imported pumpkins for Halloween decorations, but I'd never tried pumpkin bread. Paige bought a loaf, and I remember my first reaction was, "What is this deliciousness?!!!" I fell in love with this new flavor. But it wasn't until the following fall that I was able to start playing around with this new favorite ingredient on my own, and I wanted my gluten- and dairy-free version to be just as good as that first marvelous bite of pumpkin bread. After several attempts, I got the balance of pumpkin and spices that I was looking for.

This recipe makes two smaller loaves, which I love because they make an incredible gift for a Thanksgiving dinner or to bring to your neighbors, wrapped with a beautiful bow. The bread is soft, moist, and delicate, and the toppings add an extra sweet and crunchy touch. You can also make the batter into a single standard loaf, of course.

PREHEAT the oven to 350°F. Line two 5½ × 3-inch mini loaf pans with parchment paper on the bottom and up two sides, with a paper overhang. Grease the other sides lightly with coconut oil.

IN a medium bowl, combine the cassava flour, tigernut flour, arrowroot flour, shredded coconut, baking powder, pumpkin spice mix, cinnamon, and salt and mix well.

IN the bowl of a stand mixer fitted with the whisk attachment, beat the eggs until foamy, starting on low speed and slowly increasing the speed to high. With the mixer still running, slowly add the coconut sugar and mix until the sugar is dissolved and the mixture is creamy and foamy. Add the pumpkin puree and maple syrup, then the olive oil, coconut oil, and vanilla and mix until combined.

SLOWLY add the dry ingredients, scraping the sides of the bowl with a spatula when necessary.

DIVIDE the dough between the prepared pans (smoothing the tops with a spatula if needed) and sprinkle with the pumpkin seeds and chocolate chips.

BAKE for 40 minutes, until a toothpick inserted into the center comes out clean (if you're making a single loaf, bake for about 45 to 50 minutes).

TURN the loaf out onto a wire rack. Let cool completely before cutting.

See the photo on page 202.

1 teaspoon pure vanilla extract

2 tablespoons (15 g) hulled raw pumpkin seeds

1½ tablespoons (15 g) paleo 70% (such as HU brand) or 100% (such as Pascha brand) chocolate chips

banana, walnut, and goldenberry bread

MAKES 1 LOAF, WITH 10 SLICES

2 cups (235 g) superfine blanched almond flour (such as Bob's Red Mill brand)

3 tablespoons (30 g) coconut flour (such as Let's Do Organic brand)

2 teaspoons ground cinnamon

1 teaspoon Homemade Baking Powder (page 297)

½ teaspoon baking soda

⅛ teaspoon salt (see page 15)

3 large eggs, at room temperature

¾ cup plus 1 tablespoon (130 g) coconut sugar (see page 7)

1 small banana, mashed (80 to 95 g)

3 tablespoons (45 g) Almond Milk (see page 304)

1 teaspoon apple cider vinegar (see page 3)

3 tablespoons (45 g) organic extra virgin coconut oil, melted

1 tablespoon extra virgin olive oil

¾ cup (3.17 ounces/90 g) chopped walnuts or pecans

⅓ cup plus 1 tablespoon (55 g) dried goldenberries

Goldenberries are a very common fruit in Peru, and when we came to America, I thought it would be very hard to find them fresh. But I was lucky enough to find them in a couple of healthy supermarkets, and every time I go to pay for them, the cashier and people in line always ask me what they taste like and what I do with them. Of course I give them lots of ideas and mention that they're also hidden on the supermarket shelves in dehydrated form.

Dried goldenberries are sweet and sour, and a great snack all on their own. But their flavor really shines when they're mixed into this wonderfully soft, tender, and moist banana bread, which also features the satisfying crunch of walnuts. My advice is to make a double recipe and freeze the second loaf in slices (because the first one is going to disappear very quickly). It will be a lifesaver when you have impromptu visitors, need a lunch box snack, or simply experience a midafternoon banana bread craving.

I'll tell you a great secret about goldenberries: if you have a dehydrator, buy them fresh and dehydrate them yourself. But do not overdry them; dry just to the point that they're very dry on the outside and slightly moist on the inside. Dried this way, they're an amazing candy treat—so much better than gummy bears!

PREHEAT the oven to 350°F.

LINE a 4½ × 8½-inch loaf pan with parchment paper on the bottom and sides, with an overhang on the long sides for easy lifting.

IN a medium bowl, combine the almond flour, coconut flour, cinnamon, baking powder, baking soda, and salt and mix well.

IN the bowl of a stand mixer fitted with the whisk attachment, beat the eggs until foamy, starting on low speed and increasing the speed to high. Add the coconut sugar and beat until the sugar is dissolved and the mixture is creamy and foamy. Add the banana, milk, vinegar, and oils and mix well on medium speed.

LOWER the speed and add the dry ingredients little by little.

TURN off the mixer and use a spatula to fold in the walnuts and goldenberries.

POUR the batter into the prepared pan and use a spatula to smooth the top. Bake for 45 minutes, until a toothpick inserted in the center comes out clean.

TURN the loaf onto a wire rack. Let cool completely before cutting.

See the photo on page 203.

paleo molten lava cake

MAKES 4 SINGLE-SERVING CAKES

¼ cup plus 1½ tablespoons (80 g) organic extra virgin coconut oil, plus more for the ramekins

3 tablespoons (30 g) superfine blanched almond flour (such as Bob's Red Mill brand)

2 tablespoons (20 g) arrowroot flour (also known as starch or powder)

5 ounces (140 g) paleo 100% dark chocolate chips (such as Pascha brand; see page 6)

2 large eggs, at room temperature

2 egg yolks, at room temperature

½ cup plus 1 tablespoon (100 g) maple sugar (such as Coombs Family Farms brand)

½ cup (160g) pure maple syrup

4 teaspoons coffee extract (such as Flavorganics brand) or 1 teaspoon pure vanilla extract (optional)

Fresh berries, for serving

Whipped coconut cream (see Note, page 237), for serving (optional)

My Argentine friend, Flor, makes spectacular desserts, like a delicious rogel made of several layers of very thin cookies filled with dulce de leche and covered with meringue, and a divine quince pastafrola, a sweet tart filled with an amazing quince jam. When we lived in Peru, her daughter was Camila's best friend, and over time Flor became my chosen sister, my favorite partner to drink yerba mate with. She was also a spiritual teacher who taught me that maternal love is much more than giving birth to a baby; she chose to adopt one of her daughters as a form of pure and unconditional love. They are an amazing family! It was a blessing for me to accompany her on such an extraordinary journey of love and humility.

Flor is a talented cook, probably because she puts so much love into everything she does. One day she surprised us with a more than perfect molten lava cake. I spent a lot of time trying to create a paleo version of that dessert, and I think this is pretty close.

We both suffered a lot when she had to return to Argentina, but we keep in touch (as do our daughters), because when a friendship is true, neither time nor distance can break those ties. I hope one day we can see each other again—I can prepare this molten lava cake for her, and we can sit down to talk, eat, and drink a great Argentine yerba mate.

PREHEAT the oven to 425°F. Grease four 6-ounce ceramic ramekins with a little oil.

IN a small bowl, mix the almond and arrowroot flours.

FILL a medium saucepan almost halfway with water and bring it to a boil over medium-high heat.

PLACE the chocolate and coconut oil in a heatproof bowl that will fit over the saucepan without touching the water.

WHEN the water starts to boil, turn off the heat and set the bowl in the saucepan. Let the chocolate and coconut oil soften a bit, then start stirring to help them melt completely.

WHILE the chocolate is melting, in a stand mixer fitted with the whisk attachment, beat the eggs and yolks until foamy and the color begins to lighten a bit, starting on low speed and increasing the speed to high. Lower the speed, add the maple sugar and beat until foamy, increasing the speed to high.

LOWER the speed and add the maple syrup, then increase the speed to incorporate it well. Lower the speed and add the melted chocolate mixture, pouring it in slowly. Add the almond flour mixture and coffee extract (if using) and mix just to combine.

DIVIDE the batter among the prepared ramekins and bake for 14 to 16 minutes, until the surface is dry.

LET the cakes cool and rest for a couple of minutes on a wire rack.

TO serve, loosen the edges of a cake with a knife, then invert a dessert plate over the mold and carefully invert the setup. Gently lift the ramekin to unmold the cake.

SERVE immediately with fresh berries and whipped coconut cream, if you like.

See the photo on page 208.

superpowerful brownies

7 ounces (200 g) paleo 70% chocolate chips (such as HU brand)

2½ tablespoons (50 g) raw almond butter

½ cup plus 1 teaspoon (125 g) organic extra virgin coconut oil

1 tablespoon plus 1 teaspoon (12 g) cashew flour

2 tablespoons (20 g) superfine blanched almond flour (such as Bob's Red Mill Brand)

1 tablespoon (10 g) arrowroot flour (also known as starch or powder)

1 teaspoon Homemade Baking Powder (page 297)

2 teaspoons moringa powder (see page 11)

2 teaspoons adaptogenic mushroom powder (see page 2)

7.76 ounces (220 g) eggs (the weight is without the shells; start with 7 large eggs), at room temperature

1½ cups plus 1 tablespoon (250 g) coconut sugar (see page 7)

2 teaspoons pure maple syrup

1 teaspoon pure vanilla extract

2½ tablespoons (25 g) cacao nibs (see page 6)

I have a wonderful memory from many years ago when Sebas, who was sports director of the club we belonged to, had access to a beautiful little house in the country. It was located an hour from Lima, and the traffic was always crazy, so sometimes it would take us a very long time to get there. The girls were at their happiest every time we went. There were swimming pools and tennis courts, and even a tiny zoo. The truth is, I never wanted to leave that happy place, so the girls and I made it our job to convince Sebas to let them skip school on Monday so they could enjoy one more happy day in the peace of nature.

We loved to have barbecues and bake bread in the clay oven that was on the property, and a perfect and super-quick dessert was always brownies! Here's an updated and recharged version of the brownies that accompanied us on those happy weekends, now including a bunch of well-camouflaged superfoods; good fats and complete proteins are the base of this powerful treat. These brownies also contain moringa, which provides vitamins and iron; adaptogens, which are anti-inflammatory and have antistress power; and cacao, which is bursting with antioxidants. What more could you ask for in a spectacularly delicious dessert? Oh, I know—use these brownies as the base of the Cherry Cheesecake on page 217! They turn a regular cheesecake into a work of art.

Eat these while enjoying nature—that is absolute happiness!

PREHEAT the oven to 350°F. Line a 9 × 9-inch (or 8 × 8-inch) baking dish with parchment paper on the bottom and sides, with an overhang on the long sides for easy lifting.

FILL a medium saucepan almost halfway with water and bring it to a boil over medium-high heat.

PLACE the chocolate, almond butter, and coconut oil in a heatproof bowl that will fit over the saucepan without touching the water.

WHEN the water starts to boil, turn off the heat and set the bowl in the saucepan. Let the chocolate, almond butter, and coconut oil soften a bit, then start stirring to help them melt completely. Mix until smooth.

IN a medium bowl, combine the cashew flour, almond flour, arrowroot flour, baking powder, moringa powder, and mushroom powder and mix well.

IN a large bowl, combine the eggs, coconut sugar, and maple syrup. Whisk until combined, but do not overmix. Pour in the melted chocolate mixture and whisk to combine. Add the vanilla and half the dry ingredients and whisk until smooth. Add the remaining dry ingredients and whisk again until smooth.

POUR the mixture into the prepared baking dish, smooth the top with a spatula, and sprinkle with the cacao nibs.

BAKE for 35 minutes, until the surface is completely dry. If you poke the brownies with a toothpick and they still have a lot of moisture, it's no problem.

TRANSFER the brownies to a wire rack. Let cool completely. Cut into 9 brownies just like a tic-tac-toe grid. I love to eat these very cold, so as soon as they cool down, I cut them up and store them in a container in the fridge. With the amount of chocolate and coconut oil these contain, they can last a long time, even weeks, and you can freeze them, too.

AIP chocolate chip cookies

MAKES 20 COOKIES

Because of Cami's AIP diet (see page 19), her palate has changed, and sweet treats taste *very* sweet to her now (which I think is wonderful!). So, her need for sugary treats has decreased a lot, and it's weird when she asks me for something sweet. She loves citrus flavors, and her favorite dessert is berries. But sometimes she wants a baked snack, so I decided to develop some cookies that were on the less sweet side, so she wouldn't find them cloying. Even though Cami follows the AIP diet to the letter, one thing that doesn't cause her any problems (and she really enjoys) is real chocolate, but if you want to make these completely AIP-compliant by using carob chips, the result is absolutely delicious. I love baking multiple batches of these cookies and storing them in a big jar, because I know they won't last long.

PREHEAT the oven to 350°F. Line a sheet pan with a silicone baking mat or parchment paper.

IN a medium bowl, combine the glucomannan, plantain flour, tigernut flour, arrowroot flour, and baking powder and mix well.

IN the bowl of a stand mixer fitted with the paddle attachment, beat the softened coconut butter, softened coconut oil, coconut cream, and coconut sugar on high speed until well combined.

LOWER the speed and add the dry ingredients, then raise the speed and mix until well combined. Add the carob chips and mix for a couple of seconds, until distributed throughout.

USE your hands to form small balls and flatten them to form the cookies (my cookies are fairly small and I get about 20 per batch). Allow 2 inches of space between the cookies on the pan. Sprinkle flaky salt on top, if using.

BAKE for about 14 minutes, until the tops are cracked and the edges are slightly golden.

TRANSFER the cookies to a wire rack to cool completely, then enjoy!

1½ teaspoons glucomannan (konjac root powder; see page 9)

¼ cup plus 2 tablespoons (66 g) plantain flour (see page 8)

¼ cup plus 1 tablespoon (45 g) sifted tigernut flour (see page 16)

2 tablespoons (20 g) arrowroot flour (also known as starch or powder)

1 teaspoon Homemade Baking Powder (page 297)

¼ cup (2.65 ounces) plus 2 teaspoons (75 g) slightly softened coconut butter (such as Nutiva brand)

3 tablespoons (47 g) slightly softened organic extra virgin coconut oil

3½ tablespoons (70 g) coconut cream without guar gum (such as Let's Do Organic brand; see page 28), solid part only

½ cup plus 2 tablespoons (100 g) coconut sugar (see page 7)

2.5 ounces (70 g) carob chips (such as Aussie brand) or paleo 70% chocolate chips (such as HU brand; not AIP-compliant)

Flaky salt (see page 15), for sprinkling (optional)

AIP lúcuma cookies

¼ cup plus 2 tablespoons (66 g) plantain flour (see page 8)

¼ cup plus 1 tablespoon (45 g) sifted tigernut flour (see page 16)

2 tablespoons (20 g) arrowroot flour (also known as starch or powder)

2 tablespoons (20 g) lúcuma powder (see page 9)

1½ teaspoons glucomannan (konjac root powder; see page 9)

1 teaspoon Homemade Baking Powder (page 297)

3½ tablespoons (70 g) coconut cream without guar gum (such as Let's Do Organic brand, see page 28), solid part only

¼ cup (2.65 ounces) plus 2 teaspoons (75 g) slightly softened coconut butter (such as Nutiva brand)

3 tablespoons (47 g) slightly softened organic extra virgin coconut oil

½ cup plus 2 tablespoons (100 g) coconut sugar (see page 7)

Melted chocolate (paleo 70% cacao, such as HU brand; not AIP-compliant; optional)

I love when I can eat a dessert and feel good about it. Eating dessert can sometimes leave you feeling a bit guilty, like, *Oh, it's so good, it can't be healthy.* But after I created Camila's chocolate chip cookies (see the previous recipe), I was happy to look for more ways to make cookies and other sweets I felt great about eating and feeding my family. I love lúcuma fruit in all its forms: fresh, in flour, in smoothies, in coffee, in desserts—and it's wonderful here in cookies as well. Enjoy these heavenly cookies on their own or with a classic glass of coconut milk; pair them with a matcha tea or place them in a lunch box—cookies warm our hearts at any time of day!

PREHEAT the oven to 350°F. Line a sheet pan with a silicone baking mat or parchment paper.

IN a medium bowl, combine the plantain flour, tigernut flour, arrowroot flour, lúcuma powder, glucomannan, and baking powder and mix well.

IN the bowl of a stand mixer fitted with the paddle attachment, beat the coconut cream, coconut butter, coconut oil, and coconut sugar on high speed until combined, making sure to break up any lumps. Add the dry ingredients and mix well.

USE your hands to form small balls and flatten them to form the cookies (my cookies are fairly small and I get about 20 per batch). Allow 2 inches of space between the cookies on the pan. Bake for about 14 minutes, until the tops are cracked and the edges are slightly golden.

TRANSFER the cookies to a wire rack to cool completely.

FOR cookies that don't follow the AIP diet but offer a pretty (and delicious) twist, you can dip each baked cookie halfway into a bowl of melted chocolate. Refrigerate until the chocolate is firm.

cherry cheesecake with a brownie bottom

MAKES 12 SERVINGS

Once upon a time, in a very distant past, I used to make stunning brownies full of butter, white sugar, and wheat flour, marbled with a cheesecake loaded with cream cheese and tons of powdered sugar. They were the star of any party. Oh God, how much we have been through and how much we have learned about ingredients since those days!

Thankfully, now, my specialty is a raw dairy-free cheesecake, and I love to play with different flavors and textures. But that wonderful old brownie recipe is often on my mind, and one day it occurred to me to create a healthier version. This dessert—with powerful ingredients like moringa, cacao, coconut oil, adaptogenic mushrooms, and cheesecake made with cashews, cacao butter, and some incredible cherries—is worthy of a celebration. And you know what? It's so much tastier than my old, heavy marbled brownies.

This recipe takes two days to make, so plan accordingly.

FOR THE BASE: Make the brownie recipe in an 8-inch round pan. Since you're making only a half recipe, bake it for 20 to 23 minutes, depending on your oven. Do not cut the brownies.

REFRIGERATE the brownie base in the pan for 8 hours or overnight so that it is firm and easy to handle.

CAREFULLY unmold the brownie base and place it on a sheet pan. If you have a cake ring mold the same size as your brownie pan, place an acetate sheet around the inside perimeter of the ring and set the brownie inside. If you don't have a cake ring mold, don't worry—I don't either. Surround the brownie with an acetate sheet and secure it with masking tape. The goal is to make a well to hold the cheesecake filling on top of the brownie long enough to chill it until it firms up.

SECURE the base of the acetate to the sheet pan with masking tape, sealing any gaps between it and the pan, to prevent the filling from overflowing underneath. Return the whole setup to the fridge.

½ recipe Superpowerful Brownies (page 210; omit for a vegan option)

filling

8.8 ounces (250 g) raw cashews, soaked in water for 8 hours (this is about 1⅔ cups, but weighing is most accurate!)

One 13.5-ounce (398 g) can coconut cream without guar gum (such as Let's Do Organic brand, see page 28)

⅓ cup plus 1 tablespoon (120 g) pure maple syrup

Juice of ½ lime

3 ounces (85 g) cacao butter (such as Navitas Organics Cacao Butter Wafers)

¼ cup plus 1 tablespoon (70 g) organic extra virgin coconut oil

cherry compote

10½ ounces (300 g) frozen dark cherries

⅓ cup (100 g) pure maple syrup

1½ teaspoons tapioca flour

To decorate

3 ounces (85 g) paleo 70% dark chocolate (such as HU brand)

2 tablespoons (30 g) Almond Milk (page 304)

Fresh cherries with stems, edible flowers, fresh mint leaves, or fresh berries, for garnish

FOR THE FILLING: Rinse and dry the soaked cashews. Place them in a high-powered blender with the coconut cream, maple syrup, and lime juice. Blend until smooth. Prepare a double boiler: Fill a medium saucepan almost halfway with water and bring it to a boil over medium-high heat. Place the cacao butter and coconut oil in a heatproof bowl that will fit over the saucepan without touching the water. Melt the cacao butter and coconut oil together, then add to the blender and blend for a few more seconds, until the mixture is very smooth and lump-free.

FOR THE CHERRY COMPOTE: Combine the cherries and maple syrup in a medium saucepan and simmer over medium heat until almost no liquid remains, about 25 minutes.

IN a small bowl, dissolve the tapioca flour in 2 tablespoons (30 g) water. Pour this mixture slowly into the saucepan in a thin stream, stirring the cherry mixture well as you do it. Cook, stirring constantly, until thickened, about 1 minute. Remove from the heat and use immediately.

TO ASSEMBLE AND DECORATE: Remove the brownie mold from the fridge and add the cashew cheesecake filling. Spoon the hot cherry compote over the top, making sure it covers the cheesecake. The compote will sink into the filling here and there, which is good. But do not stir—we want clearly visible layers of compote when cutting into our cheesecake brownies.

FREEZE for 30 minutes, then refrigerate overnight.

IN the morning, melt the chocolate with the almond milk, again using the double boiler method, but as soon as the water starts to boil, turn off the heat, remove the saucepan from the heat, and set the bowl in the saucepan. Let the chocolate soften a bit, then start stirring to help it melt completely.

REMOVE the masking tape (or ring) and acetate from the cheesecake and use a cake lifter to transfer it to a beautiful plate. Pour the chocolate mixture on top (it will flow over the edges). Refrigerate for about 20 minutes, until fully firm and chilled.

GARNISH with fresh cherries (or other options) and serve.

mesquite chocolate "turrón"

MAKES 12 SERVINGS

The Peruvian chocolate turrón is a dessert that is believed to be derived from the Spanish turrón, a nougat containing almonds or other nuts that may have its source in a Muslim recipe. The turrón that is sold in Lima is definitely not as sweet as the Spanish one. The Peruvian version is made with chocolate and lots of pecans and its texture is reminiscent of both a brownie and cake.

When we were first married, Sebas wasn't a dessert lover, but he did like dark chocolate. So turrón was the perfect choice to celebrate his birthday. Of course, for me, birthday cakes had to be made at home—that's how I grew up. So I made it my mission in those first years of marriage to bake the perfect chocolate turrón. Every year, I invited his friends over, prepared the appetizers, the drinks, and the music, and received people at the door. Then, suddenly, I would remember the turrón in the oven. Sometimes I was able to save part of the cake by scraping off the burned parts, and sometimes we had to run to the supermarket to buy another one. Once my mom was visiting us over Sebas's birthday, and she made the perfect turrón for him (to keep me from burning it, of course). Everything turned out wonderfully, and Sebas was very happy because we had half the turrón left over, so he could eat it the next day. But at dawn, my mom heard noises in the dining room. She came out of her room, turned on the light, and there it was—the empty pan, and my dog, Athos, caught chocolate-snouted and ready to flee the crime scene.

cake

3 ounces (85 g) paleo 70% dark chocolate chips (such as HU brand; see page 6)

⅓ cup plus 1½ tablespoons (100 g) organic extra virgin coconut oil

⅓ cup plus 1 tablespoon (50 g) arrowroot flour (also known as starch or powder)

¼ cup plus 5 tablespoons (47 g) mesquite powder (see page 11)

¼ cup (35 g) cassava flour (see page 17)

3 tablespoons (20 g) cacao powder (see page 5)

¼ teaspoon salt (see page 15)

4 large eggs, at room temperature

¾ cup plus 2½ tablespoons (150 g) coconut sugar (see page 7)

2 tablespoons (30g) extra virgin olive oil

1¼ cups plus 2 tablespoons (150 g) chopped pecans

FOR THE CAKE: Preheat the oven to 350°F. Line a 9 × 9-inch pan with parchment paper on the bottom and sides, with an overhang on opposite sides for easy lifting.

PREPARE a double boiler: Fill a medium saucepan almost halfway with water and bring it to a boil over medium-high heat.

PLACE the chocolate and coconut oil in a heatproof bowl that will fit over the saucepan without touching the water.

chocolate ganache

3 ounces (85 g) paleo 100% dark chocolate chips (such as Pascha brand)

¼ cup (65 g) Almond Milk (page 304)

3 tablespoons (70 g) pure maple syrup

⅓ cup (40 g) pecan halves or chopped pecans, for garnish

WHEN the water starts to boil, turn off the heat and set the bowl in the saucepan. Let the chocolate and coconut oil soften a bit, then start stirring to help them melt completely.

IN a medium bowl, combine the arrowroot flour, mesquite powder, cassava flour, cacao powder, and salt and mix well.

IN a large bowl, combine the eggs and coconut sugar. Whisk lightly to combine the ingredients (do not overmix). Add the olive oil and the melted chocolate mixture and whisk to combine. Add the dry ingredients and mix well. Fold in the pecans with a spatula.

POUR the batter into the prepared pan and bake for 35 minutes, until a toothpick inserted into the center comes out clean.

TRANSFER the pan to a wire rack. Let cool completely.

FOR THE CHOCOLATE GANACHE: Prepare another double boiler. Place the chocolate, almond milk, and maple syrup in a heatproof bowl that will fit over the saucepan without touching the water.

WHEN the water starts to boil, turn off the heat and set the bowl in the saucepan. Let the chocolate soften a bit, then start stirring to help it melt completely.

TO SERVE: Transfer the turrón to a cake plate and cover it with the ganache. Decorate with pecans, then cut and serve.

profiteroles

MAKES 25 PROFITEROLES, TO SERVE 5

My mother has always had a lot of patience and an amazing skill for handicrafts, like making a five-tier cake decorated with individually constructed sugarpaste flowers for my wedding. Every year at Christmas she would decorate the house with wonderful ornamental objects and goodies she made herself. Once she even made a croquembouche, and I thought, *What an amazing piece of art!* And it was also edible?! What could be better?

Profiteroles have always seemed to me an incredible delicacy, an elegant snack eaten with tea served in a fancy cup. My paleo version can be filled with a dairy-free pastry cream and covered with chocolate ganache, or you can use whipped coconut cream (see the Note on page 237) and fresh fruit. Or try Josefina's idea, which is simply to split open the pastry and put a slice of pepperoni in it for a savory treat.

PREHEAT the oven to 450°F. Line a sheet pan with parchment paper.

IN a medium bowl, combine the almond flour, coconut flour, arrowroot flour, tapioca flour, baking powder, and salt and mix well.

IN a medium saucepan over medium-high heat, heat the coconut milk and coconut oil until just about to boil. Turn off the heat and add the dry ingredients. Use a spatula to mix well for few seconds until incorporated.

TRANSFER the dough to the bowl of a stand mixer fitted with the paddle attachment and beat on low speed for 3 minutes to cool it down.

WITH the mixer running, add the eggs in three parts. Increase the speed to high, and beat until the eggs are well incorporated.

THEN turn off the mixer. The dough should be very sticky. Let rest for 15 minutes.

¾ cup (86 g) superfine blanched almond flour (such as Bob's Red Mill brand)

2 tablespoons (15 g) coconut flour (such as Let's Do Organic brand)

¾ cup (110 g) plus 1 tablespoon arrowroot flour (also known as starch or powder)

¾ cup (100 g) tapioca flour

1 teaspoon Homemade Baking Powder (page 297)

Pinch of salt (see page 15)

½ cup (120 g) Coconut Milk (page 307) or canned organic coconut milk without guar gum (such as Native Forest's Simple)

½ cup (110 g) organic extra virgin coconut oil

4.2 ounces (110 g) eggs (this weight is without the shells; start with 2 eggs), at room temperature, lightly whisked

Pastry Cream (page 303), very cold

4½ ounces (127 g) paleo 70% dark chocolate chips (such as HU brand)

223

FILL a piping bag with the dough and attach a ⅝-inch tip. Pipe 1- to 2-inch (3 to 5 cm) rounds onto the prepared sheet pan, keeping 2½ inches (6 cm) of space between the rounds. (If you don't have a piping bag, fill a zip-top bag with the dough, cut off the end, and pipe the dough through the cut end.)

BAKE for 8 minutes, then lower the temperature to 400°F and bake for 3 to 4 more minutes, until lightly browned on the bottom.

LET the pastries cool on the sheet pan. (At this point, you can place them in a freezer bag or container and freeze them for up to 4 months. Thaw in the fridge overnight.)

FILL a piping bag with the cold pastry cream and attach a ¼-inch tip. Make a small cut in the side of a pastry, insert the tip, and pipe in pastry cream to taste. (You can also use the zip-top bag method here.) Repeat to fill the rest of the pastries.

FILL a medium saucepan almost halfway with water and bring it to a boil over medium-high heat.

PLACE the chocolate in a heatproof bowl that will fit over the saucepan without touching the water.

WHEN the water starts to boil, turn off the heat and set the bowl in the saucepan. Let the chocolate soften a bit, then start stirring to help it melt completely.

POUR a little melted chocolate over each profiterole and refrigerate for a couple of minutes so that the chocolate hardens. These are best when freshly made, but you can refrigerate before serving.

AIP plum and blackberry cobbler

MAKES 4 SERVINGS

This cobbler is sweet and tart, comforting and warm. And coconut oil, which is featured in this recipe, is the best ingredient in the world, as it is good for you both inside and out. Try oiling your pan with your hands, then put what you have left on your hands in your hair as a styling aid, or apply it as a face cream for wrinkles. I know, you might look like a crazy baker doing this, but it's pure wisdom that comes from nature. Just wash your hands when you're done. Believe me, the best beauty products are already hiding in your kitchen!

This combination of plums and blackberries is just fantastic, but you can swap out the plums for other seasonal fruit, such as peach-blueberry, apple-blueberry, apple-strawberry, mango-berry, or cherry-lemongrass.

PREHEAT the oven to 350°F. Grease a 9-inch oval baking dish with coconut oil.

FOR THE TOPPING: In a medium bowl, combine the cassava flour, tigernut slices, shredded coconut, arrowroot flour, coconut sugar, baking powder, and salt. Add the coconut oil and use a fork to mix it into a crumble.

FOR THE FILLING: Only when you are ready to make the dish, cut the plums in half, remove the pits, and cut the plum halves into ½- to ¾-inch dice. Combine them in a medium bowl with the blackberries, lime juice, coconut sugar, and arrowroot and mix to combine.

SPOON the fruit mixture into the prepared baking dish. Sprinkle with the topping, little by little, keeping the texture lumpy and making sure to completely cover the filling.

BAKE for 35 minutes, until the topping is golden brown and the filling is bubbling.

LET cool slightly before serving. Due to the amount of coconut oil in this recipe, I do not recommend reheating this cobbler; the coconut oil will melt. Eat it freshly baked or cold.

See the photo on page 226.

topping

⅓ cup plus 1½ tablespoons (100 g) organic extra virgin coconut oil, softened, plus more for the pan

¾ cup plus 1 tablespoon (120 g) cassava flour (see page 17)

¾ cup (60 g) sliced tigernuts (see page 16)

½ cup (50 g) unsweetened shredded coconut (such as Let's Do Organic brand)

3 tablespoons (30 g) arrowroot flour (also known as starch or powder)

½ cup plus 2 tablespoons (110 g) coconut sugar (see page 7)

1 teaspoon Homemade Baking Powder (page 297)

Pinch of salt (see page 15)

filling

1½ pounds (680 g) fresh plums

3½ ounces (100 g) frozen blackberries

Juice of ½ lime

3 tablespoons (35 g) coconut sugar (see page 7)

1 teaspoon arrowroot flour

lúcuma and algarrobina fudge

MAKES 16 SERVINGS

3½ tablespoons (50 g) organic extra virgin coconut oil, plus more for the pan

½ cup (165 g) pure maple syrup

¼ cup (45 g) maple sugar (such as Coombs Family Farm brand)

5 ounces (141 g) raw cashew butter

2 tablespoons (30 g) algarrobina syrup (available in Latin markets and online)

6¼ ounces (177 g) paleo 100% dark chocolate chips (such as Pascha brand)

2½ tablespoons (30 g) lúcuma powder (see page 9)

2 teaspoons adaptogenic mushroom powder (see page 2) or ashwagandha powder (see page 4; both optional but highly recommended)

Cacao nibs (see page 6), for garnish

special equipment needed

If you have a silicone loaf pan with an integrated steel rim (such as Trudeau brand), I recommend using it; the silicone makes the fudge easy to unmold, the steel rim adds structure, and you don't need to use parchment, which can add lines to the fudge.

How do we transform an indulgent and sinful dessert into one that even has some health benefits? By adding incredible ingredients such as good fats, superfoods, and the best quality chocolate we can find. In this recipe I use chocolate that is 100 percent cacao, which is super, super dark and in its most natural state. This allows us to take advantage of all its nutritional benefits (see page 6). I use maple syrup as a sweetener to bring out the flavors of the stars of the show: lúcuma (a fruit native to the Andean valleys of Ecuador, Peru, and Chile) and algarrobina (carob syrup; see page 11). Cashew butter gives it creaminess, protein, good fats, and a subtle earthy, nutty flavor. And of course I love to include extra power in my recipes; adaptogenic mushrooms or ashwagandha powder work very well here.

It has been a long path through history for cacao beans to reach our kitchens. Let's honor them in the purest way.

GREASE a 4½ × 8½-inch silicone loaf pan with coconut oil.

FILL a medium saucepan almost halfway with water, bring it to a boil over medium-high heat, and reduce the heat to medium-low.

PLACE the maple sugar and maple syrup in a heatproof bowl that will fit over the saucepan without touching the water.

WHEN the water starts to boil, set the bowl in the saucepan and stir until the sugar is completely melted. Turn the heat off and add the coconut oil, cashew butter, and algarrobina and mix and heat until smooth and creamy and well combined. Add the chocolate chips, let them soften a bit (be patient!), then stir to help them melt completely. Stir in the lúcuma powder and mushroom or ashwagandha powder (if using).

SCOOP the batter into the prepared pan, smooth the surface with a spatula, and sprinkle lightly with cacao nibs.

REFRIGERATE until firm. Unmold the fudge onto a cutting board, then make one long vertical and seven crosswise cuts, to make 16 pieces of fudge.

See the photo on page 227.

lime meringue pie

MAKES ONE 9½-INCH PIE, TO SERVE 8

When it comes to sour citrus, at home we normally use limes, not lemons. In Lima it was very rare to find lemons, and we are used to the super-acidic taste of Peruvian limes, which are between a key lime and a regular lime in size. Now, living in Georgia, we still always choose limes, and sometimes we are lucky enough to find key limes, which Camila loves to use in her salad dressings because of their extremely acidic flavor. When I thought about creating a lemon pie, I immediately went to the idea of using limes instead, along with a touch of turmeric to help develop their radiant color. I love making classic recipes, but using amazing ingredients that provide nutrients to the body and soul is so satisfying. We can eat pie and feel great at the same time.

Plan on making this early on the day you want to serve it, or preferably start it the day before.

PARBAKE the sweet pastry crust in a 9½-inch tart pan and set it aside to cool.

FOR THE LIME CURD: Off the heat, in a medium saucepan, combine the eggs, egg yolks, coconut oil, maple syrup, lime juice, turmeric, and salt and whisk until combined.

SET the pan over medium heat and stir continuously until the mixture reaches 160°F on a candy thermometer, about 13 minutes. The mixture will thicken a bit (and will thicken further upon refrigeration).

STRAIN the curd into a bowl, then pour it into the base of the pastry crust. Let cool, and then refrigerate until firm, at least 5 hours and preferably overnight.

FOR THE MERINGUE: Make the meringue when the pie is fully chilled. In a small saucepan over medium-high heat, bring the maple syrup to a boil. Turn the heat to medium-low and let simmer until the syrup reaches 240°F on a candy thermometer.

Sweet Pastry Crust (page 196)

lime curd

3 large eggs

3 large egg yolks

¼ cup plus 1 tablespoon (70 g) organic extra virgin coconut oil, melted

½ cup plus 2 tablespoons (208 g) pure maple syrup

½ cup (120 g) fresh lime juice (from about 4 limes)

Pinch of ground turmeric (see page 16)

Pinch of salt (see page 15)

meringue

½ cup pure maple syrup

2 large egg whites (at room temperature)

Pinch of cream of tartar

Fresh lime zest, for garnish

special equipment needed

candy thermometer

kitchen torch (optional)

IN a stand mixer fitted with the whisk attachment, beat the egg whites and cream of tartar until soft peaks form, starting on low speed and working up to a higher speed, 2½ to 3 minutes.

INCREASE the speed to high and pour in the hot maple syrup in a thin stream. Beat until the mixture cools (you'll feel it's cool by touching the side of the bowl), 3¾ to 4 minutes.

REMOVE the pie from the fridge and place it on a beautiful plate for serving. Fill a pastry bag with the meringue, attach a ⅝-inch tip, and decorate the pie with meringue peaks (you can also use a zip-top bag with the end cut off). If you have a kitchen torch, use it to artfully caramelize the top of the meringue. Garnish with lime zest. Refrigerate until ready to serve.

CUT into 8 slices and serve. Place any leftovers in a glass container with a lid for up to 3 days.

hazelnut-chocolate butter

MAKES 1½ CUPS

17½ ounces (496 g) raw unsalted hazelnuts (about 3½ cups)

⅓ cup (80 g) organic extra virgin coconut oil

7 ounces (200 g) paleo 70% dark chocolate chips (such as HU brand)

½ cup (150 g) pure maple syrup

Pinch of salt (see page 15)

The advertising of unhealthy products is everywhere, and children are the most susceptible. I tried to find a healthier alternative for a hazelnut spread, but after searching without any luck, I told Josefina that we were going to make it ourselves. There is a lot of personal satisfaction when you make something surprising from scratch. And the result was divine!

PREHEAT the oven to 350°F. Spread the hazelnuts on a rimmed sheet pan and roast for 10 minutes, until they are a light golden color and have a delicious aroma. Let cool for a few minutes, then rub off the skins with a clean kitchen towel.

IN a food processor or a high-powered blender, process the hazelnuts and coconut oil on high speed. It takes time, but if you are patient, the oils from the hazelnuts will emulsify into a paste and you will have a wonderful homemade hazelnut butter. (And although it gives you something extra to wash, to make it super-silky and lump free, process it first in a food processor until liquid (with many very small lumps), and then transfer to a high-powered blender to break up the little lumps. If you use a blender alone, you'll have more work as you scrape the edges many times.)

FILL a medium saucepan almost halfway with water and bring it to a boil over medium-high heat.

PLACE the chocolate, maple syrup, and salt in a heatproof bowl that will fit over the saucepan without touching the water.

WHEN the water starts to boil, turn off the heat and set the bowl in the saucepan. Let the chocolate soften a bit, then start stirring to help it melt completely.

WHILE the hazelnut butter is freshly blended and warm, scrape into the chocolate mixture, slowly and by spoonfuls, and stir with a spatula until you have creamy, shiny, and spreadable butter.

STORE in a glass jar in the fridge (you'll need to set it out at room temperature a bit before using it, though). It will easily last in the fridge for a month.

cold brew chocolate cake

MAKES 12 SERVINGS

This is one of the cakes that never lasts long at our house! Sometimes I don't even get to prepare the frosting, because by the time I'm ready to do it, the girls have already disappeared with the cake. Coffee and chocolate—a great combination for any celebration (or apparently, for my daughters, a good snack at all hours).

For this recipe it is very important that you choose creamy avocados—those that are dense and ripe and at the perfect point of maturity. Make sure your tigernut flour is very fine, but if it's not, you can process it a little in a blender or food processor so that it does not have a gritty texture in the cake (my girls are very picky about these details). This cake with a Cinnamon Vanilla Cold Brew Latte (page 257) is perfect for an afternoon with friends.

FOR THE CAKE: Preheat the oven to 350°F. Line two 8-inch cake pans with parchment paper rounds on the bottom and strips around the sides.

SIFT the cassava flour, tigernut flour, arrowroot flour, cacao powder, baking powder, baking soda, and salt into a medium bowl.

IN a small bowl, combine the coconut milk and vinegar and stir. Let stand until it has turned into "buttermilk," about 10 minutes.

IN the bowl of a stand mixer fitted with the whisk attachment, beat the eggs until foamy, starting on low speed and slowly increasing the speed to high. Lower the speed, add the coconut sugar, return the speed to high, and beat until it dissolves and the mixture is very frothy, about 1 minute. With the mixer on low speed, add the coconut buttermilk, cold brew, coffee extract (if using), and avocado oil, then increase the speed to medium and beat until combined.

LOWER the mixer speed and add the dry ingredients in three parts, incorporating each amount before adding more and stopping the mixer to scrape down the sides of the bowl as needed.

cake

½ cup plus 1 teaspoon (75 g) cassava flour (see page 17)

½ cup plus 2 tablespoons (75 g) sifted tigernut flour (see page 16)

½ cup (65 g) arrowroot flour (also known as starch or powder)

½ cup (50 g) cacao powder (see page 5)

1 teaspoon Homemade Baking Powder (page 297)

2 teaspoons baking soda

½ teaspoon salt (see page 15)

1 cup (240 g) Coconut Milk (page 307) or canned organic coconut milk without guar gum (such as Native Forest's Simple)

1 tablespoon apple cider vinegar (see page 3)

3 large eggs, at room temperature

1½ cups plus 2½ tablespoons (270 g) coconut sugar (see page 7)

1 cup (240 g) Homemade Cold Brew Coffee (page 257) or other organic cold brew coffee

1 teaspoon coffee extract (optional but highly recommended, such as Flavorganics brand)

½ cup (114 g) avocado oil or extra virgin olive oil

7 ounces (200 g) avocado, weighed after pitting and peeling, mashed (from about 2 avocados)

½ cup (160 g) pure maple syrup

2 teaspoons coffee extract (optional but highly recommended)

4½ tablespoons (45 g) cacao powder (see page 5)

2 tablespoons (30 g) organic extra virgin coconut oil

8.8 ounces (250 g) coconut cream without guar gum (such as Let's Do Organic; see page 28), solid part only, chilled (measure by weight for best results)

decorating

Chocolate bar, for grating (such as the HU or Pascha bar of your choice; optional)

Roasted whole coffee beans (optional)

Whole or sliced strawberries (optional)

DIVIDE the batter between the two prepared pans. Bake for 50 minutes, until a toothpick inserted into the center of each layer comes out clean.

SET aside to cool in the pans while you make the frosting.

FOR THE FROSTING: In a blender, blend the avocado, maple syrup, coffee extract (if using), cacao powder, and coconut oil on high speed.

IN the bowl of a stand mixer fitted with the whisk attachment, place the chilled solid part of the coconut cream and mix for a few seconds, until homogenized (don't overmix or it will turn into a curd). Add the avocado mixture and mix until combined. If the frosting is firm enough to use to frost the cake, go ahead. Otherwise, refrigerate it for a few hours, stirring occasionally, until it reaches the right consistency.

TO ASSEMBLE AND DECORATE: Place one of the cake layers on a serving plate. Dollop half of the frosting on top, smooth it out just to the edges, and place the other cake layer on top. Dollop the rest of the frosting onto the top layer and spread it out artfully in a way that pleases you.

IF desired, decorate with grated chocolate (simply refrigerate a chocolate bar and grate it on the slicing side of the grater), roasted whole coffee beans (you can eat them!), and/or strawberries.

pionono with dulce de leche

MAKES 8 SERVINGS

Organic extra virgin coconut oil, for the pan

1.7 ounces (50 g) superfine blanched almond flour (such as Bob's Red Mill brand)

0.46 ounces (13 g) coconut flour (such as Let's Do Organic brand)

0.46 ounces (13 g) tapioca flour

0.88 ounces (25 g) arrowroot flour (also known as starch or powder), plus more as needed

Pinch of salt (see page 15)

7 ounces (200 g) egg whites (measured from about 6 eggs; use the exact weight)

Pinch of cream of tartar

3 tablespoons (45 g) plus 6 tablespoons (90 g) maple sugar (such as Coombs Family Farms brand)

3.35 ounces (95 g) egg yolks (measured from about 7 eggs; use the exact weight)

1 teaspoon coconut extract (or your favorite: vanilla, coffee, almond; I like Flavorganics brand)

AIP Dulce de Leche (page 302)

Whipped coconut cream (optional; see Note)

Mixed fresh berries, for serving

Known as a jelly roll in America, a pionono, as it's called in Peru, has many names depending on the recipe, the filling, and where it is prepared, but it's generally a thin layer of cake topped with a filling and rolled into a cylinder. The classic Peruvian filling is manjar blanco (which is similar to dulce de leche and is made with cow's milk and tons of white sugar), and the cake is sprinkled with lots of powdered sugar.

I've already mentioned how picky my dad is when it comes to food. While visiting Georgia, I made my paleo version of the classic pionono, and as I was filling it, my dad commented, "That's not a real pionono. There's no gluten or cow's milk either." But my mom was super excited, waiting impatiently for me to cut the first slice. I had already told her on the phone how happy I was with this recipe, because people had told me it was even tastier than the original recipe. I cut a couple of slices and we savored it together (as cooks, and as mom and daughter, celebrating a recipe is one of our favorite kinds of moments). My dad looked at us curiously and asked, "Can I try?" After a few minutes, as he sat enjoying his second slice, his silence was his verdict. This is my paleo version of pionono, and it's so good—Brandon Stanton is a big fan, too!

PREHEAT the oven to 350°F. Brush a 10 × 15-inch jelly roll pan with coconut oil. Cover the entire surface, even the edges, with parchment paper. With the same brush, oil the parchment paper.

IN a medium bowl, combine the almond flour, coconut flour, tapioca flour, arrowroot flour, and salt. Sift the mixture twice.

IN the bowl of a stand mixer fitted with the whisk attachment, combine the egg whites and cream of tartar. Beat on low speed, slowly increasing the speed to high, until the egg whites reach stiff-peak stage, about 1½ minutes. Reduce the speed, add 3 tablespoons of the maple sugar, and beat until the sugar is dissolved, about

1½ minutes. Use a spatula to transfer the meringue to a medium bowl.

PLACE the egg yolks and remaining 6 tablespoons maple sugar in the mixer bowl and beat on low speed, slowly increasing the speed to high, until the egg mixture foams and turns clear, about 2 minutes. Add the coconut extract and beat for 30 seconds or so to combine.

TURN off the mixer and remove the bowl. Sift the flour mixture into the egg yolk mixture in 3 parts, folding the flour in with a spatula after each addition. Fold in the egg whites, taking care not to deflate them too much.

SPREAD the batter in the pan, stretching it out evenly with the help of a spatula.

BAKE 15 to 18 minutes, until a toothpick inserted into the center comes out clean.

MEANWHILE, spread a clean, plain cotton, untextured kitchen towel on the table and use a fine-mesh strainer to coat the entire surface with a thin layer of arrowroot flour.

AS soon as the pionono comes out of the oven, carefully unmold it onto the kitchen towel and roll it up from one of the short ends. Let cool completely at room temperature.

UNROLL the pionono and spread the dulce de leche all over it.

ROLL it back up and serve immediately or refrigerate until serving (no need to wrap it).

TO serve, slice the pionono to show the gorgeous rolled layers. Garnish with whipped coconut cream (if using) and fresh berries.

See the photo on page 238.

NOTE
Measuring by weight is especially important here, so be sure to bring out your scale.

NOTE
To whip coconut cream, refrigerate a can of coconut cream and whip the solid part only in a mixer until it looks homogenous and has some air. Do not overbeat because it can turn into a curd. If you like, mix in the sweetener of your choice, such as pure maple syrup (optional).

strawberry tart

MAKES ONE 9½-INCH TART, TO SERVE 6

filling
16 ounces (453 g) fresh strawberries, hulled and cut into thin slices

2 tablespoons (20 g) coconut sugar (see page 7)

Juice of ½ lime

crust
Sweet Pastry Crust (page 196), cold or at room temperature

strawberry jam
9 ounces (255 g) frozen strawberries

¾ cup plus 3 tablespoons (150 g) coconut sugar (see page 7)

assembly
1½ teaspoons tapioca flour

Pastry Cream (page 303), cooled

My dad has always loved desserts and sweets. For as long as I can remember, his nightstand drawer was full of chocolates and cookies, and he loved to get into bed to watch a movie while pulling sweet treasures out of the drawer. Over time—and I like to think it was because of my influence—he decided that all those chocolates and cookies weren't very healthy and switched to fruit. So, every time my dad wants to be coddled while he watches a movie, he asks my mom for his favorite homemade dessert: strawberry tart.

Like my dad, the girls learned that Abui would pamper them in the sweetest way by preparing an endless list of their favorite desserts. So my mom and I became mad scientists, looking for healthy replacement ingredients and formulating recipes so that she could continue providing her love through more nutritious baked goods. Here's our modified version of my mom's strawberry tart, approved by the girls—and my dad.

FOR THE FILLING: In a medium bowl, combine the fresh strawberries, coconut sugar, and lime juice. Refrigerate so that the strawberries begin to release their own juices, about 2 hours.

FOR THE CRUST: Follow the instructions in the recipe and set it aside to cool.

FOR THE STRAWBERRY JAM: While the crust is baking, in a small saucepan over medium-low heat, combine the frozen strawberries and coconut sugar. Cook, stirring occasionally, until the jam thickens, about 25 minutes. (I often double the jam recipe to have extra in the fridge to eat on bread.)

USE an immersion blender to blend the jam in the pot and break up any pieces of strawberry that may remain. Cook for a few more minutes, then remove from the heat and let the jam cool to room temperature, or refrigerate if you make it ahead.

TO ASSEMBLE: Spread a light layer of the cooled jam on the cooled pastry crust. Refrigerate while you work on the rest of the recipe, about 1 hour.

STRAIN the strawberries that you had macerating in the refrigerator and reserve the liquid in a small saucepan.

ADD the tapioca flour and ¼ cup (60 g) water to the reserved strawberry liquid in the pan. Whisk until dissolved. Set the pan over medium heat and cook until it thickens into a glaze, about 1 minute.

USE a spatula to spread the pastry cream evenly over the strawberry jam.

PLACE the strawberries in a circular pattern on top of the pastry cream.

WHILE it's still hot, pour the glaze carefully over the strawberries. Refrigerate until very cold.

SLICE and serve the tart. It will keep for 2 or 3 days at most, but at my house it's gone in an hour!

See the photo on page 239.

NOTE
This recipe takes time; it's great eaten the day it's made, but you'll need to start early.

dark cacao tart with berries

MAKES ONE 9½-INCH TART, TO SERVE 6

Sometimes in life, we think complex answers are required to solve our problems. But often the real solutions are very simple; there's so much wisdom in the simplicity of things. It's the same with ingredients; in their simplest form, we find the essence of an ingredient's flavor. Here we have the magnificence of plantain flour and the richness of chocolate in all its splendor, all highlighted by the tart sweetness of fresh berries. Simple and pure, this is a tart to share, to enjoy bite by bite with closed eyes and an open heart. And if you're going through a difficult situation, bake this tart, sit down, take a deep breath, eat a bite, and you will find a simple answer.

FOR THE CRUST: Preheat the oven to 350°F. Grease a 9½-inch tart pan with coconut oil.

IN the bowl of a stand mixer fitted with the paddle attachment, combine 2 tablespoons (30 g) water and the gelatin powder. Stir with a spoon to mix well. Add the coconut oil, coconut cream, plantain flour, coconut sugar, and baking powder. Mix on low speed, then gradually increase the speed to high until a dough comes together.

USE your hands to line the prepared tart pan with the dough, going up the sides of the pan. Prick the bottom of the dough all over with a fork.

BAKE for 23 minutes, until light golden brown.

LET the crust cool in the pan, then refrigerate it while you make the filling.

FOR THE FILLING: Fill a medium saucepan almost halfway with water and bring it to a boil over medium-high heat.

PLACE the coconut cream and coconut sugar in a heatproof bowl that will fit over the saucepan without touching the water.

crust

2 teaspoons gelatin powder from grass-fed beef

¼ cup plus 1 teaspoon (2.3 ounces/65 g) slightly softened organic extra virgin coconut oil, plus more for the pan

2.1 ounces (60 g) coconut cream without guar gum (such as Let's Do Organic; see page 28), solid part only, chilled (this is ¼ cup, but weighing is more accurate)

1 cup plus 1 tablespoon (150 g) plantain flour (see page 8)

2½ tablespoons (30 g) coconut sugar (see page 7)

1 teaspoon Homemade Baking Powder (page 297)

filling

3.5 ounces (100 g) coconut cream without guar gum (such as Let's Do Organic brand; see page 28), solid part only (this is ⅓ cup plus 1 tablespoon plus 1 teaspoon, but weighing is more accurate)

3 tablespoons plus 1 teaspoon (40 g) coconut sugar (see page 7)

5.5 ounces (156 g) paleo 70% dark chocolate chips or chunks (such as HU brand)

Pinch of salt (see page 15)

6 ounces (170 g)
fresh blackberries

6 ounces (170 g)
fresh raspberries

6 ounces (170 g)
fresh blueberries

Fresh mint leaves or edible
flowers (optional)

WHEN the water starts to boil, reduce the heat to medium-low and set the bowl in the saucepan. Stir until the sugar is dissolved. Turn off the heat, add the chocolate and salt, let it soften a bit, then start stirring to help it melt completely.

POUR the mixture into the chilled tart crust and spread it out evenly. Refrigerate for at least 4 hours, until the chocolate hardens.

COVER the tart with the fresh berries, being creative with your decorating. Garnish with fresh mint leaves or edible flowers, if desired.

blue spirulina marshmallows

MAKES 30 MARSHMALLOWS

A long time ago, when Cami and Gala were very young, I threw them a dual birthday party where I wanted everything I served to be homemade and healthy. I made a three-tiered cake, fruit sorbets, cake pops, sandwiches, and so on. I worked really hard learning how to make homemade marshmallows for just this occasion. I wanted them to be perfect so the kids wouldn't be able to tell the difference between my healthy marshmallows and the conventional (junk) party candy. When the day of the party arrived, I had achieved my goal—they loved the food! But then they complained about the absence of soda. You can't make everyone happy, right? But most important, my daughters had an incredible party that they really enjoyed, and the homemade marshmallows were their favorite treat of the day.

In this recipe, I've incorporated vibrant color, from an incredibly nutritious ingredient called blue spirulina. So here you have not only a delicious, homemade recipe—but one loaded with antioxidants.

Plan ahead when making this, as the marshmallows must rest overnight.

Arrowroot flour (also known as starch or powder), for dusting

1 tablespoon blue spirulina (see page 4)

3 tablespoons (30 g) gelatin from grass-fed beef

½ cup plus 1 tablespoon (180 g) pure maple syrup

2 teaspoons coconut (or almond or vanilla) extract (such as Flavorganics brand)

special equipment needed
candy thermometer

LINE a 9 × 9-inch baking dish with plastic wrap and sprinkle it with sifted arrowroot flour to prevent the marshmallows from sticking.

IN the bowl of a stand mixer fitted with the whisk attachment, combine the spirulina with ½ cup plus 2 tablespoons (150 g) room-temperature water. Whisk by hand until dissolved (so as not to generate foam at this stage). Then, with the mixer on low speed, sprinkle in the gelatin. Turn off the mixer and let the gelatin hydrate.

MEANWHILE, in a medium saucepan over medium-high heat, bring the maple syrup and ¼ cup plus 2 tablespoons (90 g) water to a boil. Lower the heat to medium and let simmer until it reaches 240°F on a candy thermometer.

WHEN the syrup has reached 240°F, turn the mixer on low speed and begin adding the maple syrup in a thin stream while increasing the speed to high. Add the coconut extract and continue to beat on high speed until the mixture is completely cool and fluffy, about 7 minutes.

QUICKLY scrape the mixture into the prepared pan, distributing it evenly with a spatula. Let it cool and dry out for a couple hours, until a little firm, then sprinkle some arrowroot flour on top. Cover the pan with plastic wrap and let it rest at room temperature overnight.

IN the morning, remove the top piece of plastic wrap and sprinkle a little more sifted arrowroot over the marshmallows. Using scissors, cut the marshmallow into 1- to 2-inch cubes—or play around and make different sizes and shapes.

STORE the marshmallows for up to 5 days in the fridge, in a glass container with a paper towel on the bottom and on the top to keep them fresh.

passion fruit super gummy candies

MAKES ABOUT 13 DOZEN BEAR-SIZE GUMMIES

6 ounces (170 g) frozen passion fruit pulp (such as Pitaya Foods brand)

¼ cup plus 1 teaspoon (85 g) pure maple syrup

1 teaspoon camu camu powder (see page 6)

1 teaspoon tapioca flour

4½ tablespoons (45 g) gelatin from grass-fed beef

3 probiotic capsules (such as Seed or Klaire brand; optional but highly recommended, of course!)

special equipment needed

small silicone gummy or chocolate molds

Unlike with conventional gummies, you can let your kids eat as many of these as they want. The vitamin C that camu camu and passion fruit provide, along with the amazing power of probiotics, makes these gummies a kind of fun medicine for children (and adults). As a mom, I feel reassured knowing my family is eating the healthiest (and most flavorful) gummies I can give them. You can find frozen passion fruit pulp in any Latin market and many other stores, and always remember to choose the best probiotics you can find (look in particular for those without any added fillers). Keep these fresh—and easily accessible—by storing them in the fridge.

Lots of different molds for gummies or chocolates are available online. At home we like the classic bears, but we also like to try fun shapes and different sizes—see what appeals to you and your kids!

IN a blender, combine the passion fruit pulp, maple syrup, camu camu powder, tapioca flour, and ½ cup plus 2 teaspoons (130 g) water. Blend on high speed until smooth.

POUR the mixture into a medium saucepan and let it stand for a few minutes to take the chill off. Sprinkle in the gelatin and whisk well to prevent lumps from forming. Let stand until the gelatin absorbs the liquid, about 5 minutes.

PLACE the saucepan over medium heat to melt the gelatin, stirring constantly. Before the liquid starts to bubble, remove the pan from the heat.

LET the mixture cool in the pan, and when you can put your finger in without burning it, you can add the probiotic capsules (if using). Open the capsules, sprinkle in the powder, and whisk until incorporated.

FILL the molds using the droppers that come in the package. (If the liquid firms up, it can be gently reheated unless you've used probiotics.) Refrigerate until firm, preferably overnight (but I prepare myself for a refrain of "Mom, are they ready?"). Remove the gummies from the molds and store them in the fridge for up to 5 days.

grain-free cherry bars

MAKES 8 BARS

crust

½ cup plus 1½ tablespoons (85 g) cassava flour (see page 17)

⅓ cup (45 g) superfine blanched almond flour (such as Bob's Red Mill brand)

¼ cup (40 g) arrowroot flour (also known as starch or powder)

1 cup (105 g) chopped walnuts or pecans (you can use your food processor to chop them faster)

2 teaspoons Homemade Baking Powder (page 297)

¼ teaspoon salt (see page 15)

¼ teaspoon ground cinnamon

½ cup plus 1½ tablespoons (100 g) coconut sugar (see page 7)

½ cup (125 g) organic extra virgin coconut oil, melted

filling

1 pound (453 g) frozen cherries

2 tablespoons (20 g) coconut sugar

1 teaspoon fresh orange juice

1 teaspoon arrowroot flour

One of the things I enjoy most about our restaurant is our relationship with our customers. Nelson (who is now a dear friend, along with his wife, Kelly) has been one of our most regular customers since we opened. He doesn't have any food restrictions; he just likes to eat healthy and feel good. During our first few months, when we didn't have many customers, I had a lot of time to create new recipes in the kitchen, and Nelson spent many hours in the dining room working on his laptop while he enjoyed our food. So naturally, he became my prime tester for new recipes. Every new dessert I made, he tried, and I always complained because he'd say every time, "This is so good, Cristy!" Of course I was eager to hear ways to improve each recipe, but he loved us too much to say anything critical.

The very first bar recipe I developed was made of apples, and as usual he praised it, but that time I agreed with him; it really was very good, so we immediately included it on the menu. This is my version of that delicious bar, but made with cherries, one of my favorite fruits.

These bars should be eaten cold because of the amount of coconut oil they contain. Enjoy them with a Blue Limonada (page 270) or Hibiscus and Pineapple Peel Drink (page 271).

And remember to plan ahead for the overnight chilling!

PREHEAT the oven to 350°F. Line the bottom and sides of a 9 × 9-inch baking pan with parchment paper, with an overhang on two sides for easy lifting.

FOR THE CRUST: In a medium bowl, combine the cassava flour, almond flour, arrowroot flour, walnuts, baking powder, salt, cinnamon, and coconut sugar and stir well. Add the melted coconut oil and stir until the mixture is evenly coated in oil.

FOR THE FILLING: In another medium bowl, combine the cherries, coconut sugar, orange juice, and arrowroot flour. Mix well.

SCOOP two-thirds of the crust mixture into the prepared pan and press firmly out to the edges to make a bottom crust. Pour the cherry filling on top and spread it out evenly. Sprinkle with the remaining crust mixture, completely covering the filling.

BAKE for 45 minutes, until the crust is golden brown and the filling is bubbling.

SET the pan on a wire rack to cool, then refrigerate overnight. In the morning, remove the parchment paper, transfer the bar block to a cutting board, and cut into 8 rectangular bars.

VARIATION
grain-free apple bars

In place of the cherries, use 1¼ pounds (567 g) peeled, cored, and small-diced Gala or Granny Smith apples.

In place of the orange juice, use fresh lime juice.

Add 1 teaspoon ground cinnamon to the filling mixture.

drinks

lucumoka

¾ cup (180 g) brewed espresso or strongly brewed coffee

¾ cup (180 g) Almond Milk (page 304)

1½ tablespoons (18 g) lúcuma powder (see page 9)

1 tablespoon cacao powder (see page 5)

1½ tablespoons sweetener (such as maple sugar or coconut sugar; see page 7) or 4 drops pure liquid monk fruit (such as NOW Foods brand)

There's nothing better than cozying up on the sofa on a cold afternoon with a sweet, hot latte, enjoying the stillness and peace that a roaring fireplace provides. A good mix of superfoods, like lúcuma and cacao, and a freshly made almond milk are enough to connect us with the wonders that nature gives us.

Lúcuma is a native fruit of the Andes, a golden treasure that can be found in every corner of Peru. There is no juice store, bakery, or restaurant (fancy or humble) that doesn't have it on its menu. It's a star wherever it goes; a superfood not only for its nutritional benefits but for its exquisite flavor. It's terrific paired with chocolate—mocha with lúcuma is always a winner. Peruvians use fresh lúcuma (this is one of the ingredients I miss the most) to make smoothies, desserts, and ice cream, among other treats. It can be found worldwide in powder form and sometimes as frozen pulp in Latin markets.

IN a blender, combine the espresso or coffee, almond milk, lúcuma, cacao, and sweetener and blend on high speed until very smooth.

POUR the mixture into a small saucepan and heat just until hot. Don't let it boil—the fats and liquid in the almond milk could separate—and don't use the microwave.

SERVE hot, then sit in front of the fireplace with a blanket and enjoy a cozy afternoon. Or serve it over ice on a hot day.

maca power coffee

MAKES 1 SERVING

I love how maca smells, and its toasty, caramel flavor takes an ordinary cold brew to another level. This was breakfast for Sebas and me when we first opened the bakery and didn't have time to make something heartier. Our work rhythm in those days was very intense; we started at dawn and didn't stop until very, very late at night. During the day we were unable to take breaks or even to sit down for a few minutes. And more than the physical exhaustion was the emotional tiredness. We had gotten used to the lack of sleep—it is incredible how the body can withstand extreme situations when it enters a state of survival—but keeping our spirit energized was increasingly difficult. So when we arrived at the restaurant in the morning, and while Sebas cleaned the place, the first thing I did was make this powerful coffee. Then, with coffee in hand and a lot of hope in our hearts, we started a new day, dreaming of a better future.

1 cup (240 g) Homemade Cold Brew Coffee (page 257)

1 tablespoon raw almond butter

1 tablespoon MCT oil (see page 10)

2 teaspoons maca powder (omit for children; see page 9)

6 drops pure monk fruit extract (such as NOW Foods brand)

1 or 2 scoops unflavored collagen protein or bone broth powder (such as Bulletproof Collagen Protein or PaleoValley Bone Broth Protein) or vegan collagen-building protein peptides (such as Sunwarrior brand; optional)

IN a blender, combine the cold brew, almond butter, MCT oil, maca, monk fruit, and collagen peptides (if using) and blend on high speed until very smooth.

SERVE cold over ice or hot by pouring the mixture into a small saucepan and heating it just until hot. Don't let it boil—and don't use the microwave, as it can cause the milk to curdle.

LUCUMOKA

MACA POWER COFFEE

CINNAMON VANILLA COLD BREW LATTE

MATCHA MORNING

homemade cold brew coffee

MAKES 2 QUARTS (2 L), 8 SERVINGS

I'm not a big fan of hot brewed coffee, but when I'm in the bakery and I make myself a cold brew coffee, it lasts five minutes, if that. The thickness of the grind, the steeping time, and the quality of coffee and water affect the characteristics of cold-brewed coffee. It generally has a milder, subtler flavor than traditionally brewed coffee, with less acidity. When you use freshly ground, freshly roasted coffee, your cold brew will be more intense and flavorful.

2⅓ cups (175 g) freshly coarse-ground coffee

special equipment needed
nut milk bag (or a cheesecloth bag)

PLACE the freshly ground coffee in a large container with a lid. Add 2 quarts (2 L) water and stir well so that the coffee absorbs the water. Cover with a lid and let stand at room temperature for 24 hours.

STRAIN the coffee with a nut milk bag. Store in the fridge for up to 1 week.

cinnamon vanilla cold brew latte

MAKES 1 SERVING

Try this drink when you need to pamper yourself with a super-refreshing flavored coffee latte, and you also want to feel great, energetic, and light. I created this recipe (and its hot version), but I am only the author; the real artist preparing it is Sebas, who transmits his genuine pleasure to each cup he makes.

Homemade almond milk has a natural sweetness, but if you want to give it a boost, pure maple syrup is fantastic!

Ice cubes

¾ cup (180 g) Homemade Cold Brew Coffee (above)

1 teaspoon pure vanilla extract

¼ teaspoon ground cinnamon

¼ cup (60 g) Almond Milk (page 304)

Pure maple syrup (optional)

FILL a glass with ice and pour in the cold brew coffee. Add the vanilla, cinnamon, and almond milk, then sweeten with maple syrup if you'd like. Stir and sip.

matcha morning

1 medium (3½ ounces/100 g) frozen banana

1 cup (240 g) Almond Milk (page 304; use Coconut Milk, page 307, for the AIP diet)

1 pitted Medjool date, finely chopped or soaked in hot water to soften

¾ cup (25 g) baby spinach

1 teaspoon matcha powder

1 or 2 scoops collagen protein or bone broth powder (such as Bulletproof Collagen Protein or PaleoValley Bone Broth Protein) or vegan collagen-building protein peptides (such as Sunwarrior brand optional)

Matcha is a finely ground powder of specially grown green tea leaves. Legend tells the story of how Emperor Shen Nung, the father of Chinese medicine and agriculture, accidentally discovered green tea in 2732 BC. He was on one of his expeditions somewhere in southern China, and while he and his helpers were boiling water on a break, the wind blew and dropped some dry leaves into the water. Curious, they tasted the resulting liquid, and that night the emperor had more energy than ever. He collected more of the leaves to bring with him and share along his journey, and that is how delicious green tea came to be. During the Tang dynasty of China, between 618 and 907, the first seeds of tea plants were brought to Japan, and over time the whole world would come to benefit from this green treasure.

The most known categories of matcha are culinary and ceremonial. Ceremonial-grade matcha has a beautiful, vibrant green color and is not bitter at all. It's the best choice to drink as a tea. Culinary grade is the most used in the preparation of smoothies and baked goods. Sometimes, when we need to increase our energy, just as Shen Nung did, we want a plain matcha, just tea. But other times we want that same energy but combined with other powerful ingredients. This smoothie has a harmonious balance between sweet and strong, with the antioxidant and energetic power of matcha and the sweetness of almonds and bananas. Perfect for morning.

IN a high-powered blender, combine the banana, almond milk, date, spinach, matcha, and collagen peptides (if using). Blend on high speed until very smooth. Serve in a glass and exclaim, "Good morning!"

spiced green banana drink

MAKES 4 SERVINGS

I was in the kitchen of our small restaurant in Lima, experimenting for the first time with green banana flour by making some cookies. It took a lot of effort to get the flour because it wasn't easy to find on the Peruvian coast at that time. One of the bakers who worked with us told me that in the Peruvian jungle, they have a comforting drink made with green bananas and spices, and it can be served alone or with milk, cold or hot. I wanted to try making it, and since we didn't have fresh green bananas on hand, I decided to try using the flour I had been experimenting with. The result was great! So on winter days when my body asks for a hot spiced drink, I remember this satisfying, comforting, and super-nutritious alternative. Green banana flour has become one of my favorite ingredients in baking, but it's just as good in a drink.

Note that plantain flour is not a good substitute here because it lacks the sweetness and color we want.

10 whole cloves

4 cinnamon sticks

8 whole allspice berries

2 whole star anise pods

2 inches of orange peel (avoid the pith)

3 tablespoons (33 g) green banana flour (not plantain flour; see page 8)

Maple syrup, coconut sugar (page 7), or monk fruit extract, to taste

Almond Milk (page 304), to taste

IN a medium saucepan, combine 4 cups (1 L) water, the cloves, the cinnamon, allspice, star anise, and orange peel. Bring to a boil over medium-high heat, lower the heat to medium, and simmer until the mixture is reduced by the width of at least one finger. Strain the mixture and return the liquid to the pan.

IN a small bowl, dissolve the green banana flour in ⅓ cup (80 g) water.

RETURN the pan to medium-high heat. When the liquid starts to boil, add the banana flour mixture in a thin stream and whisk, stirring constantly, until slightly thickened, about 2 minutes.

SERVE hot in a mug, sweeten, and add a splash of almond milk.

magic mango smoothie

MAKES 1 SERVING

6 ounces (170 g) frozen mango

6 ounces (170 g) frozen papaya

1 teaspoon diced peeled fresh turmeric (see page 16)

½ teaspoon diced peeled fresh ginger

1 tablespoon MCT oil (see page 10)

2 tablespoons (30 g) fresh lime juice (from 1 lime)

Pinch of freshly ground black pepper

1 cup (240 g) Coconut Milk (page 307)

Tropical flavors drive me crazy in the best way—they are fresh, intense, and take you away to a quiet beach where you're stretched out on the sand drinking from a hollowed-out co-conut, surrounded by freshly harvested fruits. With this recipe, your trip to paradise comes with anti-inflammatory benefits thanks to the combination of ginger, turmeric, and black pepper. Please don't omit the black pepper (even if you follow the AIP diet), as it increases the benefits of the turmeric 2,000 percent.

IN a high-powered blender, combine the mango, papaya, turmeric, ginger, MCT oil, lime juice, black pepper, and coconut milk and blend on high speed until smooth, while imagining the peace that a trip to the beach offers.

SERVE in a coconut bowl or a beachy glass and enjoy!

VARIATION

For more of an ice cream–like consistency, you can freeze nut milks in ice cube trays and use the cubes to prepare smoothies. Here you can use ½ cup (120 g) fresh coconut milk and a couple of frozen coconut milk cubes and use the tamper to blend the mixture quickly into an ice cream texture before it warms up too much.

aloe smoothie

MAKES 1 SERVING

When I was a young girl participating in the science fair, all the girls chose to include aloe vera in their projects: shampoo, cream, gel, soap, face masks, and so on. Aloe was always very popular! When I had the mumps, my mom rubbed it around my neck and covered it with a cloth to help reduce inflammation. In the markets of Peru, people add the pulp to juices almost instinctively, as if they've always known that aloe has amazing health benefits for anything and everything, no scientific studies needed. It's ancient wisdom that is passed from generation to generation.

This recipe is one of the most popular at the restaurant, and customers always ask me what brand of liquid aloe I use. The answer is . . . well, none! We use only real aloe leaves. I always recommend freezing many packs at once, to make it easy to prepare a delicious smoothie anytime.

Note that this recipe requires overnight soaking of the aloe and freezing of the ingredients.

2 ounces (60 g) frozen aloe pulp, from 1 aloe leaf (see page 3)

6½ ounces (185 g) frozen pineapple chunks

2 pitted Medjool dates, finely chopped or soaked in hot water to soften

1 tablespoon goji berries (omit for the AIP diet)

¾ cup (180 g) freshly squeezed orange juice

NOTE
You can make multiple freezer packs and have these smoothies ready to make at a moment's notice. In a small freezer bag, combine 1 serving of the aloe, pineapple, chopped dates, and goji berries. Freeze solid. To make a smoothie, pour the contents of the bag into the blender and add the orange juice and water. Blend on high until very smooth and serve.

FOR THE ALOE PULP: To process the aloe vera leaf, place the leaf standing upright in a container such as a pitcher or a high-sided bowl. Fill halfway with water and let it soak overnight at room temperature. This releases the aloin, which is toxic when consumed.

THE next day, wash and peel the aloe leaf with a knife. Cut the pulp into 2-ounce pieces and freeze it in bags, keeping the pieces separated in the bag for ease of removal, or see the Note about freezing individual servings.

FOR THE SMOOTHIE: Place 1 piece of frozen aloe pulp, the frozen pineapple, dates, goji berries, orange juice, and 2 tablespoons plus 2 teaspoons (40 g) of water in a high-powered blender. Blend on high speed until very smooth. Serve immediately.

guayusa green smoothie

MAKES 3 SERVINGS

3 tablespoons (15 g) dried guayusa leaves (see page 8)

2 cups (480 g) boiling water

17 ounces (500 g) frozen pineapple chunks

1 ounce (30 g) kale

1 ounce (30 g) spinach

0.4 ounce (10 g) fresh mint (or peppermint) leaves

Juice of 3 limes (6 tablespoons/90 g)

2 pumps liquid chlorophyll (such as MaryRuth's; optional)

2 pitted Medjool dates, finely chopped or soaked in hot water to soften (optional)

When I was a young girl, my family lived in Bariloche, Argentina, for two years. Those were the happiest days of my childhood, and there I learned how to drink yerba mate, a traditional herbal tea consumed in some South American countries, including Argentina, Uruguay, Paraguay, and Brazil. Thanks to his Argentine heritage, Sebas is a yerba mate lover, too, so we like to sit down, talk, and share a yerba mate, which is served in a mate—a vessel traditionally made from a type of calabash squash that goes through a curing process—with witha bombilla, a kind of straw with a filter at the bottom so that the drinker doesn't accidentally sip the leaves.

Recently I discovered the guayusa leaf, a relative of yerba mate that has the same energizing power and equally excellent flavor. I decided to create a new drink with guayusa, cold and blended with fruits and greens. If you have liquid chlorophyll, add it—I love not only the wonderful color it brings but also its detoxifying power.

COMBINE the guayusa leaves and boiling water in a teapot. Put the lid on and let the tea infuse for about 15 minutes.

STRAIN the tea and refrigerate until cold (or make it into ice cubes).

IN a high-powered blender, combine the guayusa tea, pineapple, kale, spinach, mint leaves, lime juice, liquid chlorophyll (if using), and dates (if using). Blend on high speed until very smooth. Serve immediately.

SPICED GREEN BANANA DRINK

MAGIC MANGO SMOOTHIE

ALOE SMOOTHIE

GUAYUSA GREEN SMOOTHIE

mesquite smoothie

MAKES 1 SERVING

2 pitted Medjool dates, finely chopped or soaked in hot water to soften

2 tablespoons (21 g) mesquite powder (see page 11)

1 teaspoon adaptogenic mushroom powder (see page 2)

1 cup (240 g) Almond Milk (page 304; use Coconut Milk, page 307, for the AIP diet)

1 medium (3½ ounce/100 g) banana, frozen in chunks

½ cup (70 g) ice cubes

If you're not in a chocolaty mood but want a drink that's like a hug and that will make you happy, mesquite is your go-to ingredient. It gives this creamy banana smoothie a delightfully rich and amazingly earthy flavor.

Served very cold and creamy, this smoothie is even perfect for dessert. Feel free to add more mesquite (I can never get enough) and adaptogenic mushrooms to suit your preference. You can also turn it into a smoothie bowl by adding fresh bananas and some Chocolate Granola (page 43).

IN a high-powered blender, combine the dates, mesquite powder, mushroom powder, almond milk, banana, and ice cubes and blend on high speed until very smooth and creamy.

lúcuma algarrobina smoothie

MAKES 1 SERVING

Algarrobina has an unforgettable intense, caramel-chocolaty flavor that can enhance any drink. It's an energy booster, and in the Peruvian markets, the ladies who sell juices at street stalls will add it to any smoothie. It's a perfect replacement for molasses, which is almost impossible to find in Lima. My mom (brilliantly!) uses algarrobina in place of molasses in her gingerbread cookie recipe.

This recipe features both algarrobina and lúcuma, two superfoods that when paired are a nutrient bomb and packed with flavor. It's one of our most popular smoothies at the restaurant and one of my personal favorites when I'm in a rush and need something to fuel me for several hours. Just take a trip to a Latin market and I'm sure you will find both ingredients.

Dates always take a little longer to break up in the blender, so if you're hoping to produce an ice cream–like texture, you can chop them into small pieces before blending or soak them in hot water until soft.

5 ounces (141 g) frozen lúcuma pulp (see page 9)

1½ cups (7½ ounces/212 g) ice cubes

1½ teaspoons algarrobina syrup (see page 11)

2 pitted Medjool dates, finely chopped or soaked in hot water to soften

½ cup (120 g) Almond Milk (page 304; use Coconut Milk, page 307, for the AIP diet)

IN a high-powered blender, combine the lúcuma pulp, ice cubes, algarrobina, dates, and almond milk and blend on high speed until smooth. Serve very cold.

LÚCUMA ALGARROBINA SMOOTHIE

STRAWBERRY TIGERNUT SMOOTHIE

SALAD-ON-THE-GO SMOOTHIE

GREEN JUICE

strawberry tigernut smoothie

MAKES 1 SERVING

One time Sebas had to travel to Egypt to install some furniture in a casino, so I investigated which common ingredients were sold in the local markets and gave him a shopping list. At the top of the list was tigernuts. When he returned, he brought me dresses, scarves, perfumes, decorative papers with Egyptian symbols—but I kept looking at the suitcase. Where were the tigernuts? Sebas made an excuse, saying, "But those things were sold everywhere! I didn't think they were that important."

Years later, a friend who traveled constantly to America would bring me things that could be ordered there but not in Peru. She brought me tigernuts when Cami was starting the AIP diet, and the first thing we made was this amazing tigernut milk, which later served as the base for endless smoothies.

So I waited a long time to try this exotic (to me) ingredient, but I was finally able to experience my dream!

I am not a two- or three-ingredient smoothie person; I take advantage of every smoothie as an opportunity to include as much great nutrition as possible for my girls! But in this case, the high amount of vitamin C from camu camu and the brain power offered by MCT oil is enough, because I don't want to get in the way of the subtle delight of strawberries and the splendid and exotic flavor of my precious tigernuts, which are truly spectacular in their most natural state.

tigernut milk
1 cup (150 g) raw whole tigernuts (such as Anthony's brand; see page 16)

smoothie
6 ounces (170 g) frozen strawberries

5½ ounces (155 g) frozen banana chunks

1 teaspoon camu camu powder (see page 6)

1½ cups (375 g) Tigernut Milk

1 tablespoon MCT oil (see page 10)

special equipment needed
nut milk bag (or a cheesecloth bag)

FOR THE TIGERNUT MILK: Soak the tigernuts in a bowl of water at room temperature for 12 to 24 hours, covering the bowl with a kitchen towel. Drain and rinse well.

IN a high-powered blender, combine the soaked tigernuts and 3 cups (720 g) water and blend on high speed until very smooth. Strain the milk with a nut milk bag. This will yield about 3 cups (720 g). Refrigerate or freeze into ice cubes to keep it on hand.

FOR THE SMOOTHIE: In a high-powered blender, combine the strawberries, banana, camu camu, tigernut milk, and MCT oil and blend on high speed until smooth and creamy.

salad-on-the-go smoothie

MAKES 1 SERVING

4 ounces (113 g) frozen ¾-inch-diced zucchini

1.8 ounces (51 g) frozen diced avocado

4½ ounces (127 g) frozen diced pineapple

1 romaine lettuce leaf

½ ounce (14 grams) baby spinach

½ ounce (14 grams) spring salad mix

0.17 ounce (5 g) fresh peppermint leaves

1 teaspoon moringa powder (see page 11)

½ cup (120 ml) fresh orange juice

1 tablespoon chia seeds (optional; omit for the AIP diet)

When I first began venturing into healthy cooking, I was invited to teach a cooking class for the children at my daughters' school. Of course, the first thing I thought to make was a green smoothie, something that was uncommon to serve at the time (except at my house). Most of the children took to the idea of adding vegetables to a drink incredibly well, but one girl was reluctant even to try the smoothie. When she saw how happy the other children were, she accepted just one taste. She took a sip, then another, and then, with a big smile, asked for a full glass. That night I hardly slept—I was so excited about teaching those children the joys of nutrition and was beyond proud to have elicited a smile from that little girl.

My green smoothies have grown in complexity over time. This recipe is full of veggies and low in sugar and contains a superpowerful ingredient: moringa. This amazing plant is one of my favorite green nutrient superfoods, and it's very easy to find in powder form at healthy supermarkets or online stores. But if you're lucky enough to find fresh leaves, you can use them here, as well as in stews, soups, or salads.

IN a high-powered blender, combine the zucchini, avocado, pineapple, romaine, spinach, spring mix, peppermint, moringa, and orange juice. Blend on high speed until smooth. Pour into a glass.

IF you are using chia seeds, just put them directly in the glass and stir to combine. Let stand 10 minutes, until the seeds expand and the texture becomes gelatin-like. This makes them easier to digest. Serve very cold.

green juice

MAKES SEVEN 1-CUP SERVINGS

I've always thought of green juice extract as so supercharged with nutrition that it's almost like an intravenous injection. Your body takes advantage of its benefits and assimilates them almost that quickly. I have experimented a lot with different combinations of fruits and vegetables, and I never get tired of making and drinking cold-pressed juices. When you have a big family like mine, making large quantities is part of the job, but it's truly worth the effort; the taste of a freshly made extract is way beyond that of a commercial juice from the store. This recipe is light, fresh, and detoxifying—full of energy and happiness—and provides incredible satisfaction when you make it for those you love most.

Feel free to multiply this recipe so that you have a lot of this green extract on hand in the fridge; cold-press juicers keep the nutrients and enzymes intact for up to 72 hours. (But if you're using a centrifugal juicer, drink it immediately.)

PROCESS all the ingredients in a cold-press juicer and serve. Use the leftover pulp as compost for your garden.

10½ ounces (300 g) cucumber

16½ ounces (470 g) peeled (but not cored) pineapple

7 ounces (200 g) celery

5½ ounces (155 g) spinach

2.2 pounds (1 kg) Granny Smith apples (5 to 7 apples)

3 lemons

1 bunch (60 g) carrot greens

½ ounce (15 g) parsley (leaves and some stems)

0.28 ounces (8 g) fresh peppermint leaves

1 lime

special equipment needed

cold-press juicer (preferred; see page 22) or centrifugal juicer

blue limonada

MAKES 1 SERVING

1 teaspoon butterfly pea flower powder (see page 5)

1 tablespoon pure maple syrup

Ice cubes

3 tablespoons (45 g) fresh lime juice (from 1½ limes)

2 tablespoons (30 g) frozen mixed berries (optional but highly recommended)

VARIATION

blue limonada soda

Combine the butterfly pea flower powder, maple syrup, and 1 tablespoon of water in a milk frother and froth until dissolved. Fill a glass with ice, add the blue mixture, then fill the glass with sparkling water and the lime juice.

This drink is something of a magic trick that everyone loves, so it's terrific for when you have guests over for lunch. Like any magic trick, it has a preamble and a mystery, but in this case, the secret is revealed. After letting your guests enjoy the spectacle of the mysterious color-changing liquid, you'll let them in on the secret of the magical and beautiful blue butterfly pea flower. And there's no need to restrict the big reveal to special guests—it's a beautiful drink for a family summer lunch in the garden.

IN a blender, combine the butterfly pea flower powder, maple syrup, and 1 cup (240 g) water. Blend on high speed until smooth.

GATHER your audience. Fill a clear glass with ice and pour in the blue liquid. Pour or squeeze in the lime juice while saying the magic word—*abracadabra!*—and watch your limonada magically transform into a wonderful purple color.

ADD some frozen berries (which serve doubly as ice and garnish) and enjoy!

hibiscus and pineapple peel drink

MAKES ABOUT TWELVE 8-OUNCE SERVINGS

Hibiscus flower is a terrific ingredient. It has hypotensive and anticholesterol benefits, and offers antioxidant and antibacterial properties, too. But one of the other ingredients in this drink might surprise you—pineapple peel! We normally throw it away, but it offers just as many benefits as the other ingredients, if not more, including fiber, magnesium, and bromelain, a digestive enzyme that supports the function of the small intestine and has anti-inflammatory properties. It also works as a natural diuretic and, most important, adds an incredible flavor to drinks.

When you cut up a whole pineapple, don't toss the peel and the core—freeze them. That way, you'll always have this amazing ingredient on hand to boil and convert into flavorful drinks! We keep a large pitcher of this drink in the fridge (unsweetened) so that the girls always have a cold "flavored" (and sugar-free) drink available at any time of the day.

PEEL and core the pineapple. Reserve the fresh fruit for another use and discard the spiky top (or save a few leaves for garnish).

IN a large saucepan over medium-high heat, combine the pineapple peel and core, apple peels, cinnamon sticks, cloves, hibiscus flowers, and 5 quarts (5 L) water. Bring to a boil, lower the heat, and let simmer until the water level is reduced by at least 3 fingers (this concentrates the flavors). Strain into a pitcher and set aside to cool (discard the solids).

IF you want to add sweetener, it is better to do so while the liquid is still hot. I personally like to leave it as is, so our family's favorite drink isn't training us to want sweetness.

REFRIGERATE until very cold. Now you and your family always have a refreshing and healthy drink on hand! Garnish with a pineapple leaf and/or edible flowers if you'd like for a beautiful effect.

1 whole pineapple

Peel from 1 green apple

Peel from 1 red apple

4 cinnamon sticks

10 whole cloves

¾ cup (25 g) organic dried hibiscus flowers

Sweetener of your choice, such as raw unfiltered honey or pure maple syrup (optional)

Pineapple leaf or edible flowers, for garnish (optional)

NOTE
You can also reduce the mixture to two-thirds the amount. You can serve it unreconstituted with lots of ice—and a pretty garnish if you like!

fruity black tea

1½ tablespoons (6 g) diced dried apples or apple chips (such as Bare brand)

⅓ cup (8.5 g) freeze-dried berries (such as Trader Joe's brand)

1 tablespoon English breakfast black tea leaves

½ teaspoon (0.15 g) organic dried rose petals

2 cups (480 g) boiling water

I love fruity teas, and every time I check a box of organic tea in stores, I always find the phrase "organic natural flavor." But what does that even mean? Where does it come from? How is it made? I need to know more, and those boxed teas weren't cutting it. I believe that nature always has the answers, so I turn to real ingredients to make the safest and most delicious fruity tea.

This recipe is my favorite version, using real fruit and black tea, and is as delicious cold as it is hot. Nothing is more refreshing in the summer than making a big pitcher of this tea and keeping it in the fridge for anytime use. Just add ice cubes and orange, lime, and apple slices to serve.

I've said it before, but this recipe illustrates clearly why it's important to have a gram scale in the kitchen. I consider it crucial to making recipes using ingredients that are high in volume, low in weight, and tricky to put in a spoon or cup.

COMBINE the apples, berries, tea leaves, and rose petals in a teapot with an infuser or a heat-resistant glass pitcher. Add the boiling water, cover with a lid, and set aside to infuse for 8 minutes. Strain and serve.

IT'S really convenient to combine multiples of the dry ingredients in a glass container for future use. Then, any time you want to make a tea, just add a portion of the mix (0.7 ounces/19.6 grams) to the tea infuser and pour in the boiling water.

BLUE LIMONADA

HIBISCUS AND PINEAPPLE PEEL DRINK

FRUITY BLACK TEA

ALGARROBINA COCKTAIL

algarrobina cocktail

⅓ cup (3 ounces/85 g) Peruvian pisco (omit for the AIP diet)

1½ tablespoons (36 g) algarrobina syrup, plus more for serving (find it at Latin markets or online; see page 11)

⅓ cup (2.8 ounces/80 g) Almond Milk (page 304; use Coconut Milk, page 307, for the AIP diet)

1 tablespoon aquafaba (see page 3) or 1 raw egg white (omit both for the AIP diet; use egg white for the paleo diet)

4 pitted Medjool dates, finely chopped or soaked in hot water to soften

1 cup (160 g) ice cubes

Ground cinnamon, to garnish

The emblematic cocktails of Peru are the pisco sour and algarrobina, both of which contain pisco. They are essential to any party, especially formal occasions such as engagement parties, weddings, baby showers, and baptisms. If there are children or pregnant women present, their drinks are made without pisco so that everyone can have a glass in hand for toasting. When it comes to cocktails, my favorites have always been on the sweeter side, so algarrobina is my preference. Every time Sebas and I went to a wedding or a business event, I had to run after the waiter with the cocktail tray to find a glass of algarrobina, as the drink would disappear so quickly—apparently it was everyone else's favorite, too.

The original algarrobina recipe is made with evaporated cow's milk, so of course I created a healthy, dairy-free version. With the pisco omitted, it's a gorgeous mocktail for those who don't want alcohol.

IN a high-powered blender, combine the pisco, algarrobina, almond milk, aquafaba or egg white, dates, and ice cubes. Blend until well mixed and foamy.

DRIZZLE a little bit of algarrobina around the insides of two glasses (optional, for a pretty presentation). Divide the cocktail mixture between the glasses and sprinkle ground cinnamon on top.

peach mocktail

MAKES 3 SERVINGS

One day back in Peru, I accompanied Sebas to get his hair cut at a new place. The truth is, I'm not patient at all when it comes to the hair salon—I must be the only one who really hates the "pleasure" of having my hair done. After five minutes I got bored and decided to go for a walk to look at the surrounding businesses. I found a bar that caught my attention because its menu included many herbal elements. I decided that wasting my time at the bar was much more entertaining than watching a bunch of men have their hair and beards groomed. So I sat down and ordered a drink with unusual ingredients—and there I met a shrub for the first time.

I was impressed not only by the taste but the process of making it, which the bartender kindly explained to me. I thought, *This doesn't even need the vodka!* I imagined the exciting possibilities behind it, using the right organic ingredients.

So I learned how to make a shrub, and I learned how to cut Sebas's hair, and now I'm his official hairdresser and his mocktail maker.

Note that the peach shrub needs two days advance prep to do its thing!

peach shrub

2 fresh peaches, halved (thawed frozen peaches are okay in a pinch)

Raw unfiltered honey, as needed, by weight

Apple cider vinegar, as needed, by weight (see page 3)

mocktail

½ cup (100 g) roughly chopped peeled fresh peach

2 basil leaves

Ice cubes

Juice of 2 limes (4 tablespoons/60 g)

6 tablespoons (90 g) peach shrub

Unflavored kombucha (such as GT's brand, Original)

FOR THE PEACH SHRUB: Brown the peach halves face down in a skillet over medium-high heat (without any oil), to lightly caramelize.

ROUGHLY chop the peaches and weigh them in a 36-ounce glass jar. Take note of the weight.

WITH a muddler, crush the peaches to break them up a little. Do not make a puree; we just want to help them release their flavor. Add honey of the same weight as the peaches. Close the jar and leave it at room temperature for 24 hours.

OPEN the jar and add that same weight of vinegar. Cover the jar and refrigerate until the next day. Strain and store in a glass jar in the fridge until use.

VARIATION

peach cocktail

Fill three 16-ounce glasses with ice. Divide the peach puree among the glasses and add 2 tablespoons (1 ounce) of the peach shrub, one-third of the lime juice, and ¼ cup (2 ounces) bourbon or Peruvian pisco. Fill each glass with ½ cup sparkling water.

TO MAKE THE MOCKTAIL: Place the fresh peach in a container and puree it with an immersion blender. Add the basil and blend the leaves into small, pretty pieces.

FILL three 16-ounce glasses with ice. Divide the peach puree among the glasses and add 2 tablespoons (1 ounce) of the peach shrub, and one-third of the lime juice to each glass. Fill each glass with ¾ cup unflavored kombucha.

camila's daily noni dose

MAKES 1 SERVING

Noni is a tropical fruit from the Pacific Islands, Southeast Asia, Australia, and India that has been used for thousands of years as a food source and for medicinal purposes. Our experience at home with noni has been incredible; Camila takes it frequently to relieve and prevent the symptoms of allergic rhinitis and as a natural detoxifier. She has gotten used to the taste over time, with the help of added grapefruit juice, though I must warn you, the smell of noni is very unpleasant. But just like Camila, you will get used to it and be able to enjoy its incredible health benefits.

⅓ cup (80 g) noni juice (see page 12)

1 cup (240 g) fresh grapefruit juice

MIX the noni juice and grapefruit juice in a glass. Pinch your nose and drink.

dragon fruit pisco sour

MAKES 4 SERVINGS

¾ cup (6 ounces/180 g) Peruvian pisco

⅓ cup (2½ ounces/80 g) fresh lime juice

⅓ cup (2½ ounces/80 g) pure maple syrup

1 large raw egg white, at room temperature (or 1 tablespoon of aquafaba, for a vegan drink)

7 ounces (200 g) frozen pink dragon fruit (such as Pitaya Foods brand)

1½ cups (210 g) ice cubes

Angostura bitters, to taste

Pisco is a Peruvian spirit that has been granted an appellation, or des denominación de origen. It is distilled from eight specific types of grapes called "criollas" that are native to Peru. The pisco sour cocktail was born in the 1920s, when, according to historians, the Morris Bar in downtown Lima announced the pisco sour as one of its specialties. However, other cocktail history buffs maintain that the authentic pisco sour originated in the bar of the Maury Hotel, also in downtown Lima. That's where they enriched the traditional pisco sour by adding egg white and angostura bitters. The drink became very popular, and it was soon served in the most elegant hotels and bars in Lima. Today it's the most emblematic cocktail of Peru. And I must say, Sebas is an expert at preparing the tastiest pisco sour right at home in Georgia!

The traditional pisco sour recipe is made with pisco, simple syrup, ice, Peruvian limes (similar to key limes), egg white, and angostura bitters. My version adds dragon fruit, which gives it a beautiful color and provides nutrients such as iron, vitamin C, and fiber.

IN a high-powered blender, combine the pisco, lime juice, maple syrup, egg white, dragon fruit, and ice cubes and blend on high speed until very smooth.

DIVIDE the mixture among four glasses and add a few drops of angostura bitters on top of each.

condiments and pantry

chia balsamic dressing

MAKES 1 CUP

½ cup (120 g) balsamic vinegar (look for balsamic vinegar of Modena IGP with at least 20% grape must and at least 6% acidity)

½ cup plus 2 tablespoons plus 2 teaspoons (160 g) extra virgin olive oil

4 teaspoons (20 g) raw unfiltered honey

Salt (see page 15), to taste

2 teaspoons chia seeds

A quality balsamic vinegar, containing only organic cooked grape must or cooked grape must and organic wine vinegar, will always make a difference in a good balsamic vinaigrette. The chia seeds here give the dressing a crunchy touch and a creamier texture, in addition to healthy omega-3 fatty acids, polyunsaturated fatty acids, dietary fiber, protein, vitamins, and minerals. Give the chia a few minutes to activate and puff up before you serve.

IN a medium bowl, combine the balsamic vinegar, olive oil, honey, and salt. Mix briskly with a wire whisk until the honey and salt are dissolved.

WHILE stirring, gradually mix in the chia seeds, continuing to stir until the seeds begin to absorb liquid and swell up. This will ensure that they do not stick together.

TRANSFER to a jar with a lid and refrigerate for 15 minutes before using. The dressing keeps for 3 days in the fridge, but I like to use it when the chia seeds are freshly activated.

hibiscus dressing

MAKES 1 CUP

Normally when making a tea with hibiscus flowers, we discard them after the tea is steeped. In this recipe, we blend the flowers into a kind of puree that gives the dressing an incredible consistency. I love the glorious pink color that results, in addition to the great health benefits provided by the flower itself.

½ cup (15 g) organic dried hibiscus flowers

3 tablespoons (45 g) red wine vinegar

⅓ cup plus 3 tablespoons (105 g) extra virgin olive oil

½ teaspoon salt (see page 15)

1 tablespoon plus 1 teaspoon (28 g) raw unfiltered honey

1 tablespoon fresh lime juice

1 teaspoon Roasted Garlic Paste (page 294) or ¼ teaspoon garlic powder

IN a small saucepan over medium heat, combine the hibiscus flowers and 1 cup (240 g) water. Bring the mixture to a boil, lower the heat, and simmer until the flowers soften and only a couple of tablespoons of concentrated liquid are left in the pan. Set the pan aside to cool for a bit.

TRANSFER the contents of the pan to a blender and add the vinegar, olive oil, salt, honey, lime juice, garlic paste, and 2 tablespoons (30 g) water. Blend on high speed until smooth.

IF you prefer a super-smooth dressing, strain it after blending. Store in a jar in the fridge for up to 3 days.

dill coconut yogurt dressing

MAKES 1½ CUPS

¾ cup (240 g) Coconut Yogurt (page 50)

Juice from 1 lime (about 2 tablespoons/30 g)

1 teaspoon dried dill (or 2 teaspoons minced fresh dill)

1 teaspoon salt (see page 15)

¼ cup (60 g) extra virgin olive oil

This recipe is the perfect replacement for mayonnaise in AIP salad dressings because it doesn't contain eggs or nuts. It's easy, creamy, and loaded with probiotics, and it makes you feel satisfied, happy, and full of energy. Use fresh dill if you have it.

Remember that the homemade Coconut Yogurt recipe is not very sweet, so if you use store-bought yogurt instead, look for one without any sweetener.

IN a medium bowl, combine the yogurt, lime juice, dill, salt, olive oil, and ½ cup (120 g) water. Whisk until smooth and emulsified. Store in a jar in the fridge for 2 to 3 days.

Chia Balsamic dressing

Dill Coconut Yogurt dressing

Hibiscus dressing

Mustard-orange
Vinaigrette

mustard-orange vinaigrette

MAKES 1¼ CUPS

½ cup plus 1 tablespoon (135 g) fresh orange juice

2 tablespoons (42 g) whole-grain mustard

½ cup plus 1 tablespoon (129 g) walnut oil

Salt (see page 15), to taste

I love a whole-grain mustard, especially if it's made from quality real ingredients. The combination of orange and mustard in this dressing is just amazing—just be sure to use fresh squeezed juice, as the flavor is totally different from boxed juices.

Besides tasting exquisite, walnut oil, which comprises 70 percent of the walnut, is an antioxidant, an anti-inflammatory, and an immunomodulator. Composed primarily of polyunsaturated fatty acids, walnut oil helps prevent memory decline and is beneficial for gut health.

IN a medium bowl, combine the orange juice, mustard, walnut oil, and salt. Whisk until emulsified. Store in a jar in the fridge and use within 2 days, to keep the orange juice fresh.

AIP turmeric dressing

MAKES 1 CUP

This is one of our favorite dressings to use at home, as it pairs well with a wide range of dishes. I usually triple the recipe and keep it in a big jar in the fridge so that I always have a wonderful dressing on hand for last-minute salads. I love knowing that in addition to being delicious, the dressing provides my family with powerful anti-inflammatory benefits.

The AIP diet does not allow seeds, including black pepper, but pepper enormously enhances the anti-inflammatory power of turmeric. For those who have an autoimmune disease, these benefits are strong enough to make me go against the general "no pepper on the AIP diet" rule. So you'll notice that whenever I include turmeric in my recipes, black pepper is always there to enhance its benefits.

⅓ cup plus 2 tablespoons (95 g) extra virgin olive oil

¼ cup plus 1 tablespoon (75 g) apple cider vinegar (see page 3)

1 teaspoon turmeric powder (see page 16)

2 tablespoons (50 g) raw unfiltered honey

1¼ teaspoons salt (see page 15)

½ teaspoon garlic powder

⅛ teaspoon freshly ground black pepper

IN a blender or a glass jar with a lid, combine the olive oil, vinegar, turmeric, honey, salt, garlic powder, pepper, and 3 tablespoons (45 g) water. Blend very well or cover and shake the jar vigorously until the mixture is emulsified. If you want the consistency to be thicker, omit or reduce the amount of water.

THIS dressing stores well in the fridge for several days. Remove the dressing 30 minutes before serving and shake again before using.

AIP Turmeric dressing

Goldenberry dressing

Pomegranate Molasses dressing

Mango Chutney

goldenberry dressing

When I was a child, goldenberries grew like weeds at my aunt's house—we even used them as we played. Back then few people focused much on certain native ingredients. *Physalis peruviana* is a plant native to Peru (where we call it aguaymanto), and the history of its cultivation dates back to the Incas. It's commonly known as cape gooseberry or goldenberry in English, and it's from the nightshade family, so it's not allowed on the AIP diet.

Goldenberries are highly antioxidant, are believed to prevent obesity-induced insulin resistance, and have considerable potential in the treatment of allergic asthma. Their flavor is sweet and sour—perfect to include in a wide variety of dishes, both desserts and savory fare. They're the perfect addition to any salad, juice, or jam and can even be used in ceviche.

1½ cups (200 g) fresh goldenberries

½ cup (120 g) extra virgin olive oil

½ teaspoon salt (see page 15)

¼ teaspoon freshly ground black pepper

2 teaspoons fresh lime juice

2 teaspoons raw unfiltered honey

COMBINE the goldenberries, olive oil, salt, pepper, lime juice, and honey in a cylindrical container and use an immersion blender to blend until smooth.

IF desired, strain to remove the hard-to-digest seeds.

STORE in a jar in the fridge for up to 2 days.

pomegranate molasses dressing

MAKES 1 CUP

¼ cup plus 1 tablespoon (105 g) pomegranate molasses

¾ cup (180 g) extra virgin olive oil

2 tablespoons plus 2 teaspoons (40 g) apple cider vinegar

1½ teaspoons salt (see page 15)

Pinch of ground allspice (omit for the AIP diet)

Pomegranate molasses is a viscous syrup commonly used in some Middle Eastern, African, and Mediterranean cuisines to provide a sweet and slightly acidic flavor. To make it, pure pomegranate juice is boiled until concentrated into a thick syrup. It's very easy to make at home, but you can also find great brands at the store; just make sure that its only ingredient is 100 percent organic pomegranate juice. Pomegranate molasses is also desirable for its antioxidant properties.

IN a glass jar with a lid, combine the pomegranate molasses, olive oil, vinegar, salt, allspice, and 2 tablespoons (30 g) water. Shake the jar vigorously until the contents are emulsified. Store in the fridge for 4 to 5 days.

mango chutney

MAKES 2 CUPS

I honestly don't know when my chutney obsession started, but it was many years ago.

Do you remember my mentioning those magazines that my mom collected that featured recipes from all over the world? They included versions of chutney that inspired me to dabble in these flavor blends, and mango was always my favorite. Doesn't your mouth water at the thought of a perfect slice of toast with mango chutney? Or a juicy pork chop with the chutney on top?

What if you double the recipe and make someone happy? A jar of chutney will always be a loving gift.

IN a medium saucepan, combine the mango, vinegar, maple syrup, coconut sugar, shallots, ginger, garlic, crushed red pepper, salt, and cayenne.

IN a cast-iron pan over medium-high heat, toast the mustard, coriander, cumin, fennel, fenugreek, and caraway seeds without any oil, stirring constantly to avoid burning (which happens very quickly). As soon as the seeds begin to give off their aromas, remove them from the heat and transfer them to a mortar. Grind them with a pestle, coarsely or into a fine powder, according to your preference (you can use a spice grinder but it will be a finer grind; the mortar's coarser grind is great in this chutney).

TRANSFER the spice mixture to the saucepan, turn the heat to medium-high, and bring the mixture to a boil. Simmer for 30 minutes, then reduce the heat to medium and let the chutney cook down until it has the consistency of jam, about 20 more minutes, stirring occasionally.

LET the chutney cool, then store it in a glass jar in the fridge for up to 1 month.

5 cups (28 ounces/800 g) ½-inch-diced fresh or frozen mango

1⅓ cups (320 g) apple cider vinegar (see page 3)

½ cup plus 1 tablespoon (200 g) pure maple syrup

¾ cup (140 g) coconut sugar (see page 7)

2 tablespoons (30 g) small-diced shallots

2 tablespoons (20 g) peeled and minced fresh ginger

2 teaspoons minced garlic

½ teaspoon crushed red pepper

¼ teaspoon salt (see page 15)

Pinch of cayenne

½ teaspoon mustard seeds

½ teaspoon coriander seeds

½ teaspoon cumin seeds

½ teaspoon fennel seeds

½ teaspoon fenugreek seeds

½ teaspoon caraway seeds

cashew mayonnaise

MAKES 2 CUPS

1 cup (150 g) raw
unsalted cashews

3 tablespoons (45 g) fresh lime
juice (from about 1½ limes)

½ teaspoon salt
(see page 15)

¼ teaspoon garlic powder

1 tablespoon extra
virgin olive oil

I love mayonnaise, especially when it is well made with avocado oil or olive oil, but I'm always a little bit nervous about using raw egg. Looking for an egg-free alternative, I chose cashews, a miraculous, super-versatile, nutrient-packed ingredient perfect for creating a thick cream to mimic the texture of mayonnaise. Plus it's absolutely delicious. You can use it as is or create amazing salad dressings by adding your favorite herbs and spices.

Note that the cashews need to be soaked for at least 8 hours, so plan ahead!

SOAK the cashews in a bowl of water at room temperature for 8 to 12 hours, covering them with a kitchen towel. (Soaking makes them more digestible.) Drain and rinse well.

IN a high-powered blender, combine the cashews with 1 cup (240 g) water, the lime juice, salt, garlic powder, and olive oil and blend on high speed into a silky cream.

TRANSFER the mayonnaise to a glass container and refrigerate it, preferably overnight, before use. The mayonnaise will be very creamy—both dense and light, and not as heavy as a traditional mayonnaise made with oil. The mayonnaise will last 5 days in the refrigerator.

horseradish quinoa mayonnaise

MAKES 1 CUP

¾ cup cooked white quinoa (see how to cook quinoa on page 168)

2 teaspoons Garlic-Herb Paste (page 294) or garlic powder

1 tablespoon lime juice (from about ½ lime)

1 teaspoon prepared horseradish sauce

¼ cup (60 g) extra virgin olive oil

Horseradish is a root vegetable that is used as both a spice and a condiment. It has been cultivated since ancient times, and according to Greek mythology, the oracle of Delphi told Apollo that horseradish was worth its weight in gold.

Modern horseradish sauce consists of the root grated and mixed with vinegar, and it is used primarily to season meats, although it has lots of other uses. In Peru we don't have this delicious root, so when I tried it in America, the first thing that came to mind was mayonnaise! So I decided to create this recipe by adding a subtle hint of garlic flavor.

IN a blender, combine the cooked quinoa, garlic paste, lime juice, horseradish sauce, and ¾ cup (180 g) water and blend on high speed until smooth.

WITH the blender running, pour in a thin stream of the olive oil until the mayonnaise emulsifies.

STORE in a jar in the fridge overnight before use. The mayonnaise will keep, refrigerated, for up to 3 days.

roasted garlic paste

8 to 10 whole garlic heads

3 tablespoons (45 g) extra virgin olive oil, plus more for drizzling

Salt (see page 15), to taste

¼ teaspoon freshly ground black pepper (omit for the AIP diet)

VARIATION
garlic-herb paste

Combine 1 tablespoon dried rosemary and 1 tablespoon dried oregano in a spice grinder or mortar and grind into a coarse powder. Measure out 4 teaspoons of the ground spice mixture and process it in the roasted garlic mixture in the last step.

This roasted garlic paste can be used to season almost any savory dish. At the restaurant, we use it to season our Peruvian ham, marinating it for hours and giving it incredible flavor. If you're making a stew, stir-fry, soup, or roasted chicken, just add a teaspoon of this to the rest of your seasoning for a heavenly boost of flavor.

Always keep a jar of this garlic paste on hand in the fridge, and not just for seasoning—you can even spread it on toast and top with some vegetables and greens. And the garlic-herb variation below is terrific in Cauliflower Rice with Chicken (page 181) or Horseradish Quinoa Mayonnaise (page 293). Delicious!

PREHEAT the oven to 350°F.

CUT off the top third or so of the garlic head, like taking off its hat. You want the tops of the garlic bulbs to peek out and await their olive oil bath.

PLACE the garlic bulbs in a baking dish lined with parchment paper. Drizzle generously with olive oil and sprinkle with salt. Cover them with another piece of parchment paper to keep the steam in, which prevents the garlic from drying out and allows even cooking.

ROAST the garlic for about 60 minutes (depending on the size of the garlic heads) or until tender, very soft, and with a light golden color.

LET cool a little, then remove the pulp from the roasted garlic bulbs with the help of a knife, one by one. The pulp must be soft and tender, ready to convert into a puree.

PLACE 5.6 ounces (160 g) of the roasted garlic pulp (you can store any extra in a jar covered with olive oil for a later use) in a mortar. (You can also use an immersion blender, but the texture from grinding in a mortar is much better.) Add the 3 tablespoons (45 g) olive oil, pepper, and salt and crush with a pestle into a smooth paste.

PLACE the roasted garlic paste in a glass jar and add a thin layer of oil on top to help preserve it. Store in the fridge for 2 to 3 weeks.

Cashew Mayo

Quinoa Mayo

Garlic-Herb Paste

Poblano Sauce

poblano sauce

MAKES 1⅓ CUPS

4 small poblano
peppers (400 g)

2 tablespoons (40g) Roasted
Garlic Paste (page 294)

¼ cup (60 g) extra
virgin olive oil

½ teaspoon salt (see page 15)

2 tablespoons (16 g)
chopped fresh cilantro

Poblano peppers are delicious prepared lots of ways, but they are spectacularly tasty when roasted. Combine them with roasted garlic paste—and boom! This poblano sauce can be eaten with everything, or even alone by the spoonful if you're as big a fan as I am. It's perfect with meat, chicken, baked potatoes, fried yuca, and rice. Use it where you might use a chimichurri or even a mayonnaise.

TO roast the poblano peppers, place a whole pepper directly on the flame of a gas burner until the skin on the bottom has blackened, then turn it over and blacken the other side. Repeat until the entire poblano skin is completely black. They have to be very black all over in order to produce the amazing smoky flavor we need for the sauce. Remove from the heat, wrap in a clean kitchen towel, and let sit for about 10 minutes so that the pepper "sweats." Repeat with the rest of the peppers. (Alternatively, you can broil on high for 5 to 8 minutes, depending on the size of the pepper. Flip and broil another 5 to 8 minutes, until blackened.)

WHEN the peppers are cool enough to handle, peel the peppers under running water. Remove the seeds and place the peppers in a mortar (you know how much I love the texture that a mortar gives!). Add the garlic paste, olive oil, salt, and cilantro and use a pestle to mash everything into a creamy sauce.

STORE in the fridge for up to 3 days.

homemade baking powder

MAKES 1 CUP

As you know by now, I like to be in control of the ingredients in my kitchen, and I extend this to making my own homemade baking powder. Most commercial baking powders are full of ingredients that I believe to be unsafe, such as aluminum, cornstarch, and other mysterious components I don't even know how to pronounce. The ratio I use is 2 parts cream of tartar to 1 part baking soda, but this mixture can become very compact, so to help keep it airy and easy to use, I add arrowroot flour, which absorbs moisture.

In the bakery, I make and use a giant jar of this baking powder to ensure that my customers receive only the best (and most pronounceable) ingredients. Baking powder does expire, so when I make this recipe, I find the closest expiration date on the ingredients and make that the expiration date for my baking powder.

This baking powder works wonderfully as a one-to-one swap for commercial baking powder in your recipes.

½ cup (130 g) cream of tartar (such as Anthony's brand)

¼ cup (70 g) baking soda

2 tablespoons (20 g) arrowroot flour (also known as starch or powder)

COMBINE the cream of tartar, baking soda, and arrowroot flour in a jar, seal it, and shake to mix well. Put a nice label on it and write "Homemade Baking Powder." Be proud! Now you are a magician in your kitchen.

PUMPKIN SPICE MIX

HOMEMADE PROTEIN POWDER MIX

AIP DULCE DE LECHE

PASTRY CREAM

pumpkin spice mix

MAKES ½ CUP

You may be wondering why I want to make my own pumpkin spice if I can buy a good organic one already made. Well, the truth is that the flavor and aroma of a homemade mix is absolutely better than a commercial one, and you know what? You put all your love into it. So enjoy mixing and smelling these incredible aromas, because that's what cooking is all about—enjoying yourself while becoming a food alchemist.

I have included volume measurements, but it's much better to weigh the ingredients. Place a small container on a gram scale and measure each ingredient into it, then combine the ingredients separately in a jar. (This makes it easier not to overmeasure an ingredient into the jar.) Seal the jar and shake to mix well. Store in a cool, dry place.

3 tablespoons plus 1 teaspoon (20 g) ground cinnamon

1 tablespoon plus 2 teaspoons (9 g) ground ginger

1¾ teaspoons (5 g) ground cloves

1 teaspoon (3 g) ground allspice

¼ teaspoon (0.5 g) freshly grated nutmeg

homemade protein powder mix

MAKES 10 SERVINGS (¼ CUP PLUS 2 TABLESPOONS/60 G PER SERVING)

1½ cups (150 g) pumpkin seed protein powder (such as Sprout Living brand)

½ cup plus 2 tablespoons (140 g) sacha inchi protein powder (such as HerbaZest brand; see page 14)

1 cup (100 g) MCT oil powder (omit if you want to use MCT liquid in your smoothies; see page 10)

¼ cup plus 3 tablespoons (70 g) flaxseed meal

⅓ cup (50 g) maca powder (omit for children; see page 9)

3½ tablespoons (38 g) adaptogenic mushroom powder (see page 2)

¼ cup (30 g) moringa powder (see page 11)

3 tablespoons (20 g) camu camu powder (see page 6)

Every time I read the label of any protein powder from the store, I find some ingredient that does not seem appropriate or healthy. So instead of buying premade, I make my own version with ingredients I like and trust. I love to increase the nutritional benefits of any smoothie or hot drink by adding this protein mix, which boasts about 23 grams of protein for every 60 grams of mixture. In addition to nourishment, it provides satiety and energy. Enjoy it in my Magic Mango Smoothie (page 260) or Strawberry Tigernut Smoothie (page 267), among others.

COMBINE all the ingredients in a glass container with a lid. Seal and shake to blend well. Store in a cool, dry place. Consult the expiration dates on the packages; the closest date is the expiration date for this mix.

cashew parmesan

MAKES 1 CUP PLUS 3 TABLESPOONS

Going dairy-free doesn't mean depriving yourself. You can enjoy incredible flavors and feel good at the same time. This parmesan is so tasty—full of good fats and proteins from the cashews—and you can choose your favorite texture of grind. I personally like it coarsely ground, to have some crunchy notes, but you can grind it more finely if you prefer. It is super useful to add on top of any pasta or zoodles, to use as a topping on avocado toast (you can also add some chopped nori sheets for an incredible pairing), or in our Leek, Onion, and Bacon Quiche (page 170). You can sprinkle it on top of any stew, a fried egg, or even on a salad. I make a double recipe and keep it in a glass jar to always have on hand.

1 cup (150 g) raw unsalted cashews

2 teaspoons nutritional yeast

½ teaspoon salt (see page 15)

IN a food processor, combine the cashews, nutritional yeast, and salt and pulse until coarsely ground. Store in a glass jar in a cool, dry place for up to 1 month.

AIP dulce de leche

MAKES 2 CUPS

3⅓ cups (800 g) coconut cream without guar gum (from about two 13.5-ounce/398 g cans; such as Let's Do Organic brand; see page 28)

1¼ cups (200 g) coconut sugar (see page 7)

1½ teaspoons acacia fiber (see page 1)

Dulce de leche is a Latin American confectionery prepared by slowly heating sugar and cow's milk over a period of several hours. This results in a very thick sauce that can be used in pastries or as a dessert itself. It goes by different names depending on where it is produced. In Peru it is called manjar blanco, which means "white delicacy"; in Argentina it is called dulce de leche; in other places it is called arequipe or cajeta. But ultimately, they are all milk and sugar, with different colors and consistencies.

This dairy-free version made with coconut milk has nothing to be ashamed of in comparison to traditional dulce de leche. The acacia fiber provides a nice consistency, though it is necessary for the mixture to rest overnight to thicken fully. Serve it with pancakes, waffles, crepes, toast, or just by the spoonful!

IN a medium saucepan, combine the coconut cream and coconut sugar. Sprinkle with the acacia fiber and stir until completely dissolved (this won't take long).

BRING to a boil over medium-high heat, then lower the heat to medium and let the mixture boil until it thickens, 30 to 40 minutes, stirring around the edges only occasionally. It's done when you can scrape a spoon through the mixture along the bottom and see the bottom of the pot. Set aside to cool.

REFRIGERATE in a covered glass jar overnight to thicken. Store in the fridge for up to 2 weeks.

pastry cream

MAKES 1⅓ CUPS

I love how quick and easy this recipe is. You can use this pastry cream to fill a tart, a pie, or Profiteroles (page 223), or you can eat it as is with a spoon. Serve it in a glass with lots of berries on top and relax; without any dairy or white sugar, this dessert will make you feel great.

¾ cup (180 g) plus 2 tablespoons (30 g) Almond Milk (page 304)

6 large egg yolks

1 tablespoon tapioca flour

¾ cup (180 g) coconut cream without guar gum (such as Let's Do Organic brand; see page 28), solid part only

⅓ cup (110 g) pure maple syrup

IN a small bowl, mix 2 tablespoons (30 g) of the almond milk, the egg yolks, and the tapioca flour.

IN a saucepan, combine the remaining ¾ cup (180 g) almond milk, the coconut cream, and the maple syrup.

SET the saucepan over medium heat and cook, stirring, until smooth. Before it starts to boil, pour in the egg yolk mixture, stirring quickly. Cook on medium heat until the mixture is thick, stirring constantly, about 10 minutes.

STRAIN the mixture into a bowl and let cool. Lay a piece of parchment paper over the cream so it does not form a skin when cooling.

REFRIGERATE overnight for best results. The pastry cream will keep in the fridge for about 3 days.

almond milk

MAKES 4 CUPS (1 L)

2 cups (300 g) raw
unsalted almonds

special equipment needed

nut milk bag (or a
cheesecloth bag)

NOTE

Here's a tip to save time
when making this recipe and
to always have sprouted and
activated almonds on hand
(not just for milk, but as a
snack or to use in any recipe).
Soak a large batch of almonds,
drain and rinse them well,
and spread them out in a
dehydrator tray. Dehydrate
at 115°F for 18 to 24 hours
(until they are completely
dry). Store them in a glass
container in a cool, dry place.

Although I am a huge fan of coconut milk, almond milk is my favorite when it comes to a cold brew with lots of ice and a touch of maple syrup, or a spiced hot milk on a winter night. It's always advisable to soak nuts and seeds to activate them before consumption, as it makes them more digestible and improves our ability to absorb minerals.

This recipe makes a super-creamy almond milk—the best consistency for use as creamer for your coffee or matcha, or as a base for a powerful smoothie. But if you want it thinner, you can add up to an equal amount of water to the finished almond milk.

Note that there are several nut milk makers on the market, and they do the trick when you're in a rush, but no flavor (or creaminess) compares to an almond milk made by squeezing it out of a nut milk bag. And when it comes to packaged nut milk, read the list of ingredients, as a real almond milk should include only water and activated (sprouted) almonds.

SOAK the almonds in a bowl of water at room temperature for 8 to 12 hours (or overnight), covering the bowl with a kitchen towel. Drain and rinse well.

IN a high-powered blender, combine the almonds with 4 cups (1 L) water and blend on high speed until the brown skins of the almonds are as tiny as possible; the creaminess of your milk will depend on the power of your blender and how long you blend it. Make sure the resulting pulp is as fine as possible, so your milk comes out super creamy.

STRAIN the milk using a nut milk bag.

THE best way to preserve your milk and always have a supply on hand is to freeze it. Fill an ice cube tray with the milk, remove the cubes from the tray, and store them in a freezer bag or container. You can use the cubes directly in smoothies, or heat them in a saucepan (without letting them boil) for hot drinks. The almond milk will last 2 to 3 days in the refrigerator.

coconut milk

MAKES 5 CUPS (1.25 L)

An interesting thing can happen when you make coconut milk—when it's refrigerated, the fat separates quickly from the liquids, forming a hard layer on the surface. That hard layer is the coconut cream. This separation is great when you're looking for homemade coconut cream. But when you want a homogeneous, liquid, ready-to-pour coconut milk to add to your coffee or use in a recipe, making it with boiling water is the best option, as it takes much longer for the cream to solidify.

With Cami following the AIP diet, I use a lot of coconut milk in my kitchen—plus I simply love the taste of coconut in any form. A homemade creamy coconut milk is a treasure, and for a different twist, you can toast the coconut before making the milk. However you do it, you'll have a milk to enjoy plain, with cinnamon, with a splash of maple syrup, or in a spectacular latte.

3 cups (300 g) unsweetened shredded coconut (such as Let's Do Organic brand)

4 cups (1 L) boiling water

1 cup (240 g) cold water

special equipment needed

nut milk bag (or a cheesecloth bag)

PLACE the shredded coconut in a large bowl and add the boiling water. Cover the bowl and let it cool down a bit.

WHEN the temperature drops enough that you can touch the mixture with your hands, add the cold water and pour everything into a high-powered blender. Blend on high speed until the mixture is a smooth puree.

STRAIN the mixture using a nut bag.

THE best way to preserve your milk and always have a supply on hand is to freeze it. Fill an ice cube tray with the milk, remove the cubes from the tray, and store them in a freezer bag or container. You can use the cubes directly in smoothies, or heat them in a saucepan (without letting them boil) for hot drinks. The coconut milk will last 2 to 3 days in the refrigerator.

acknowledgments

THANK YOU—YES, YOU! Because this book would not exist if it weren't for you. You changed my life, you made me believe in miracles, you make me wake up every morning and live in gratitude, you saved my life, and you gave my daughters the opportunity to have a better future. You are part of my life. Thank you for connecting with my story as much as I connect with yours, because we are all one.

SEBAS. The adventure of life is perfect by your side. Thank you for making my life better; thank you for making me better.

Thank you for always believing in me, for holding me each of the many times I thought I was falling apart. Thank you for always showing me the bright side of everything and everyone, and for always reminding me that everything was going to be fine, even when you yourself were fighting against tiredness and despair.

Thank you for loving me despite my putting so much coconut in your meals. Thank you for washing up my messes in the kitchen late at night, and thank you for making so many sacrifices just to make me happy.

Thank you for your criticism and wonderful suggestions for each recipe; thank you for completing my recipes, and for completing me. Thank you for believing in all my crazy projects and letting me be obsessive and perfectionistic; for cleaning the clean tables one more time just to make me happy. Thank you for our wonderful life together.

MY LOVELY DAUGHTERS. My beloved daughters, my babies, thank you, my loves, for enduring everything you have at such a young age. Thank you for having faced life with so much courage, with so much love, and with so much strength. I have no words to say how proud I am of you.

CAMILA, life has hit you very hard, but your heart and your courage are unbelievable. You have gone through many things, always teaching us so much in every situation, with that deep smile that comes from your beautiful soul. You are brilliant, intelligent, determined, obsessive, and perfectionistic (like me, sorry) and have the sweetest heart in the world. You are my hero; you have so much power inside you to create! Thanks for teaching me so much.

GALA, my little Galosa, my left and right hand, thank you, mi vida, for sharing so much with me in the kitchen, for teaching me to trust that everything will be fine and that you won't set the kitchen on fire. You have matured faster than you should have, you took on responsibilities that weren't yours, and you did wonderfully! You are pure drive—determined, relentless, incredibly resilient, strong, and full of love. Thank you for your funny sarcasm and all your jokes, and thank you for filling our lives with so much joy and fun.

JULIETA, my sweet Tochi, my little worker, thank you for always being willing to help, for doing everything with so much love, for lighting up our lives with your sweet smile and contagious laughter. Thank you, my daughter, for peeling so many ginger roots; for your delicious, creative, and beautiful food; for washing so many dishes; and for your more than perfect drawings. Thank you for your pure heart of gold that always thinks about how to make others happy.

JOSEFINA, my beautiful Chacha, my little storm, my strong, determined, brilliant, sweet baby. Thank you, my love, for your patience while I wrote this cookbook; thank you for the strongest hugs and kisses in the world; thank you for always listening to me and teaching me so much at the same time! Thank you for being such a critical tester, pushing me to repeat and repeat recipes to get your approval. Thank you for being my meditation partner, and my little treasure.

HEBE, oh! my brave, loving, sensitive, and brilliant baby. Thank you, my little Monada, for filling my days with kisses, hugs, and the many times you say "I love you, Mama" and melt my heart; for being my little helper in the kitchen and the most beautiful cook who loves to appear in my videos. Thank you for your patience in waiting for me every night to do our meditation together before bed and for giving me the purest love there is. I feel so blessed to be your mom.

MOM AND DAD. Thanks for making me strong, for trusting me, and for giving me the perfect life path. Thank you, Mom, for teaching me that the kitchen is the heart of the home, for transmitting your passion for cooking to me, and for getting excited about every successful recipe I make. Thank you for helping me with so many tips and for all the tests you helped me do, for having spent the most beautiful five months in Roswell, for believing in me even when I didn't, and for giving me wings to find myself. Thank you, Dad, for so many life lessons learned. Thank you for planting those questions that have marked my life. It is true that there are no

bad or good decisions in life; everything happens for a reason. Thank you for your wisdom and for your critical palate, for those wonderful and deeply enjoyable months that we spent together, and for creating new miracles together. I can't wait to hug you again!

BRANDON. Thank you, my dear friend, for being there every time I need you and every time fear attacked me, and for your advice on every important decision. Thank you for believing in me and my food, for changing our lives, and for making our dreams come true. Thank you for your beautiful heart and for being part of our family.

DIANA AND DANIELA. My sisters, thank you for always being there for me, because I know I can count on you at any time and for anything. I love you so much!

GRAZZIA, PAOLA. My chosen sisters, my dear soul friends, thank you for always being with me. Our bond is stronger and deeper than distance and time. I love you!

CASSIE. Thank you for believing I could write a book in English without even knowing how to conjugate verbs correctly. Thank you for believing in my food and making me feel like a real chef. Thank you for your loving patience in editing for so long with me, for letting me make so many mistakes, and for teaching me along the way how to organize everything with such detail and love; thank you for helping me turn my boring science texts into light and understandable stories. Thank you for making this book a dream come true.

BRIAN. Thank you for betting on me and guiding me in this unknown world of publishing; thank you for taking care of me and teaching me how to navigate each stage of the birth of this book.

310

JIMENA. "Hello, Jime, we don't know each other, but we have many friends in common. Do you want to fly to my house in Roswell for two weeks to take the photos for my cookbook?" Thank you, my dear Jime, for accepting this tremendous madness and for making the sacrifice of leaving your family in Lima for two weeks to dedicate yourself to this project with so much love and dedication. Thank you for those incredible days we spent together, and for the most beautiful photos that this cookbook could have.

ROSTAM. Thank you, dear friend, for betting on this dream, and for helping me to help others through my recipes and my kitchen. Thank you for believing in my vision and mission, for your love and support, and for being part of our family.

CARLOS, DANIEL. There are no words to describe the gratitude and deep love I have for you. I will never forget your words, "It's not us; it's God acting through us," which I later heard, in exactly the same words, from Brandon. You supported us when we needed it most and pushed us to have faith in others, in humanity, in God, and in ourselves.

NANETTE. Oh, my dear friend, you are my chosen sister. Thank you for helping me test my recipes, for your advice, for your criticism, and for all your love. Thank you for that orange juice that gives us precious time together.

ANACE. You are my angel. I would not have survived the most difficult times of my life if it had not been for your wise advice, your spiritual guidance, and the space you gave me to breathe and gather strength. Thank you for accepting my cakes and desserts as small compensation for something that changed my life. Thank you so much; I always carry you in my heart.

MY RESTAURANT TEAM. I feel so blessed to have an amazing team in the restaurant kitchen.

JANET, you are a wonderful baker and person; thank you for following my complicated recipes to the letter; thank you for giving me the peace of mind that everything will be baked to perfection when I'm not there and for being such a good person with such a big heart.

DIEGO, it's always your fault when a dish comes out perfectly served, when a pizza comes out with the spinach in the right place, when the ham is cooked to perfection, when a golden milk is at the precise temperature. Thanks for being here!

ROSI, thank you for being the sweetest lady who runs from one place to another, ensuring everything is impeccable and the drinks are perfectly made, with the right ingredients and lots of love.

THE ROSWELL COMMUNITY. From the day we opened our restaurant doors and met for the first time, the community in Roswell, Georgia, gave us the warmest welcome. We never thought we'd feel as at home and as loved as we felt from that first day. You are incredible. Infinite thanks for making us feel so welcomed, for supporting us and getting excited about all our projects, and for being our family.

OUR FRIENDS AND FAMILY. Thanks to Diego and Mapi, Santiago and Paige, Ilonka, Sergio and Hilda, Rosalba, Eliana, and Nico and Julie, who lent us money to buy our bakery in Roswell. Thank you for trusting and betting on us; without you we would not have reached America.

CRISTINA S. Thank you for pampering me and helping me through our worst years. Thank you for running to the supermarket a hundred times to buy the wrong ingredients and going back a hundred more for the right ones.

universal conversion chart

OVEN TEMPERATURE EQUIVALENTS

250°F = 120°C

275°F = 135°C

300°F = 150°C

325°F = 160°C

350°F = 180°C

375°F = 190°C

400°F = 200°C

425°F = 220°C

450°F = 230°C

475°F = 240°C

500°F = 260°C

MEASUREMENT EQUIVALENTS

Measurements should always be level unless directed otherwise.

⅛ teaspoon = 0.5 mL

¼ teaspoon = 1 mL

½ teaspoon = 2 mL

1 teaspoon = 5 mL

1 tablespoon = 3 teaspoons = ½ fluid ounce = 15 mL

2 tablespoons = ⅛ cup = 1 fluid ounce = 30 mL

4 tablespoons = ¼ cup = 2 fluid ounces = 60 mL

5⅓ tablespoons = ⅓ cup = 3 fluid ounces = 80 mL

8 tablespoons = ½ cup = 4 fluid ounces = 120 mL

10⅔ tablespoons = ⅔ cup = 5 fluid ounces = 160 mL

12 tablespoons = ¾ cup = 6 fluid ounces = 180 mL

16 tablespoons = 1 cup = 8 fluid ounces = 240 mL

index

CRISTY'S KITCHEN. Copyright © 2023 by Huh Natural & Real Food Corp. Foreword © 2023 by Brandon Stanton. All rights reserved. Printed in the United States of America. No part of this book may be used or reproduced in any manner whatsoever without written permission except in the case of brief quotations embodied in critical articles and reviews. For information, address HarperCollins Publishers, 195 Broadway, New York, NY 10007.

HarperCollins books may be purchased for educational, business, or sales promotional use. For information, please email the Special Markets Department at SPsales@harpercollins.com.

FIRST EDITION

Designed by Alison Bloomer

Photographs by Jimena Agois except page 105 (Traditional Leche de Tigre Cups), by Cristina Kisner

Illustrations by Julieta Gracey Kisner

Library of Congress Cataloging-in-Publication Data has been applied for.

ISBN 978-0-06-321468-2

23 24 25 26 27 LBC 5 4 3 2 1